WEBSTER'S TRAVELERS PHRASE BOOK

---◆---

SPANISH

---◆---

G. & C. MERRIAM CO.

SPRINGFIELD, MASSACHUSETTS 01101

Copyright © 1971

by

G. & C. MERRIAM CO.

Standard Book Number:

87779-091-4

MADE IN U.S.A.

Preface

This Merriam-Webster phrase book offers the *quickest* language assistance to the traveler who does not speak Spanish. In any situation requiring an exchange of ideas, the greatest need is for *fast* access to the words necessary to do the job. This handy book is the answer —for businessman, student, or tourist.

All entries are listed ALPHABETICALLY by key word. For example, if you are in a restaurant and want the check, or if you are in need of funds and want to cash a check, there is no need to figure out whether the phrase you need is under *Eating, Restaurant, Money,* or *Bank.* You go directly to the word *Check* and immediately find the phrase that meets your situation. With conventional phrase books many frustrating minutes are often lost in first trying to determine under what category a phrase might be listed. This phrase book has been prepared to save time and to prevent awkward situations by putting your words where you'll find them quickest—in their alphabetical order.

At the same time, however, additional related phrases are given under many key words. If you wish to rent an automobile, you'll find the appropriate phrase under *Automobile;* but you will also find phrases to help you deal with a flat tire, ask for the next gas station, request repairs, and express a wide range of related needs. And if you plan to drive in Spain or Latin America, the special section of international road signs will be of particular interest.

IN ADDITION to the alphabetical listing of phrases, this book includes a glossary of 3000 individual words. The words in this glossary are the words most likely to be needed in the situations confronting the average traveler. Each word is listed where you expect to find it—in its alphabetical order—to speed consultation and to increase your competence.

Guide to Pronunciation

After quickly finding the necessary phrase, you will need to pronounce it easily with a minimum of hesitation. Here again, this new guide offers rapid assistance by showing pronunciation in symbols that are familiar. The pronunciation of all sentences in this book is indicated by use of the English alphabet. Capital letters are used to indicate the stressed syllables. When you become accustomed to hearing Spanish spoken, you will find it easier to imitate and your pronunciation will improve rapidly so that you will seldom need to refer to the pronunciation guide.

Vowels

Symbol	Approximate Sound	Spanish Example	
ah	f*a*ther	granja	GRAHN-*hah*
ahy	t*ie*	hay	AHY
ee	mach*i*ne	sentir	*sehn*-TEER
eh	l*a*te	freno	FREH-*noh*
oh	h*o*me	acción	*ahk*-SYOHN
oo	b*oo*t	discurso	*deess*-KOOR-*soh*
oy	b*oy*	estoy	*ehss*-TOY

Consonants

Symbol	Approximate Sound	Spanish Example	
p	*p*et	previo	PREH-*byoh*
b	*b*ed	banco	BAHN-*koh*
t	*t*ill	tonto	TOHN-*toh*
d	*d*o	descender	*dehss-sehn*-DEHR
k	*k*ing	caso	KAH-*soh*
g	*g*et	grano	GRAH-*noh*
f	*f*or	fila	FEE-*lah*
th	*th*en	maduro	*mah*-THOO-*roh*
s	*s*end	suerte	SWEHR-*teh*
z	*z*oo	rasgar	*rrahz*-GAHR
ch	*ch*ill	checque	CHEH-*keh*
m	*m*eet	momento	*moh*-MEHN-*toh*
n	*n*ot	nacional	*nah-syoh*-NAHL
l	*l*eave	luz	LOOSS
r	rolled or trilled	roca	RROH-*kah*
w	*w*it	muy	MWEE
y	*y*es	llevar	*yeh*-BAHR
h	*h*ouse	jugo	HOO-*goh*

Aboard

When can we go aboard?

¿Cuándo podemos ir a bordo?

KWAHN-*doh poh*-THEH-*mohss eer ah* BOHR-*thoh?*

Accept

Do you accept U.S. currency (travelers' checks, credit cards)?

¿Acepta usted dinero (cheques de viaje, tarjetas de crédito) de los Estados Unidos?

ah-SEHP-*tah oo*-STEHTH *dee*-NEH-*roh (*CHEH-*kehss deh bee*-AH-*heh, tahr*-HEH-*tahss deh* KREH-*thee-toh) deh lohss ess*-TAH-*thohss oo*-NEE-*thohss?*

Accident

There has been an accident.

Ha ocurrido un accidente.

ah oh-koo-RREE-*thoh oon ahk-see*-THEHN-*teh.*

Get a doctor!

¡Busquen a un médico!

BOOSS-*kehn ah oon* MEH-*thee-koh!*

Call for the police!

¡Llamen a la policía!

YAH-*mehn ah lah poh-lee*-SEE-*ah!*

Send for an ambulance!

¡Llamen una ambulancia!

YAH-*mehn* OOH-*nah ahm-boo*-LAHN-*syah!*

Take me (take him, take her) to the hospital.

Llévenme (llévenle, llévenla) al hospital.

YEH-*behn-meh (*YEH-*behn-leh,* YEH-*behn-lah) ahl ohss-pee*-TAHL.

He (She) is injured.

El (ella) está herido (herida).

EHL (EH-*yah) ehss*-TAH *eh*-REE-*thoh (eh*-REE-*thah).*

Don't move him (her).

No le (la) muevan.

noh leh (lah) MUEH-*bahn.*

He (She) has fainted.
El (ella) se ha desmayado.
EHL *(EH-yah)* seh ah dehss-mah-YAH-*thoh*.

Help me carry him (carry her).
Ayúdenme a llevarle (llevarla).
ah-YOO-*thehn-meh ah yeh*-BAHR-*leh (yeh*-BAHR-*lah)*.

I feel dizzy.
Me siento mareado (mareada).
meh SYEHN-*toh mah-reh*-AH-*thoh (mah-reh*-AH-*thah)*.

He (She) has a fracture (bruise, cut, burn).
El (ella) tiene una fractura (contusión, cortadura, quemadura).
EHL *(EH-yah)* TYEHN-*eh* OOH-*nah frahk*-TOO-*rah (kohn-too*-SYOHN, *kohr-tah*-THOO-*rah, keh-mah*-THOO-*rah)*.

He (She) is bleeding.
El (ella) está sangrando.
EHL *(EH-yah)* ehss-TAH *sahn*-GRAHN-*doh*.

Are you all right?
¿Está usted bien?
ehss-TAH *oo*-STEHTH BYEHN?

Where does it hurt?
¿Dónde le duele?
DOHN-*deh leh* DWEH-*leh?*

It hurts here.
Me duele aquí.
meh DWEH-*leh ah*-KEE.

I cannot move my _____.
No puedo mover mi _____.
noh PWEH-*thoh moh*-BEHR *mee* _____.

Please notify my husband (wife).
Por favor, informen a mi marido (esposa).
pohr fah-BOHR, *een*-FOHR-*mehn ah mee mah*-REE-*thoh (ehss*-POH-*sah)*.

Accommodate

Can you accommodate me (two, three, four)?

¿Puede usted alojarme (alojar a dos, tres, cuatro)?

PWEH-*theh oo*-STEHTH *ah-loh*-HAHR-*meh (ah-loh*-HAHR
ah dohss, trehss, KWAH-*troh)?*

Does the train to _____ have sleeping
accommodations?

¿Lleva el tren a _____ coches-cama?

YEH-*bah ehl* TREHN *ah* _____ KOH-*chehss*-KAH-*mah?*

Accompany

May I accompany you?

¿Puedo acompañarle a usted?

PWEH-*thoh ah-kohm-pah*-NYAHR-*leh ah oo*-STEHTH?

Account (Bank)

I would like to (where do I) open a checking account.

Quisiera (¿Dónde puedo) abrir una cuenta corriente.

kee-SYEH-*rah* (DOHN-*deh* PWEH-*thoh)* ah-BREER OOH-
nah KWEHN-*tah koh*-RRYEHN-*teh.*

Ache – see Hurt

Acquaintance – see also Meet

I am very happy to make your acquaintance.

Me agrada mucho conocerle (or: Mucho gusto en
conocerle).

meh ah-GRAH-*thah* MOO-*choh koh-noh*-SEHR-*leh (*MOO-
choh GOO-*stoh ehn koh-noh*-SEHR-*leh).*

Address

Please forward all mail to this address.

Haga usted el favor de enviar toda la correspondencia
a esta dirección.

AH-*gah oo*-STEHTH *ehl fah*-BOHR *deh ehn*-BYAHR TOH-
thah koh-rrehss-pohn-DEHN-*syah ah* EHSS-*tah dee-
rehk*-SYOHN.

Here is my address.

Esta es mi dirección.

EHSS-*tah ehss mee dee-rehk*-SYOHN.

What is your address (and telephone number)?

¿Cuál es su dirección (y número de teléfono)?

KWAHL *ess soo dee-rehk*-SYOHN *(ee* NOO-*meh-roh deh*
teh-LEH-*foh-noh)?*

Admission

How much is the admission?

¿Cuánto cuesta la entrada?

KWAHN-*toh* KWEHSS-*tah lah ehn*-TRAH-*thah?*

Advertise

I would like to advertise for a _____.

Quisiera anunciar un(a) _____.

kee-SYEH-*rah ah-noon*-SYAHR *oon(-ah)* _____.

Advertisement

I am answering your advertisement.

Contesto a su anuncio.

kohn-TEHSS-*toh ah soo ah*-NOON-*syoh.*

I would like to run an advertisement.

Quisiera poner un anuncio.

kee-SYEH-*rah poh*-NEHR *oon ah*-NOON-*syoh.*

Afford

I cannot afford that.

No puedo permitirme ese lujo.

noh PWEH-*thoh pehr-mee*-TEER-*meh* EH-*seh* LOO-*hoh.*

No tengo medios para eso.

noh TEHN-*goh* MEH-*thyohss* PAH-*rah* EH-*soh.*

Afternoon

I would like to arrange it for the afternoon.

Quisiera arreglarlo para la tarde.

kee-SYEH-*rah ah-rreh*-GLAHR-*loh* PAH-*rah lah* TAHR-
theh.

Again

I hope to see you again soon.

Espero verle otra vez dentro de poco.

ehss-PEH-*roh* BEHR-*leh* OH-*trah* BEHSS DEHN-*troh deh*
POH-*koh.*

Please say it again.
Por favor, dígalo otra vez.
pohr fah-BOHR, DEE-*gah-loh* OH-*trah* BEHSS.

Age
What is your age?
¿Qué edad tiene (usted)?
keh eh-THAHTH TYEH-*neh (oo*-STEHTH)?

Aid – see Help

Air
My tire(s) need(s) air.
Mi(s) llanta(s) necesita(n) aire.
mee(ss) YAHN-*tah(ss) neh-seh*-SEE-*tah(n)* AH-*ee-reh*.

Air Conditioning
Does it have air conditioning?
¿Tiene aire acondicionado?
TYEH-*neh* AH-*ee-reh ah-kohn-dee-syohn*-AH-*thoh?*

I want a room with air conditioning, please.
Por favor, quisiera una habitación con aire
    acondicionado.
pohr fah-BOHR, *kee*-SYEH-*rah* OO-*nah ah-bee-tah*-SYON
    kohn AH-*ee-reh-ah-kohn-dee-syohn*-AH-*doh.*

Air Mail – see Mail

Airplane – see Flight

Airport
The airport, please.
El aeropuerto, por favor.
ehl ah-eh-roh-PWEHR-*toh, pohr fah*-BOHR.

Airsick
I feel airsick.
Me siento mareado (mareada).
meh SYEHN-*toh mah-reh*-AH-*thoh (mah-reh*-AH-*thah).*

A la Carte
Please show me the a la carte menu.
Haga el favor de traerme el menú a la carta.
AH-*gah ehl fah*-BOHR *deh trah*-EHR-*meh ehl meh*-NOO *ah
    lah* KAHR-*tah.*

All
This is all I have (need, want).
Esto es todo lo que tengo (necesito, quiero).
EHSS-*toh ehss* TOH-*thoh loh keh* TEHN-*goh (neh-seh-*SEE-*toh,* KYEH-*roh)*.

Allergy
I am allergic to this.
Soy alérgico a esto.
*soy ah-*LEHR-*hee-koh ah* EHSS-*toh*.

All Right
It is all right.
Esta bien.
*ehss-*TAH BYEHN.

Alone
Please leave me alone.
Por favor, déjeme solo (sola).
*pohr fah-*BOHR, DEH-*heh-meh* SOH-*loh (*SOH-*lah)*.

Are you alone?
¿Está usted solo (sola)?
*ehss-*TAH *oo-*STEHTH SOH-*loh (*SOH-*lah)?*

I am alone.
Sí, estoy solo (sola).
SEE, *ehss-*TOY SOH-*loh (*SOH-*lah)*.

I am not alone.
No, no estoy solo (sola).
NOH, *noh ehss-*TOH SOH-LOH *(*SOH-*lah)*.

Ambulance
Call me an ambulance.
Llame una ambulancia.
YAH-*meh* OO-*nah ahm-boo-*LAHN-*syah*.

American
I am an American.
Soy norteamericano.
soy NOHR-*teh-ah-meh-ree-*KAH-*noh*.

Do you accept American money?

¿Acepta usted dinero norteamericano?

ah-SEHP-*tah* oo-STEHTH *dee*-NEH-*roh* NOHR-*teh-ah-meh-ree-*KAH-*noh?*

American Embassy

Please direct me (take me) to the American embassy.

Por favor, ¿puede usted dirigirme (llevarme) a la embajada norteamericana?

pohr fah-BOHR, PWEH-*theh* oo-STEHTH *dee-ree-*HEER-*meh (yeh-*BAHR-*meh)* ah lah ehm-bah-HAH-*dah* NOHR-*teh-ah-meh-ree-*KAH-*nah?*

American Express

Please direct me (take me) to the American Express office.

Por favor, ¿puede usted dirigirme (llevarme) a la oficina de American Express?

pohr fah-BOHR, PWEH-*theh* oo-STEHTH *dee-ree-*HEER-*meh (yeh-*BAHR-*meh)* ah lah oh-*fee-*SEE-*nah* deh *ah-*MEH-*ree-kan* ehss-PREHSS?

Do you accept the American Express credit card?

¿Acepta usted la tarjeta de crédito de American Express?

ah-SEHP-*tah* oo-STEHTH lah *tahr*-HEH-*tah* deh KREH-*thee-toh* deh *ah-*MEH-*ree-kahn* ehss-PREHSS?

Amount

What is the total amount?

¿Cuál es la cantidad total?

KWAHL *ehss* lah *kahn-tee-*THAHTH *toh*-TAHL?

Another

Let's have another.

Tomemos otro.

toh-MEH-*mohss* OH-*troh.*

Please get me another drink.

Por favor, tráigame otra bebida.

pohr fah-BOHR, TRAH-*ee-gah-meh* OH-*trah* beh-BEE-*thah.*

Answer

They do not answer; please try again.
No contestan; por favor, pruebe otra vez.
noh kohn-TEHSS-*tahn; pohr fah*-BOHR, PRWEH-*beh* OH-*trah* BEHSS.

Antiques

Please direct me (take me) to an antique shop.
Por favor, diríjame (lléveme) a una tienda de antigüedades.
pohr fah-BOHR, *dee*-REE-*hah-meh (*YEH-*beh-meh) ah oo-nah* TYEHN-*dah deh ahn-tee-gueh*-THAHTH-*ehss.*

I am interested in antiques.
Me interesan las antigüedades.
meh een-teh-REH-*sahn lahs ahn-tee-gueh*-THAHTH-*ehss.*

Do you sell antiques?
¿Vende usted antigüedades?
BEHN-*deh oo*-STEHTH-*ahn-tee-gueh*-THAHTH-*ehss?*

Apologize − see also Pardon, Sorry

I apologize.
Le pido perdón.
leh PEE-*thoh pehr*-THOHN.

Appointment

I would like to make an appointment for _____.
Quisiera hacer una cita para _____.
kee-SYEH-*rah ah*-SEHR OO-*nah* SEE-*tah pah-rah* _____.

Arrive

When does the plane (bus, boat, train) arrive?
¿Cuándo llega el avión (autobús, barco, tren)?
KWAHN-*doh* YEH-*gah ehl ah*-BYOHN *(ow-toh*-BOOSS, BAHR-*koh,* TREHN*)?*

When do we arrive at _____?
¿Cuándo llegamos a _____?
KWAHN-*doh yeh*-GAH-*mohss ah* _____?

Article − see Things

Asleep

My husband (wife) is asleep.

Mi marido (esposa) está dormido (dormida).

mee mah-REE-thoh (ehss-POH-sah) ehss-TAH dohr-MEE-thoh (dohr-MEE-thah).

Assistance – see Help

Authority

I will report this to the authorities.

Voy a informar a las autoridades acerca de esto.

boy ah een-fohr-MAHR ah lahss ow-toh-ree-THAH-thehss ah-SEHR-kah deh EHSS-toh.

Automobile

I want to rent an automobile, please.

Quisiera alquilar un automóvil, por favor.

kee-SYEH-rah ahl-kee-LAHR oon ow-toh-MOH-beel, pohr fah-BOHR.

Where is the next gas station (the next garage)?

¿Dónde está la estación de gasolina más cercana (el garaje más cercano)?

DOHN-deh ehss-TAH lah ehss-tah-SYOHN deh gah-soh-LEE-nah mahss sehr-KAH-nah (ehl gah-RAH-heh mahss sehr-KAH-noh)?

My car has broken down; I am out of gas.

Mi automóvil no marcha; me he quedado sin gasolina.

mee ow-toh-MOH-beel noh MAHR-chah; meh eh keh-THAH-thoh seen gah-soh-LEE-nah.

I have a flat tire.

Tengo una llanta pinchada.

TEHN-goh OO-nah YAHN-tah peen-CHAH-thah.

Can you help me?

¿Puede ayudarme usted?

PWEH-theh ah-yoo-THAHR-meh oo-STEHTH?

Can you tow (push) me to a garage?

¿Me lo puede usted remolcar (empujar) hasta un garaje?

meh loh PWEH-theh oo-STEHTH reh-mohl-KAHR (ehm-poo-HAHR) AHSS-tah oon gah-RAH-heh?

I have (I do not have) an international license.
Tengo (no tengo) una licencia internacional.
TEHN-*goh (noh* TEHN-*goh)* OO-*nah lee*-SEHN-*syah een-tehr-nah-syoh*-NAHL.

Here is my license.
Aquí tiene mi licencia.
ah-KEE TYEH-*neh mee lee*-SEHN-*syah*.

Can you recommend a good mechanic?
¿Puede recomendarme un buen mecánico?
PWEH-*theh rreh-koh-mehn*-DAHR-*meh oon bwehn meh*-KAH-*nee-koh?*

Fill it up, please.
Llénelo, por favor.
YEH-*neh-loh, pohr fah*-BOHR.

Give me _____ liters, please.
Déme _____ litros, por favor.
DEH-*meh* _____ LEE-*trohss, pohr fah*-BOHR.

The _____ does not work.
El (la) _____ no funciona.
ehl (lah) _____ *noh foon*-SYOH-*nah*.

Please check the _____.
Por favor compruebe el (la) _____.
pohr fah-BOHR *kohm*-PRWEH-*beh ehl (lah)* _____.

Can you repair it while I wait? When?
¿Puede arreglarlo mientras espero? ¿Cuándo?
PWEH-*theh ah-rreh*-GLAHR-*loh* MYEHN-*trahss ehss*-PEH-*roh?* KWAHN-*doh?*

What is wrong?
¿Qué es lo que le pasa?
keh ehss loh keh leh PAH-*sah?*

Can you wash it (now)?
¿Puede lavarlo (ahora)?
PWEH-*theh lah*-BAHR-*loh (ah*-OH-*rah)?*

There is a rattle (squeak).
Hace un ruido (chirrido).
AH-*seh oon* RWEE-*thoh (chee*-RREE-*thoh)*.

Something is leaking here.
Aquí gotea algo.
ah-KEE *goh*-TEH-*ah* AHL-*goh.*

Will you accept this credit card (travelers checks, a
personal check)?
¿Aceptaría esta tarjeta de crédito (cheques de viajero,
un cheque personal)?
ah-sehp-tah-REE-*ah* EHSS-*tah tahr*-HEH-*tah deh* KREH-
thee-toh (CHEH-*kehss deh byah*-HEH-*roh, oon* CHEH-
keh pehr-sohn-AHL)?

I am staying at _____.
Me estoy alojando en _____.
meh ehss-TOY *ah-loh*-HAHN-*doh ehn* _____.

I am a member of the Automobile Club.
Soy socio del Club de automovilistas.
soy SOH-*syoh dehl kloob deh ow-toh-moh-bee*-LEESS-
tahss.

Available

Are there any rooms (any seats) available?
¿Tiene alguna habitación (algún asiento) disponible?
TYEH-*neh ahl*-GOO-*nah ah-bee-tah*-SYOHN *(ahl*-GOON *ah*-
SYEHN-*toh) dees-poh*-NEE-*bleh?*

Awaken – see Call

Away

Go away!
¡Vayase!
BAH-*yah-seh!*

Please take it away.
Lléveselo.
YEH-*beh-seh-loh.*

Babysitter

Can you recommend an English-speaking babysitter?
¿Puede recomendarme una niñera de habla inglesa?
PWEH-*theh rreh-koh-mehn*-DAHR-*meh* OO-*nah nee*-NYEH-
rah deh AH-*blah een*-GLEH-*sah?*

Bachelor

I am a bachelor.
Soy soltero.
*soy sohl-*TEH-*roh.*

Is he a bachelor?
¿Es soltero?
*ehss sohl-*TEH-*roh?*

Back

Please show me the way back to _____.
¿Puede indicarme el camino de regreso a _____?
PWEH-*theh een-dee-*KAHR-*me ehl kah-*MEE-*noh deh*
   *rreh-*GREH-*soh ah* _____?

Please come back later.
Haga el favor de volver más tarde.
AH-*gah ehl fah-*BOHR *deh bohl-*BEHR *mahss* TAHR-*theh.*

I (do not) like to sit in the back.
(No) me gusta sentarme atrás.
(noh) meh GOOSS-*tah sehn-*TAHR-*meh ah-*TRAHSS.

When are we due back?
¿Cuándo debemos estar de vuelta?
KWAHN-*doh deh-*BEH-*mohss ehss-*TAHR *deh* BWEHL-*tah?*

Please take me back to the _____.
Por favor, lléveme de nuevo a _____.
*pohr fah-*BOHR, YEH-*beh-meh deh* NWEH-*boh ah* _____.

Bad (Unsatisfactory)

This is bad. (Please take it away.)
Esto está mal. (Por favor, lléveselo.)
EHSS-*toh ehss-*TAH MAHL. *(pohr fah-*BOHR, YEH-*beh-seh-*
   loh.)

Bags, Baggage

May I leave my bag(s) here?
¿Me permite dejar la(s) maleta(s) aquí?
*meh pehr-*MEE-*teh deh-*HAHR *lah(ss) mah-*LEH-*tah(ss)*
   *ah-*KEE?

Please help me with my bags.
Haga el favor de ayudarme con mis maletas.
AH-*gah ehl fah*-BOHR *deh ah-you*-THAHR-*meh kohn
meess mah*-LEH-*tahss.*

Please take my bags to _____.
Haga el favor de llevar mis maletas a _____.
AH-*gah ehl fah*-BOHR *deh yeh*-BAHR *meess mah*-LEH-
tahss ah _____.

Where is the baggage room?
¿Dónde está la consigna?
DOHN-*deh ehss*-TAH *lah kohn*-SEEG-*nah?*

How much baggage am I allowed?
¿A cuánto equipaje tengo derecho?
ah KWAHN-*toh eh-kee*-PAH-*heh* TEHN-*goh deh*-REH-*choh?*

Where is my baggage?
¿Dónde está mi equipaje?
DOHN-*deh ehss*-TAH *mee eh-kee*-PAH-*heh?*

I cannot find my bags.
No puedo encontrar mis maletas.
nah PWEH-*thoh ehn-kohn*-TRAHR *meess mah*-LEH-*tahss.*

I need a porter for my bags.
Necesito un mozo para llevar mis maletas.
neh-seh-SEE-*toh oon* MOH-*soh pah-rah yeh*-BAHR *meess
mah*-LEH-*tahss.*

Bank
Where is the nearest bank?
¿Dónde está el banco más próximo?
DOHN-*deh ehss*-TAH *ehl* BAHN-*koh mahss* PROHK-*see-
moh?*

At what time does the bank open (close)?
¿A qué hora se abre (cierra) el banco?
ah keh OH-*rah seh* AH-*breh* (SYEH-*rah) ehl* BAHN-*koh?*

Where can I cash this?
¿Dónde puedo cobrar esto?
DOHN-*deh* PWEH-*thoh koh*-BRAHR EHSS-*toh?*

Will you cash a personal check?

¿Me puede cambiar un cheque personal?

meh PWEH-*theh kahm*-BYAHR *oon* CHEH-*keh pehr-soh-*
NAHL?

Can I cash a money order here?

¿Puedo cobrar un giro postal aquí?

PWEH-*thoh koh*-BRAHR *oon* HEE-*roh pohss*-TAHL *ah-*
KEE?

Where is the window for cashing travelers checks?

¿Dónde está la ventanilla para cobrar los cheques de
viajero?

DOHN-*deh ehss*-TAH *lah behn-tah*-NEE-*yah pah-rah koh-*
BRAHR *lohss* CHEH-*kehss deh byah*-HEH-*roh*?

Please give me (don't give me) large bills.

Haga el favor de darme (de no darme) billetes de alta
denominación.

AH-*gah ehl fah*-BOHR *deh* DAHR-*meh (deh noh* DAHR-
meh) bee-YEH-*tehss deh* AHL-*tah deh-noh-mee-nah-*
SYOHN.

Can you change this for me, please?

¿Me puede cambiar esto, por favor?

meh PWEH-*theh kahm*-BYAHR EHSS-*toh, pohr fah*-BOHR?

I would like to change some American dollars into

_____.

Quisiera cambiar dólares norteamericanos por _____.

kee-SYEH-*rah kahm*-BYAHR DOH-*lah-rehss nohr-teh-ah-*
meh-ree-KAH-*nohss pohr* _____.

What is the rate of exchange?

¿Cuál es el tipo de cambio?

kwahl ehss ehl TEE-*poh deh* KAHM-*byoh*?

Bar

Where is the bar?

¿Dónde está el bar?

DOHN-*deh ehss*-TAH *ehl* BAHR?

Is there a bar open?

¿Hay un bar abierto?

ahy oon BAHR *ah*-BYEHR-*toh*?

When do the bars close (open)?
¿Cuándo se cierran (abren) los bares?
KWAHN-*doh seh* SYEH-*rrahn (*AH-brehn*) lohss* BAH-*rehss?*

Barber

Can you recommend a good barber?
¿Me puede recomendar un buen barbero?
meh PWEH-*theh rreh-koh-mehn-*DAHR *oon bwehn bahr-*BEH-*roh?*

I want a haircut (shave), please.
Quiero cortarme el pelo (afeitarme), por favor.
KYEH-*roh kohr-*TAHR-*meh ehl* PEH-*loh (ah-fey-*TAHR-*meh), pohr fah-*BOHR.

Not too short, please.
No demasiado corto, por favor.
*noh deh-mah-*SYAH-*thoh* KOHR-*toh, pohr fah-*BOHR.

Don't cut any off the top.
No corte nada por encima.
noh KOHR-*teh* NAH-*thah pohr ehn-*SEE-*mah.*

I part my hair on the (other) side.
Me hago la raya al (otro) lado.
meh AH-*goh lah* RAH-*yah ahl (*OH-*troh)* LAH-*thoh.*

(Don't) put on oil.
(No) ponga aceite.
(noh) POHN-*gah ah-*SAY-*teh.*

Bath

A room with bath, please.
Una habitación con baño, por favor.
OO-*nah ah-bee-tah-*SYOHN *kohn* BAH-*nyoh, pohr fah-*BOHR.

A private bath is not necessary.
No hace falta baño privado.
noh AH-*seh* FAHL-*tah* BAH-*nyoh pree-*BAH-*thoh.*

Bathing

Is bathing permitted here?
¿Está permitido bañarse?
*ehss-*TAH *pehr-mee-tee-thoh bah-*NYAHR-*seh?*

Bathing Suit

Where can I rent (buy) a bathing suit?

¿Dónde puedo alquilar (comprar) un traje de baño?

DOHN-*deh* PWEH-*thoh* ahl-kee-LAHR *(kohm-*PRAHR*) oon*
TRAH-*heh deh* BAH-*nyoh?*

Bathroom (not toilet)

Where is the bathroom?

¿Dónde está el cuarto de baño?

DOHN-*deh ehss*-TAH *ehl* KWAHR-*toh deh* BAH-*nyoh?*

Bathtub

I prefer a bathtub (to a shower).

Prefiero la bañera (en lugar de una ducha).

preh-FYEH-*roh lah bah*-NYEH-*rah (ehn loo*-GAHR *deh* OO-
nah DOO-*chah).*

Battery

Do you sell flashlight (radio, transistor, electric razor)
batteries?

¿Vende pilas de flás (de radio, de transistor, de
máquina de afeitar eléctrica)?

BEHN-*deh* PEE-*lahss deh flahss (deh* RRAH-*dyoh, deh*
trahn-SEES-*tohr, deh* MAH-*kee-nah deh ah-fey*-TAHR
eh-LEHK-*tree-kah)?*

Beach

Is there a beach nearby?

¿Hay alguna playa cerca?

ahy ahl-GOO-*nah* PLAH-*yah* SEHR-*kah?*

Beauty Parlor

Can you recommend a good beauty parlor?

¿Puede recomendarme un buen salón de belleza?

PWEH-*theh rreh-koh-mehn*-DAHR-*meh oon bwehn sah*-
LOHN *deh beh*-YEH-*sah?*

Can I make an appointment for _____?

¿Puedo hacer una cita para _____?

PWEH-*thoh ah*-SEHR OO-*nah* SEE-*tah pah-rah* _____?

I (don't) have an appointment (with) _____.

(No) tengo cita (con) _____.

(noh) TEHN-*goh* SEE-*tah (kohn)* _____.

I want a wash, cut, and set, please.
Quisiera un lavado, corte y marcado, por favor.
kee-SYEH-*rah oon lah*-BAH-*thoh,* KOHR-*teh ee mahr*-KAH-*thoh, pohr fah*-BOHR.

Trim it, please.
Córtelo un poco, por favor.
KOHR-*teh-loh oon* POH-*koh, pohr fah*-BOHR.

Not too short.
No demasiado corto.
noh deh-mah-SYAH-*doh* KOHR-*toh.*

I want a permanent (a rinse), please.
Quisiera una permanente (un lavado), por favor.
kee-SYEH-*rah* OOH-*nah pehr-mah*-NEHN-*teh (oon lah-*BAH-*thoh), pohr fah*-BOHR.

I want a facial (a manicure, a massage), please.
Quisiera un masaje facial (una manicura, un masaje), por favor.
kee-SYEH-*rah oon mah*-SAH-*heh fah*-SYAHL (OOH-*nah mah-nee*-KOO-*rah, oon mah*-SAH-*heh), pohr fah*-BOHR.

I part my hair on the (other) side (in the middle).
Me hago la raya al (otro) lado (en medio).
meh AH-*goh lah* RAH-*yah ahl (*OH-*troh)* LAH-*thoh (ehn* MEH-*thyoh).*

I wear bangs.
Llevo flequillo.
YEH-*boh fleh*-KEE-*yoh.*

I want a French twist (chignon), please.
Quisiera un moño italiano (moño, rodete), por favor.
kee-SYEH-*rah oon* MOH-*nyoh ee-tah*-LYAH-*noh (*MOH-*nyoh, roh*-DEH-*teh), pohr fah*-BOHR.

Can you wash and set (and cut) my wig (fall)? Please (don't) tease it.
¿Puede lavar y marcar (y cortar) mi peluca (pelo postizo)? Por favor, (no) lo carde.
PWEH-*theh lah*-BAHR *ee mahr*-KAHR *(ee kohr*-TAHR) *mee peh*-LOO-*kah (*PEH-*loh pohss*-TEE-*soh)? pohr fah*-BOHR, *(noh) loh* KAHR-*theh.*

The water (dryer) is too hot (cold).

El agua (secador) está demasiado caliente (frío).

ehl AH-*guah (seh-kah-*THOHR*) ehss-*TAH *deh-mah-*SYAH-
*thoh kah-*YEHN-*teh (*FREE-*oh).*

Becoming

(I'm sorry), it is (not) becoming.

(Lo siento, no) me va bien.

(loh SYEHN-*toh, noh) meh bah* BYEHN.

Bed

A room with a double bed (twin beds), please.

Una habitación con una cama doble (dos camas), por
favor.

OOH-*nah ah-bee-tah-*SYOHN *kohn* OO-*nah* KAH-*mah* DOH-
bleh (dohss KAH-*mahss), pohr fah-*BOHR.

Please (do not) make up the bed(s) now.

Por favor, (no) haga la(s) cama(s) ahora.

*pohr fah-*BOHR, *(noh)* AH-*gah lah(ss)* KAH-*mah(ss) ah-
*OH-*rah.*

Bedroom

We would like (two) separate bedrooms.

Quisiéramos (dos) cuartos separados.

*kee-*SYEH-*rah-mohss (dohss)* KWAHR-*tohss seh-pah-*RAH-
thohss.

Bellboy

Please send the bellboy up to me.

Por favor, diga al botones que suba.

*pohr fah-*BOHR, DEE-*gah ahl boh-*TOH-*nehss keh* SOO-*bah.*

Berth

I want an upper (lower) berth.

Quisiera una litera alta (baja).

*kee-*SYEH-*rah* OO-*nah lee-*TEH-*rah* AHL-*tah (*BAH-*hah).*

Better

I like this one better.

Me gusta esto más.

meh GOOSS-*tah* EHSS-*toh mahss.*

Have you anything better?

¿Tiene usted algo mejor?

TYEH-*neh oo-*STEHTH AHL-*goh meh-*HOHR?

Bicycle

Have you a bicycle repair kit?

¿Tiene usted un estuche de herramientas para
  bicicletas?

TYEH-*neh* oo-STEHTH *oon ehss*-TOO-*cheh deh eh-rrah*-
  MYEHN-*tahss pah-rah bee-see*-KLEH-*tahss?*

Where can I rent (buy) a bicycle?

¿Dónde puedo alquilar (comprar) una bicicleta?

DOHN-*deh* PWEH-*thoh ahl-kee*-LAHR *(kohm*-PRAHR*)* OO-
  nah bee-see-KLEH-*tah?*

Where can my bicycle be repaired?

¿Dónde pueden arreglarme la bicicleta?

DOHN-*deh* PWEH-*then ah-rreh*-GLAHR-*meh lah bee-see*-
  KLEH-*tah?*

Big

This is too big.

Esto es demasiado grande.

EHSS-*toh ehss deh-mah*-SYAH-*thoh* GRAHN-*deh.*

This is not big enough.

Esto no es bastante grande.

EHSS-*toh noh ehss bahss*-TAHN-*teh* GRAHN-*deh.*

I want something bigger.

Me gustaría algo mas grande.

meh goo-stah-REE-*ah* AHL-*goh mahss* GRAHN-*deh.*

Bill (currency)

Can you change this bill?

¿Puede usted cambiarme este billete?

PWEH-*theh* oo-STEHTH *kahm*-BYAHR-*meh* EHSS-*teh bee*-
  YEH-*teh?*

Bill (of charges)

The bill, please.

La cuenta, por favor.

lah KWEHN-*tah, pohr fah*-BOHR.

Blanket

May I have another blanket, please?

¿Me puede dar otra manta, por favor?

meh PWEH-*theh dahr* OH-*trah* MAHN-*tah, pohr fah*-
  BOHR?

Bleed – see Accident

Board

When can we board?
¿Cuándo podemos subir a bordo?
KWAHN-*doh poh*-THEH-*mohss soo*-BEER *ah* BOHR-*thoh?*

Are meals served on board?
¿Se sirven comidas a bordo?
seh SEER-*behn koh*-MEE-*thahss ah* BOHR-*thoh?*

Boardinghouse (Pension)

Can you recommend a boardinghouse?
¿Puede recomendarme una pensión?
PWEH-*theh rreh-koh-mehn*-DAHR-*meh* OO-*nah pehn*-
SYOHN*?*

Boat

Where can I rent a boat?
¿Donde puedo alquilar un barco?
DOHN-*deh* PWEH-*thoh ahl-kee*-LAHR *oon* BAHR-*koh?*

I wish to rent a boat.
Quisiera alquilar un barco.
kee-SYEH-*rah ahl-kee*-LAHR *oon* BAHR-*koh.*

When does the boat leave for _____?
¿Cuándo sale el barco para _____?
KWAHN-*doh* SAH-*leh ehl* BAHR-*koh pah-rah* _____?

Book

I would like a book of tickets.
Quisiera un carnet de billetes.
kee-SYEH-*rah oon kahr*-NEH *deh bee*-YEH-*tehss.*

Do you have a book about _____?
¿Tiene usted un libro sobre _____?
TYEH-*neh oo*-STEHTH *oon* LEE-*broh soh-breh* _____?

I would like to book passage on _____ to _____.
Quisiera reservar pasaje el _____ hasta _____.
kee-SYEH-*rah rreh-sehr*-BAHR *pah*-SAH-*heh ehl* _____
AHSS-*tah* _____.

Bookstore

Where is there a bookstore?
¿Dónde hay una librería?
DOHN-*deh ahy* OO-*nah lee-breh*-REE-*ah?*

Border

How far is it to the border?
¿A qué distancia está la frontera?
*ah keh deess-*TAHN-*syah ehss-*TAH *lah frohn-*TEH-*rah?*

When do we arrive at the border?
¿Cuándo llegamos a la frontera?
KWAHN-*doh yeh-*GAH-*mohss ah lah frohn-*TEH-*rah?*

Borrow

May I borrow _____?
¿Puede prestarme _____?
PWEH-*theh prehss-*TAHR-*meh* _____?

Boss

Where is the boss?
¿Dónde está el jefe?
DOHN-*deh ehss-*TAH *ehl* HEH-*feh?*

Both

I want (I like) both.
Quiero (me gustan) ambos.
KYEH-*roh (meh* GOOSS-*tahn)* AHM-*bohss.*

Bother

Stop bothering me.
No me fastidie más.
*noh meh fahss-*TEE-*thyeh* MAHSS.

They are (he is) bothering me.
Me están (está) molestando.
*meh ehss-*TAHN *(ehss-*TAH) *moh-lehss-*TAHN-*doh.*

Bottle — see Wine

Brand

Is this a good brand?
¿Es una buena marca?
ehss OO-*nah* BWEH-*nah* MAHR-*kah?*

What is the best brand?
¿Cuál es la mejor marca?
*kwahl ehss lah meh-*HOHR MAHR-*kah?*

Break

The _____ is broken. (Please have it fixed.)

Se ha roto el (la) _____. (Por favor, arréglenlo.)

seh ah ROH-*toh ehl (la)* _____. *(pohr fah-*BOHR, *ah-*
RREH-*glehn-loh.)*

Breakfast

When is breakfast (lunch, dinner) served?

¿Cuándo se sirve el desayuno (el almuerzo, la cena)?

KWAHN-*doh seh* SEER-*beh ehl deh-sah-*YOO-*noh (ehl ahl-*
MWEHR-*soh, lah* SEH-*nah)?*

I want breakfast (lunch, dinner) in my room.

Quisiera tomar el desayuno (el almuerzo, la cena) en
mi habitación.

*kee-*SYEH-*rah toh-*MAHR *ehl deh-sah-*YOO-*noh (ehl ahl-*
MWEHR-*soh, lah* SEH-*nah) ehn mee ah-bee-tah-*SYOHN.

Is breakfast included?

¿Está incluído el desayuno?

*ehss-*TAH *een-kloo-*EE-*thoh ehl deh-sah-*YOO-*noh?*

Bring

Please bring a _____.

Haga el favor de traer un (una) _____.

AH-*gah ehl fah-*BOHR *deh trah-*EHR *oon (*OO-*nah)* _____.

I did not bring a _____.

No traje un (una) _____.

noh TRAH-*heh oon (*OO-*nah* _____).

Building

What is that building?

¿Qué es ese edificio?

keh ehss EHSS-*eh eh-thee-*FEE-*syoh?*

Bus

When does the bus leave for _____?

¿Cuándo sale el autobús para _____?

KWAHN-*doh* SAH-*leh ehl ow-toh-*BOOSS *pah-rah* _____?

How much is the bus fare?

¿Cuánto cuesta el pasaje del autobús?

KWAHN-*toh* KWEHSS-*tah ehl pah-*SAH-*heh dehl ow-toh-*
BOOSS?

Where is the bus stop (station)?
¿Dónde está la parada (estación) del autobús?
DOHN-*deh ehss*-TAH *lah pah*-RAH-*thah (ehss-tah*-SYOHN)
dehl ow-toh-BOOSS

Which bus goes to _____?
¿Qué autobús va a _____?
keh ow-toh-BOOSS *bah ah* _____?

Business

I am here on business.
Estoy aquí de negocios.
ehss-TOY *ah*-KEE *deh neh*-GOH-*syohss*.

Where is the business district?
¿Dónde está el centro comercial?
DOHN-*deh ehss*-TAH *ehl* SEHN-*troh koh-mehr*-SYAHL?

Busy

I am busy.
Estoy ocupado (ocupada).
ehss-TOY *oh-koo*-PAH-*thoh (oh-koo*-PAH-*thah)*.

Are you busy?
¿Está usted ocupado (ocupada)?
ehss-TAH *oo*-STEHTH *oh-koo*-PAH-*thah (oh-koo*-PAH-
thah)?

The line is busy.
La línea está ocupada.
lah LEE-*neh-ah ehss*-TAH *oh-koo*-PAH-*thah*.

Buy

Where can I buy _____?
¿Dónde puedo comprar _____?
DOHN-*deh* PWEH-*thoh kohm*-PRAHR _____?

I wish to buy _____.
Quisiera comprar _____.
kee-SYEH-*rah kohm*-PRAHR _____.

Cab – see Taxi

Cabin

Where is cabin number _____?
¿Dónde está el camarote número _____?
DOHN-*deh ehss*-TAH *ehl kah-mah*-ROH-*teh* NOO-*meh-roh*
_____?

Cablegram – see Telegram

Call

I want to put a call through to _____.
Quisiera hacer una llamada a _____.
kee-SYEH-rah ah-SEHR OO-nah yah-MAH-thah ah _____.

Please call me at _____.
Haga el favor de llamarme a las _____.
AH-*gah ehl fah*-BOHR *deh yah*-MAHR-*meh ah lahss*

_____.

How much is a call to _____?
¿Cuánto cuesta una llamada a _____?
KWAHN-*toh* KWEHSS-*tah* OO-*nah yah*-MAH-*thah ah*
_____?

What is this (that) called?
¿Cómo see llama esto (aquello)?
KOH-*moh seh* YAH-*mah* EHSS-*toh (ah*-KEH-*yoh)?*

Camera

Do you rent cameras?
¿Se puede alquilar cámaras fotográficas?
seh PWEH-*theh ahl-kee*-LAHR *ah-pah*-RAH-*tohss foh-toh-*
GRAH-*fee-kahss?*

I need film for this camera.
Necesito película para esta cámara.
neh-seh-SEE-*toh peh*-LEE-*koo-lah pah-rah* EHSS-*tah* KAH-
mah-rah.

Something is the matter with this camera.
Esta cámara tiene algo que no funciona.
EHSS-*tah* KAH-*mah-rah* TYEH-*neh* AHL-*goh keh noh foon-*
SYOH-*nah.*

Can you fix it?
¿Puede arreglarla?
PWEH-*theh ah-rreh*-GLAHR-*lah?*

Please direct me to a camera shop.
Haga el favor de indicarme dónde hay una tienda de
cámaras.
AH-*gah ehl fah*-BOHR *deh een-dee*-KAHR-*meh* DOHN-*deh*
OO-*nah* TYEHN-*dah deh* KAH-*mah-rahss.*

Camp

May we camp in your field?

¿Podemos acampar en su terreno?

poh-THEH-*mohss ah-kahm*-PAHR *ehn soo teh*-RREH-*noh?*

Is there a campsite nearby?

¿Hay un campamento cerca?

ahy oon kahm-pah-MEHN-*toh* SEHR-*kah?*

Can

Can you help me?

¿Puede ayudarme?

PWEH-*theh ah-yoo*-THAHR-*meh?*

Cancel

Please cancel my reservation.

Haga el favor de anular mi reserva.

AH-*gah ehl fah*-BOHR *deh ah-noo*-LAHR *mee rreh*-SEHR-
bah.

Is the flight cancelled?

¿Se ha anulado el vuelo?

seh ah ah-noo-LAH-*thoh ehl* BWEH-*loh?*

Candle

Do you have candles?

¿Tiene usted velas?

TYEH-*neh oo*-STEHTH BEH-*lahss?*

Car — see Automobile

Card, Calling

May I have your calling card?

¿Me puede dar una tarjeta de visita?

meh PWEH-*theh dahr* OO-*nah tahr*-HEH-*tah deh bee*-SEE-
tah?

Card, Post

I wish to buy some postcards.

Quisiera comprar tarjetas postales.

kee-SYEH-*rah kohm*-PRAHR *tahr*-HEH-*tahss pohss*-TAH-
lehss.

Careful

Please be careful.
Por favor, tenga cuidado.
*pohr fah-*BOHR, TEHN-*gah kwee-*THAH-*thoh.*

Please handle this with care.
Por favor, trate esto con cuidado.
*pohr fah-*BOHR, TRAH-*teh* EHSS-*toh kohn kwee-*THAH-
thoh.

Carry

Please carry this (my bags).
Haga el favor de llevar esto (mis maletas).
AH-*gah ehl fah-*BOHR *deh yeh-*BAHR EHSS-*toh (meess*
*mah-*LEH-*tahss).*

Cash

Can you cash this check?
¿Puede cambiar este cheque?
PWEH-*theh kahm-*BYAHR EHSS-*teh* CHEH-*keh?*

Cashier

Where is the cashier?
¿Dónde está el cajero?
DOHN-*deh ehss-*TAH *ehl kah-*HEH-*roh?*

Casino

Please direct me (take me) to a casino.
Por favor, diríjame (lléveme) a un casino.
*pohr fah-*BOHR, *dee-*REE-*hah-meh* (YEH-*beh-meh) ah*
*oon kah-*SEE-*noh.*

Castle

Are there tours of the castle?
¿Se organizan visitas al castillo?
*seh ohr-gah-*NEE-*sahn bee-*SEE-*tahss ahl kahss-*TEE-*yoh?*

Catalog

May I have one of your catalogs?
¿Podría darme uno de sus catálogos?
*poh-*THREE-*ah* DAHR-*meh* OO-*noh deh sooss kah-*TAH-
loh-gohss?

Catch

I have to catch a train.

Tengo que tomar el tren.

TEHN-*goh keh toh*-MAHR *ehl* TREHN.

Cathedral

Please take me (direct me) to the cathedral.

Por favor, lléveme (diríjame) a la catedral.

pohr fah-BOHR, YEH-*beh-meh (dee*-REE-*hah-meh) ah lah
    kah-teh-DRAHL.

Chamber of Commerce

Please direct me (take me) to the chamber of
    commerce.

Por favor, diríjame (lléveme) a la camara de comercio.

pohr fah-BOHR, *dee*-REE-*hah-meh* (YEH-*beh-meh) ah lah
    KAH-*mah-rah deh koh*-MEHR-*syoh*.

Change

Can you change this?

¿Me puede cambiar esto?

meh PWEH-*theh kahm*-BYAHR EHSS-*toh?*

May I have some change?

¿Puede darme cambio?

PWEH-*theh* DAHR-*meh* KAHM-*byoh?*

Please change the sheets today.

Por favor, cambie las sábanas hoy.

pohr fah-BOHR, KAHM-*byeh lahss* SAH-*bah-nahss oy.*

Where must I change for _____?

¿Dónde debo cambiar para ir a _____?

DOHN-*deh* DEH-*boh kahm*-BYAHR *pah-rah eer ah* _____?

Chapel – see Church

Charge

Why do you charge for this?

¿Por qué me ha cobrado esto?

pohr KEH *meh ah koh*-BRAH-*thoh* EHSS-*toh?*

Is there a service charge?

¿Se cobra el servicio?

seh KOH-*brah ehl sehr*-BEE-*syoh?*

What is the admission charge?
¿Cuánto cuesta la entrada?
KWAHN-*toh* KWEHSS-*tah lah ehn*-TRAH-*thah?*

What is the charge per (minute, hour, day, week,
    kilogram, kilometer)?
¿Cuánto cuesta por (minuto, hora, día, semana,
    kilógramo, kilómetro)?
KWAHN-*toh* KWEHSS-*tah pohr (mee*-NOO-*toh,* OH-*rah,*
    DEE-*ah, seh*-MAH-*nah, kee*-LOH-*grah-moh, kee*-LOH-
    meh-troh)?

Cheap
I would prefer something cheaper.
Preferiría algo mas barato.
preh-fehr-eer-EE-*ah* AHL-*goh mahss bah*-RAH-*toh.*

Check
The check, please.
La cuenta, por favor.
lah KWEHN-*tah, pohr fah*-BOHR.

Will you cash a check?
Le ruego que me cambie un cheque.
leh RRWEH-*goh keh meh* KAHM-*byeh oon* CHEH-*keh.*

Here is the check for my baggage.
Aquí está el comprobante de mi equipaje.
ah-KEE *ehss*-TAH *ehl kohm-proh*-BAHN-*teh deh mee eh-
    kee*-PAH-*heh.*

Would you accept a travelers check?
¿Aceptaría un cheque de viajero?
ah-sehp-tah-REE-*ah oon* CHEH-*keh deh byah*-HEH-*roh?*

Checkout
What is the checkout time?
¿A qué hora se debe salir (del hotel)?
ah keh OH-*rah seh* DEH-*beh sah*-LEER *(dehl oh*-TEHL)?

Child
Are children allowed?
¿Se permiten niños?
seh pehr-MEE-*tehn* NEE-*nyohss?*

Chilly — see cold

Christian

Are you a Christian?
¿Es usted cristiano?
ehss oo-STEHTH *kreess-*TYAH*-noh?*

I am a Christian.
Soy cristiano.
*soy kreess-*TYAH*-noh.*

Church

I would like to attend church services.
Quisiera asistir a un servicio religioso.
*kee-*SYEH*-rah ah-sees-*TEER *ah oon sehr-*BEE*-syoh rreh-
lee-*HYOH*-soh.*

When are church services held?
¿Cuándo se celebran los servicios religiosos?
KWAHN*-doh seh seh-*LEH*-brahn lohss sehr-*BEE*-syohss
rreh-lee-*HYOH*-sohss?*

Cigarette

A pack of cigarettes, please.
Un paquete de cigarrillos, por favor.
*oon pah-*KEH*-teh deh see-gah-*RREE*-yohss, pohr fah-*
BOHR.

Citizen

Are you a citizen of _____?
¿Es usted ciudadano de _____?
ehss oo-STEHTH *syoo-thah-*THAH*-noh deh* _____?

I am a citizen of the United States.
Soy ciudadano de los Estados Unidos.
*soy syoo-thah-*THAH*-noh deh lohss ehss-*TAH*-thoss oo-
NEE-thohss.*

Clean

This is not clean.
Esto no está limpio.
EHSS*-toh noh ehss-*TAH LEEM*-pyoh.*

I want this cleaned.
Quiero que limpien esto.
KYEH*-roh keh* LEEM*-pyehn* EHSS*-toh.*

Clerk

I wish to speak to the room clerk.
Quisiera hablar con el encargado de la habitación.
kee-SYEH-*rah ah*-BLAHR *kohn ehl ehn-kahr*-GAH-*thoh deh lah ah-bee-tah*-SYOHN.

Climate — see Weather

Climb

Can one climb at this time of year?
¿Se puede escalar en esta época del año?
seh PWEH-*theh ehss-kah*-LAHR *ehn* EHSS-*tah* EH-*poh-kah dehl* AH-*nyoh?*

How long does it take to climb _____?
¿Cuánto tiempo se tarda en escalar _____?
KWAHN-*toh* TYEHM-*poh seh* TAHR-*thah ehn ehss-kah*-LAHR_____?

I cannot climb stairs.
No puedo subir las escaleras.
noh PWEH-*thoh soo*-BEER *lahss ehss-kah*-LEH-*rahss.*

Close

Are you closed? (When do you open?)
¿Está cerrado? (¿Cuándo se abre?)
ehss-TAH *seh*-RRAH-*thoh?* (KWAHN-*doh seh* AH-*breh?*)

When does it close (open)?
¿Cuándo cierran (abren)?
KWAHN-*doh* SYEH-*rrahn(*AH-*brehn)?*

Close the door (the window), please.
Cierre la puerta (la ventana), por favor.
SYEH-*rreh lah* PWEHR-*tah (lah behn*-TAH-*nah), pohr fah*-BOHR.

Clothing

What kind of clothing should be worn?
¿Qué tipo de ropa se debe llevar?
keh TEE-*poh deh* RROH-*pah seh* DEH-*beh yeh*-BAHR?

Can you recommend a good clothing store?
¿Puede recomendarme un buen almacén de ropa?
PWEH-*theh rreh-koh-mehn*-DAHR-*meh oon bwehn ahl-mah*-SEHN *deh* RROH-*pah?*

Coach

Are there any coach seats available?

¿Hay algún asiento disponible en el autocar?

ahy ahl-GOON *ah*-SYEHN-*toh deess-poh*-NEE-*bleh ehn ehl ow-toh*-KAHR?

Coast

How far is the coast from here?

¿A qué distancia está la costa?

ah keh deess-TAHN-*syah ehss*-TAH *lah* KOHSS-*tah?*

How long does it take to reach the coast?

¿Cuánto tiempo se tarda en llegar a la costa?

KWAHN-*toh* TYEHM-*poh seh* TAHR-*thah ehn yeh*-GAHR *ah lah* KOHSS-*tah?*

Coat

Should I wear a coat (coat and tie)?

¿Debo llevar abrigo (chaqueta y corbata)?

DEH-*boh yeh*-BAHR *ah*-BREE-*goh (chah*-KEH-*tah ee kohr*-BAH-*tah)?*

Cocktail

Do you serve cocktails?

¿Se sirven cocteles?

seh SEER-*behn kohk*-TEH-*lehss?*

Would you like a cocktail?

¿Le gustaría un coctel?

leh gooss-tah-REE-*ah oon kohk*-TEHL?

Cold

This is cold.

Esto está frío.

EHSS-*toh ehss*-TAH FREE-*oh.*

I am cold.

Tengo frío.

TEHN-*goh* FREE-*oh.*

Color

I do not like the color.

No me gusta el color.

noh meh GOOSS-*tah ehl koh*-LOHR.

Do you have other colors?
¿Tiene usted otros colores?
TYEH-*neh* oo-STEHTH OH-*trohss koh-*LOH-*rehss?*

Do you have a brighter (darker) color?
¿Tiene usted un color más vivo (más oscuro)?
TYEH-*neh* oo-STEHTH *oon koh-*LOHR *mahss* BEE-*boh*
  (*mahss ohss-*KOO-*roh*)?

Come
Please come back later.
Por favor, vuelva más tarde.
*pohr fah-*BOHR, BWEHL-*bah mahss* TAHR-*theh.*

Come here, please.
Venga aquí, por favor.
BEHN-*gah ah-*KEE, *pohr fah-*BOHR.

Come in.
Entre.
EHN-*treh.*

Companion
I am traveling with a companion.
Estoy viajando con un compañero.
*ehss-*TOY *byah-*HAHN-*doh kohn oon kohm-pah-*NYEH-*roh.*

Have you seen my companion?
¿Ha visto usted a mi compañero?
ha BEESS-*toh* oo-STEHTH *ah mee kohm-pah-*NYEH-*roh?*

Company
I am traveling on company business.
Estoy en viaje de negocios por cuenta de la compañía.
*ehss-*TOY *ehn* BYAH-*heh deh neh-*GOH-*syohss pohr*
  KWEHN-*tah deh lah kohm-pah-*NYEE-*ah.*

What company are you with?
¿Con qué compañía trabaja?
*kohn keh kohm-pah-*NYEE-*ah trah-*BAH-*hah?*

Compartment
I would like a compartment.
Quisiera un compartimiento.
*kee-*SYEH-*rah oon kohm-pahr-tee-*MYEHN-*toh.*

Complain

I have a complaint.

Tengo una queja.

TEHN-*goh* OO-*nah* KEH-*hah*.

Confirm

Can you confirm my reservation on flight number
_____?

¿Me puede usted confirmar mi reserva en el vuelo
número _____?

meh PWEH-*theh* oo-STEHTH *kohn-feer-*MAHR *mee rreh-*
SEHR-*bah ehn ehl* BWEH-*loh* NOO-*meh-roh* _____?

Consulate

Please direct me to the U.S. consulate (embassy).

Haga el favor de dirigirme al consulado (a la
embajada) de los Estados Unidos.

AH-*geh ehl fah-*BOHR *deh dee-ree-*HEER-*meh ahl kohn-*
*soo-*LAH-*thoh (ah lah ehm-bah-*HAH-*thah) deh lohss*
*ehss-*TAH-*thohss* oo-NEE-*thohss*.

Contents

What are the contents (ingredients) of this dish?

¿Cuáles son los ingredientes de este plato?

KWAH-*lehss sohn lohss een-greh-*THYEHN-*tehss deh* EHSS-
teh PLAH-*toh*?

Convention

I am attending a convention.

Estoy asistiendo a un congreso.

*ehss-*TOY *ah-seess-*TYEHN-*doh ah oon kohn-*GREH-*soh*.

Cook

Can you recommend a good cook?

¿Puede recomendarme una buena cocinera?

PWEH-*theh rreh-koh-mehn-*DAHR-*meh* OO-*nah* BWEH-
*nah koh-see-*NEH-*rah*?

I want it thoroughly cooked.

Lo quiero muy bien cocido.

loh KYEH-*roh mwee byehn koh-*SEE-*thoh*.

Must this be cooked before being eaten?
¿Hay que cocinar esto antes de comerlo?
ahy keh koh-see-NAHR EHSS-toh AHN-tehss deh koh-MEHR-loh?

Correct
That is (not) correct.
Eso (no) es exacto.
eh-soh (noh) ehss ehg-SAHK-toh.

Correspond
I would like to correspond with you.
Quisiera mantener correspondencia con usted.
kee-SYEH-rah mahn-teh-NEHR koh-rrehss-pohn-DEHN-syah kohn oo-STEHTH.

May I have your address?
¿Me puede dar su dirección?
meh PWEH-theh dahr soo dee-rehk-SYOHN?

Cost
How much does it cost (per liter, per kilogram)?
¿Cuánto cuesta (por litro, por kilógramo)?
KWAHN-toh KWEHSS-tah (pohr LEE-troh, pohr kee-LOH-grah-moh)?

It costs too much.
Cuesta demasiado.
KWEHSS-tah deh-mah-SYAH-thoh.

Costly
It is too costly.
Es demasiado caro.
ehss deh-mah-SYAH-doh KAH-roh.

Costume
Where do the people wear native costume?
¿Dónde lleva la gente trajes nacionales?
DOHN-deh YEH-bah lah HEHN-teh TRAH-hehss nah-syoh-NAH-lehss?

Cot – see Bed

Cotton

Do you have any made of cotton?

¿Tiene alguno hecho de algodón?

TYEH-*neh* ahl-GOO-*noh* EH-*choh deh* ahl-goh-THOHN?

Country

What country are you from?

¿De qué país viene usted?

*deh keh pah-*EESS BYEH-*neh* oo-STEHTH?

Can this be taken out of country?

¿Se puede sacar esto del país?

seh PWEH-*theh sah-*KAHR EHSS-*toh dehl pah-*EESS?

Credit Card

What credit cards do you honor?

¿Qué tarjetas de credito acceptan ustedes?

*keh tahr-*HEH-*tahss deh* KREH-*thee-toh* ah-SEHP-*tahn*
oo-STEH-*thehss?*

Cup

Please bring me another cup(ful).

Por favor, tráigame otra taza (llena).

*pohr fah-*BOHR, TRAH-*ee-gah-meh* OH-*trah* TAH-
*sah (*YEH-*nah).*

Currency

Do you accept U.S. currency?

¿Aceptan ustedes dinero de los Estados Unidos?

ah-SEHP-*tahn* oo-STEH-*thehss* dee-NEH-*roh deh lohss*
ehss-TAH-*thohss* oo-NEE-*thohss?*

Where can I exchange currency?

¿Dónde puedo cambiar dinero?

DOHN-*deh* PWEH-*thoh kahm-*BYAHR *dee-*NEH-*roh?*

Current - see also Electricity

Are there any dangerous currents here?

¿Hay alguna corriente peligrosa aquí?

*ahy ahl-*GOO-*nah koh-*RRYEHN-*teh peh-lee-*GROH-*sah*
*ah-*KEE?

Customhouse

Where is the customhouse?

¿Dónde está la aduana?

DOHN-*deh ehss-*TAH *lah ah-*THWAH-*nah?*

Customs

Where is the customs office?
¿Dónde está la oficina de aduanas?
DOHN-*deh ehss*-TAH *lah oh-fee*-SEE-*nah deh ah*-THWAH-*nahss?*

Do we have to go through customs?
¿Tenemos que pasar la aduana?
teh-NEH-*mohss keh pah*-SAHR *lah ah*-THWAH-*nah?*

Cut – see Accident

Cycle – see also Bicycle, Hostel

We are (I am) cycling to _____.
Vamos (voy) en bicicleta a _____.
BAH-*mohss (boy) ehn bee-see*-KLEH-*tah ah* _____.

How long does it take to cycle to _____?
¿Cuánto tiempo se tarda en llegar en bicicleta a _____?
KWAHN-*toh* TYEHM-*poh seh* TAHR-*thah ehn yeh*-GAHR
ehn bee-see-KLEH-*tah ah* _____?

Are there accommodations for cyclists along the way?
¿Hay alojamiento para ciclistas en el camino?
ahy ah-loh-hah-MYEHN-*toh pah-rah see*-KLEESS-*tahss
ehn ehl kah*-MEE-*noh?*

Dance

May I have this dance?
¿Me hace usted el honor de bailar conmigo?
meh AH-*seh oo*-STEHTH *ehl oh*-NOHR *deh bah-ee*-LAHR
kohn-MEE-*goh?*

Where can we go to dance?
¿Dónde podemos ir a bailar?
DOHN-*deh poh*-THEH-*mohss eer ah bah-ee*-LAHR?

Dangerous

Is it dangerous?
¿Es peligroso?
ehss peh-lee-GROH-*soh?*

Date

What is the date today?
¿A qué fecha estamos hoy?
ah keh FEH-*chah ehss*-TAH-*mohss oy?*

Do you have a date?
¿Tiene usted una cita?
TYEH-*neh* *oo*-STEHTH OO-*nah* SEE-*tah?*

Day

What is the rate per day?
¿Cuál es la tarifa diaria?
*kwahl ehss lah tah-*REE-*fah* DYAH-*ryah?*

Declare

I have nothing to declare.
No tengo nada que declarar.
noh TEHN-*goh* NAH-*thah keh deh-klah-*RAHR.

Deep

Is it very deep?
¿Es muy profundo?
*ehss mwee proh-*FOON-*doh?*

How deep is it?
¿Qué profundidad tiene?
*keh proh-foon-dee-*THAHTH TYEH-*neh?*

Delay

Has there been a delay?
¿Ha habido algún retraso?
*ah ah-*BEE-*thoh ahl-*GOON *rreh-*TRAH-*soh?*

Will there be a delay?
¿Habrá retraso?
*ah-*BRAH *rreh-*TRAH-*soh?*

Deliver

Please deliver this to this address.
Por favor, entregue esto a esta dirección.
*pohr fah-*BOHR, *ehn-*TREH-*geh* EHSS-*toh ah* EHSS-*tah dee-rehk-*SYOHN.

Dentist

Can you recommend a good (English-speaking) dentist?
¿Puede usted recomendarme un buen dentista (de habla inglesa)?
PWEH-*theh oo-*STEHTH *rreh-koh-mehn-*DAHR-*meh oon bwehn dehn-*TEESS-*tah (deh* AH-*blah een-*GLEH-*sah)?*

Can you give me an appointment as soon as possible?
¿Podría verme lo más pronto posible?
poh-THREE-*ah* BEHR-*meh loh mahss* PROHN-*toh poh*-SEE-
bleh?

I (don't) have an appointment.
(No) tengo una cita con el dentista.
(noh) TEHN-*goh* OO-*nah* SEE-*tah kohn ehl dehn*-TEESS-
tah.

I have a terrible toothache.
Me duelen mucho las muelas.
meh DWEH-*lehn* MOO-*choh lahss* MWEH-*lahss.*

I have lost a filling.
He perdido un empaste.
eh pehr-THEE-*thoh oon ehm*-PAHSS-*teh.*

The filling is loose.
El empaste está flojo.
ehl ehm-PAHSS-*teh ehss*-TAH FLOH-*hoh.*

Can you put in a temporary filling?
¿Me puede poner un empaste temporal?
meh PWEH-*theh poh*-NEHR *oon ehm*-PAHSS-*teh tehm-*
poh-RAHL?

Please don't pull it unless it is absolutely necessary.
Por favor, no lo extraiga si no es absolutamente
necesario.
pohr fah-BOHR, *noh loh ehss*-TRAH-*ee-gah see noh ehss*
ahb-soh-loo-tah-MEHN-*teh neh-seh*-SAH-*ryoh.*

Please (don't) use novocaine.
Por favor, (no) use novocaína.
pohr fah-BOHR, *(noh)* OO-*seh noh-boh-kah*-EE-*nah.*

When can you give me another appointment?
¿Cuándo puedo verle de nuevo?
KWAHN-*doh* PWEH-*thoh* BEHR-*leh deh* NWEH-*boh?*

Deposit
Is a deposit required?
¿Se exige fianza?
seh ehg-SEE-*heh* FYAHN-*sah?*

How much deposit is required?
¿Cuánto se pide de fianza?
KWAHN-*toh seh* PEE-*theh deh* FYAHN-*sah?*

Dessert

What do you have for dessert?
¿Qué tiene para postre?
keh TYEH-*neh pah-rah* POHSS-*treh?*

Is dessert included?
¿Se incluye el postre?
*seh een-*KLOO-*yeh ehl* POHSS-*treh?*

Dining Car

Where is the dining car?
¿Dónde está el comedor?
DOHN-*deh ehss-*TAH *ehl koh-meh-*THOR?

Does the train have a dining car?
¿Tiene el tren comedor?
TYEH-*neh ehl* TREHN *koh-meh-*THOR?

Dining Room

Where is the dining room?
¿Dónde está el comedor?
DOHN-*deh ehss-*TAH *ehl koh-meh-*THOR?

Dinner

When is dinner served?
¿Cuándo se sirve la cena?
KWAHN-*doh seh* SEER-*beh lah* SEH-*nah?*

Will you have dinner with me?
¿Quiere cenar conmigo?
KYEH-*reh seh-*NAHR *kohn-*MEE-*goh?*

Direct

What is the most direct route to _____?
¿Cuál es el camino más directo a _____?
*kwahl ehss ehl kah-*MEE-*noh mahss dee-*REHK-*toh ah*
_____?

Please direct me to _____.
Por favor, diríjame a _____.
*pohr fah-*BOHR, *dee-*REE-*hah-meh ah* _____.

Direction

In which direction is _____?

¿En qué dirección está _____?

ehn keh dee-rehk-SYOHN ehss-TAH _____?

Dirty

This is dirty. (Please bring me another.)

Esto está sucio. (Por favor, tráigame otro.)

EHSS-*toh ehss*-TAH SOO-*syoh. (pohr fah*-BOHR, TRAH-*ee-gah-meh* OH-*troh.)*

Discount

Is there a discount for students?

¿Hay descuento para estudiantes?

ahy dehss-KWEHN-*toh pah-rah ehss-too*-THYAHN-*tehss?*

Dish

What is in this dish?

¿Qué hay en este plato?

keh ahy ehn EHSS-*teh* PLAH-*toh?*

Which dish do you recommend?

¿Qué plato me recomienda?

keh PLAH-*toh meh rreh-koh*-MYEHN-*dah?*

Is this dish served hot or cold?

¿Se sirve este plato caliente o frío?

seh SEER-*beh* EHSS-*teh* PLAH-*toh kah*-YEHN-*teh oh* FREE-*oh?*

Disinfected

Please have this disinfected.

Por favor, desinfecte esto.

pohr fah-BOHR, *deh-seen*-FEHK-*teh* EHSS-*toh.*

Distance

What is the distance to _____?

¿A qué distancia está _____?

ah keh deess-TAHN-*syah ehss*-TAH _____?*

District

Please take me to the _____ district.

Por favor, lléveme al distrito _____.

pohr fah-BOHR, YEH-*beh-meh ahl dee*-STREE-*toh* _____.

Disturb

Please do not disturb me until _____.
Por favor, no me moleste hasta _____.
*pohr fah-*BOHR, *noh meh moh-*LEHSS-*teh* AHSS-*tah*
_____.

He is disturbing me.
Me está molestando.
*meh ehss-*TAH *moh-lehss-*TAHN-*doh.*

Divorced

I am divorced (about to be divorced).
Estoy divorciado (a punto de divorciarme).
*ehss-*TOY *dee-bohr-*SYAH-*thoh (ah* POON-*toh deh dee-
bohr-*SYAHR-*meh).*

Dock

When will the ship dock?
¿Cuándo llegará el barco (al muelle)?
KWAHN-*doh yeh-gah-*RAH *ehl* BAHR-*koh (ahl* MWEH-
yeh)?

Is our baggage on the dock?
¿Está nuestro equipaje en el muelle?
*ehss-*TAH NWEHSS-*troh eh-kee-*PAH-*heh ehn ehl* MWEH-
yeh?

Doctor — see also Accident, Medical

Can you recommend a good doctor?
¿Puede recomendarme un buen doctor?
PWEH-*theh rreh-koh-mehn-*DAHR-*meh oon bwehn dohk-*
TOHR?

I would like to see the doctor (dentist).
Quisiera ver al doctor (dentista).
*kee-*SYEH-*rah behr ahl dohk-*TOHR *(dehn-*TEESS-*tah).*

Send for a doctor.
Llame a un doctor.
YAH-*meh ah oon dohk-*TOHR.

Dog

Are dogs allowed?
¿See permiten perros?
*seh pehr-*MEE-*tehn* PEH-*rrohss?*

Dollar

How much (how many) can I get for a dollar?
¿Cuánto (cuántos) me darán por un dólar?
KWAHN-*toh* (KWAHN-*tohss*) *meh dah*-RAHN *pohr oon*
   DOH-*lahr?*

How many _____ can I exchange for one dollar?
¿Cuántos _____ me darán a cambio de un dólar?
KWAHN-*tohss* _____ *meh dah*-RAHN *ah* KAHM-*byoh deh*
   oon DOH-*lahr?*

Door

Please open (close) the door.
Por favor, abra (cierre) la puerta.
pohr fah-BOHR, AH-*brah* (SYEH-*rreh*) *lah* PWEHR-*tah.*

I cannot unlock (lock) my door.
No puedo abrir (cerrar con llave) la puerta.
noh PWEH-*thoh ah*-BREER *(seh*-RRAHR *kohn* YAH-*beh)*
   lah PWEHR-*tah.*

Double Bed

Do you have a room with a double bed?
¿Tiene una habitación con cama doble?
TYEH-*neh* OO-*nah ah-bee-tah*-SYON *kohn* KAH-*mah* DOH-
   bleh?

Dozen

How much is a dozen?
¿Cuánto cuesta una docena?
KWAHN-*toh* KWEHSS-*tah* OO-*nah doh*-SEH-*nah?*

I'll take a dozen.
Tomaré una docena.
toh-mah-REH OO-*nah doh*-SEH-*nah.*

Draft

There is a draft.
Hay una corriente de aire.
ahy OO-*nah koh*-RRYEHN-*teh deh* AH-*ee-reh.*

Dressed

I am not dressed.
No estoy vestido (vestida).
noh ehss-TOY *behss*-TEE-*thoh* (*behss*-TEE-*thah*).

Dresses

I wish to look at dresses.

Quiero ver vestidos.

KYEH-*roh behr behss*-TEE-*thohss.*

Dressing Room

Where is the men's (women's) dressing room?

¿Dónde está el tocador para cabelleros (señoras)?

DOHN-*deh ehss*-TAH *ehl toh-kah*-THOHR *pah-rah kah-bah*-YEH-*rohss (seh*-NYOH-*rahss)?*

Dressing (Salad)

Oil and vinegar; garlic; roquefort cheese.

Aceite y vinagre; ajo; queso roquefort.

ah-SAY-*teh ee bee*-NAH-*greh;* AH-*hoh;* KEH-*soh rohk*-FOHR.

Drink

Where can I get something to drink?

¿Dónde puedo tomar algo para beber?

DOHN-*deh* PWEH-*thoh toh*-MAHR AHL-*goh pah-rah beh*-BEHR*?*

What do you have to drink?

¿Qué tiene usted para beber?

keh TYEH-*neh oo*-STEHTH *pah-rah beh*-BEHR*?*

Would you like a drink?

¿Quiere una copita?

KYEH-*reh* OO-*nah koh*-PEE-*tah?*

Drive

Please drive me to _____.

Por favor, condúzcame a _____.

pohr fah-BOHR, *kohn*-DOOSS-*kah-meh ah* _____.

Please drive more carefully (drive slowly).

Por favor, conduzca con más cuidado (conduzca lentamente).

pohr fah-BOHR, *kohn*-DOOSS-*kah kohn mahss kwee*-THAH-*thoh (kohn*-DOOSS-*kah lehn-tah*-MEHN-*teh).*

Can you drive?

¿Sabe usted conducir?

SAH-*beh oo*-STEHTH *kohn-doo*-SEER*?*

Driver

I want to hire a driver.

Quiero contratar un chófer.

KYEH-*roh kohn-trah-*TAHR *oon* CHOH-*fehr.*

Driver's License

I have (I do not have) an international driver's license.

Tengo (no tengo) un carnet de conducir (carnet de manejar) internacional.

TEHN-*goh (noh* TEHN-*goh) oon kahr-*NEH *deh kohn-doo-*SEER *(kahr-*NEH *deh mah-neh-*HAHR) *een-tehr-nah-syoh-*NAHL.

Drugstore

Please direct me (take me) to a drugstore.

Por favor, diríjame (lléveme) a la farmacia.

*pohr fah-*BOHR, *dee-*REE-*hah-meh (*YEH-*beh-meh) ah lah fahr-*MAH-*syah.*

Dry Clean — see Laundry

Duty

Must I pay duty on this?

¿Debo pagar un impuesto sobre esto?

DEH-*boh pah-*GAHR *oon* eem-PWEHSS *toh* SOH-*breh* EHSS-*toh?*

What is the duty on this?

¿Cuál es el impuesto sobre esto?

kwahl ehss ehl eem-PWEHSS-*toh* SOH-*breh* EHSS-*toh?*

Early

It is too early.

Es demasiado temprano.

*ehss deh-mah-*SYAH-*thoh tehm-*PRAH-*noh.*

Have we come too early?

¿Hemos llegado demasiado temprano?

EH-*mohss yeh-*GAH-*thoh deh-mah-*SYAH-*thoh tehm-*PRAH-*noh?*

Eat

What do you have to eat?

¿Qué tiene usted para comer?

keh TYEH-*neh oo-*STEHTH *pah-rah koh-*MEHR?

Where can I get something to eat?
¿Dónde me pueden dar algo de comer?
DOHN-*deh meh* PWEH-*thehn dahr* AHL-*goh deh koh-*MEHR?

Do you want to eat now?
¿Quiere usted comer ahora?
KYEH-*reh* oo-STEHTH *koh-*MEHR *ah-*OH-*rah?*

Either
Either one will do.
Cualquiera de los dos es suficiente.
*kwahl-*KYEH-*rah deh lohss dohss ehss soo-fee-*SYEHN-*teh.*

Electricity
Is there an electrical outlet here?
¿Hay un enchufe electrico aquí?
*ahy oon ehn-*CHOO-*feh eh-*LEHK-*tree-koh ah-*KEE?

Elevator
Is there an elevator here?
¿Hay un ascensor aquí?
*ahy oon ahss-sehn-*SOHR *ah-*KEE?

Embassy – see Consulate

Emergency
This is an emergency.
Se trata de una emergencia.
seh TRAH-*tah deh* OO-*nah eh-mehr-*HEHN-*syah.*

Engaged (busy)
I am engaged.
Estoy ocupado (ocupada).
*ehss-*TOY *oh-koo-*PAH-*thoh (oh-koo-*PAH-*thah).*

Engaged (to be married)
I am engaged to be married.
Estoy comprometido (comprometida) a casarme.
*ehss-*TOY *kohm-proh-meh-*TEE-*toh (kohm-proh-meh-*TEE-*thah) ah kah-*SAHR-*meh.*

English
Do you speak English?
¿Sabe usted hablar inglés?
SAH-*beh* oo-STEHTH *ah-*BLAHR *een-*GLEHSS?

I need an English-speaking guide.
Necesito un guía de habla inglesa.
neh-seh-SEE-toh oon GHEE-ah deh AH-blah een-GLEH-sah.

I speak only English.
Solamente hablo inglés.
soh-lah-MEHN-teh AH-bloh een-GLEHSS.

Is there a church service in English?
¿Se celebra algún servicio religioso en inglés?
seh seh-LEH-brah ahl-GOON sehr-BEE-syoh rreh-lee-HYOH-soh ehn een-GLEHSS?

Enough

That is enough.
Eso es bastante.
EH-soh ehss bahss-TAHN-teh.

Is that enough?
¿Es eso bastante?
ehss EH-soh bahss-TAHN-teh?

It isn't hot enough.
No está suficientemente caliente.
noh ehss-TAH soo-fee-SYEHN-teh-mehn-teh kah-YEHN-teh.

I've had enough, thank you.
Ya no puedo más, gracias.
yeh noh PWEH-thoh mahss, GRAH-syahss.

I do not have enough money with me.
No tengo bastante dinero conmigo.
noh TEHN-goh bahss-TAHN-teh dee-NEH-roh kohn-MEE-goh.

Entrance

Where is the entrance to _____?
¿Dónde está la entrada de _____?
DOHN-deh ehss-TAH lah ehn-TRAH-thah deh _____?

Envelope

May I have an envelope.
¿Me puede dar un sobre?
meh PWEH-theh dahr oon SOH-breh?

Equipment

Do you rent equipment for _____?

¿Alquila usted equipo para _____?

ahl-KEE-*lah* oo-STEHTH *eh*-KEE-*poh pah-rah* _____?

Error

I think that there is an error here.

Creo que hay un error aquí.

KREH-*oh keh ahy oon eh*-RROHR *ah*-KEE.

Escort

May I escort you home?

¿Puedo acompañarle a casa?

PWEH-*thoh ah-kohm-pah*-NYAHR-*leh ah* KAH-*sah?*

Evening

See you this evening.

Hasta esta tarde.

AHSS-*tah* EHSS-*tah* TAHR-*theh.*

Excess

What is the rate for excess baggage?

¿Cuánto cuesta el exceso de peso?

KWAHN-*toh* KWEHSS-*tah ehl ehss*-SEH-*soh deh* PEH-*soh?*

Is my baggage in excess of the weight allowance?

¿Tiene mi equipaje un exceso de peso?

TYEH-*neh mee eh-kee*-PAH-*heh ehss*-SEH-*soh deh* PEH-*soh?*

Exchange

What is the rate of exchange for the dollar?

¿Cuál es el tipo de cambio para el dólar?

KWAHL *ehss ehl* TEE-*poh deh* KAHM-*byoh pah-rah ehl* DOH-*lahr?*

Can I exchange this?

¿Puedo cambiar esto?

PWEH-*thoh kahm*-BYAHR EHSS-*toh?*

I would like to exchange these dollars for _____.

Quisiera cambiar estos dólares por _____.

kee-SYEH-*rah kahm*-BYAHR EHSS-*tohss* DOH-*lah-rehss pohr* _____.

Excursion

I would like to buy an excursion ticket.
Quisiera comprar un billete de excursión.
kee-SYEH-rah kohm-PRAHR oon bee-YEH-teh deh ehss-koor-SYOHN.

What is the schedule for the excursion boat?
¿Cuál es el horario para el barco de excursión?
kwahl ehss ehl oh-RAH-ryoh pah-rah ehl BAHR-koh deh ehss-koor-SYOHN?

How long does the excursion last?
¿Cuánto tiempo dura la excursión?
KWAHN-toh TYEHM-poh DOO-rah la ehss-koor-SYOHN?

Excuse

Excuse me!
¡Discúlpeme!
dees-KOOL-peh-meh!

Exit

Where is the exit?
¿Dónde está la salida?
DOHN-deh ehss-TAH lah sah-LEE-thah?

Expensive

It is too expensive.
Es demasiado caro.
ehss deh-mah-SYAH-thoh KAH-roh.

Do you have anything less expensive.
¿Tiene usted algo menos caro?
TYEH-neh oo-STEHTH AHL-goh MEH-nohss KAH-roh?

Express Train

Where do I catch the express train to _____?
¿Dónde tomo el tren expreso para _____?
DOHN-deh TOH-moh ehl TREHN ehss-PREH-soh pah-rah _____?

Is this the express train?
¿Es éste el tren expresso?
ehss EHSS-teh ehl TREHN ehss-PREH-soh?

Fade
Will this color fade?

Pierde esto su color?

PYEHR-*theh* EHSS-*toh soo koh*-LOHR?

Family
Do you have family rates?

¿Tiene tarifas familiares?

TYEH-*neh tah*-REE-*fahss fah-mee*-YAH-*rehss?*

Far
How far is it (to _____)?

¿Qué distancia hay (hasta _____)?

keh dees-TAHN-*syah ahy (*AHSS-*tah _____)?*

Fare
How much is the fare (to _____)?

¿Cuál es el precio de billete (hasta _____)?

kwahl ehss ehl PREH-*syoh deh bee*-YEH-*teh (*AHSS-*tah*
_____)?

Fast
Don't go so fast, please.

No vaya tan rapido, por favor.

noh BAH-*yah tahn* RRAH-*pee-thoh, pohr fah*-BOHR.

Fat
There is too much fat on this. (Take it back, please.)

Hay demasiado grasa en esto. (Lléveselo, por favor.)

ahy deh-mah-SYAH-*thoh* GRAH-*sah ehn* EHSS-*toh.*
  (YEH-*beh-seh-loh, pohr fah*-BOHR.)

Fee
What is your fee?

¿Qué honorario cobra usted?

keh oh-noh-RAH-*ryoh* KOH-*brah oo*-STEHTH?

What is the admission fee?

¿Cuánto cuesta la entrada?

KWAHN-*toh* KWEHSS-*tah lah ehn*-TRAH-*thah?*

Ferry
Is there a ferry service to _____?

¿Hay servicio de trasbordador hasta _____?

ahy sehr-BEE-*syoh deh trahss-bohr-thah*-THOHR AHSS-
  tah _____?

When does the ferry leave?

¿A qué hora sale el trasbordador?

ah keh OH-*rah* SAH-*leh ehl trahss-bohr-thah-*THOHR?

What is the fare for the ferry?

¿Cuánto cuesta el billete para el trasbordador?

KWAHN-*toh* KWEHSS-*tah ehl bee-*YEH-*teh pah-rah ehl*
*trahss-bohr-thah-*THOHR?

Fill

Please fill the glass (the bath, the tub, the cup, the
tank, the bottle).

Por favor, llene el vaso (el baño, la taza, el tanque, la
botella).

*pohr fah-*BOHR, YEH-*neh ehl* BAH-*soh (ehl* BAH-*nyoh, lah*
TAH-*sah, ehl* TAHN-*keh, lah boh-*TEH-*yah).*

Filling

I have lost a filling from my tooth.

Se me ha caído un empaste del diente.

*seh meh ah kah-*EE-*thoh oon ehm-*PAHSS-*teh dehl* DYEHN-
teh.

Film

Please develop this film.

Por favor, revele esta película.

*pohr fah-*BOHR, *rreh-*BEH-*leh* EHSS-*tah peh-*LEE-*koo-lah.*

When will the film be ready?

¿Cuándo estará lista la película?

KWAHN-*doh ehss-tah-*RAH LEES-*tah lah peh-*LEE-*koo-*
lah?

Do you have film for this camera?

¿Tiene película para esta cámara?

TYEH-*neh peh-*LEE-*koo-lah pah-rah* EHSS-*tah* KAH-*mah-*
rah?

Find

Please find my _____.

Por favor, búsqueme mi _____.

*pohr fah-*BOHR, BOOSS-*keh-meh mee* _____.

I cannot find my _____.
No puedo encontrar mi _____.
noh PWEH-*thoh ehn-kohn-*TRAHR *mee* _____.

Finish

Please wait until I finish.
Por favor, espere hasta que termine.
*pohr fah-*BOHR, *ehss-*PEH-*reh* AHSS-*tah keh tehr-*MEE-*neh.*

Have you finished?
¿Ha usted terminado?
*ah oo-*STEHTH *tehr-mee-*NAH-*thoh?*

Fire

Please light a fire in the fireplace.
Por favor, encienda el fuego en la chimenea.
*pohr fah-*BOHR, *ehn-*SYEHN-*dah ehl* FWEH-*goh ehn lah chee-meh-*NEH-*ah.*

The fire has gone out.
El fuego se ha apagado.
ehl FWEH-*goh seh ah ah-pah-*GAH-*thoh.*

Fishing

I would like to go fishing.
Me gustaría ir de pesca.
*meh gooss-tah-*REE-*ah eer deh* PEHSS-*kah.*

Where can I rent (buy) fishing gear?
¿Dónde puedo alquilar (comprar) equipo de pesca?
DOHN-*deh* PWEH-*thoh ahl-kee-*LAHR *(kohm-*PRAHR*) eh-*KEE-*poh deh* PEHSS-*kah?*

Fit – see also Shopping

It does not fit me.
No me viene bien.
noh meh BYEH-*neh byehn.*

Fix

Can fix it?
¿Lo puede arreglar?
loh PWEH-*theh ah-rreh-*GLAHR*?*

Flag
What flag is that?
¿Qué bandera es esa?
*keh bahn-*DEH-*rah ehss* EH-*sah?*

Flat (Tire) – see also Automobile
Can you fix a flat?
¿Puede arreglar un pinchazo?
PWEH-*theh ah-rreh-*GLAHR *oon peen-*CHAH-*soh?*

Please fix (help me fix) this flat.
Por favor, arregle (ayúdeme a arreglar) este pinchazo.
*pohr fah-*BOHR, *ah-*RREH-*gleh (ah-*YOO-*theh-meh ah ah-
rreh-*GLAHR*)* EHSS-*teh peen-*CHAH-*soh.*

Flight
When does the next flight leave for _____?
¿A qué hora sale el próximo vuelo a _____?
ah keh OH-*rah* SAH-*leh ehl* PROHK-*see-moh* BWEH-*loh ah
_____?*

Could I make a reservation on flight number _____ to
_____?
¿Podría hacer una reserva en el vuelo número _____ a
_____?
*poh-*THREE-*ah ah-*SEHR OO-*nah rreh-*SEHR-*bah ehn ehl*
BWEH-*loh* NOO-*meh-roh* _____ *ah* _____?

Are there any seats on flight number _____ to _____?
¿Hay algún asiento libre en el vuelo número _____ a
_____?
*ahy ahl-*GOON *ah-*SYEHN-*toh lee-breh ehn ehl* BWEH-*loh*
NOO-*meh-roh* _____ *ah* _____?

Is there a connecting flight for _____?
¿Hay vuelo de enlace a _____?
ahy BWEH-*loh deh ehn-*LAH-*seh ah* _____?

Is a meal served on this flight?
¿Se sirve comida en este vuelo?
seh SEER-*beh koh-*MEE-*thah ehn* EHSS-*teh* BWEH-*loh?*

Floor
On what floor is my room?
¿En qué piso está mi habitación?
ehn keh PEE-*soh ehss-*TAH *mee ah-bee-tah-*SYOHN?

I want to move to a higher (lower) floor.
Quisiera mudarme a un piso más alto (más bajo).
kee-SYEH-rah moo-THAHR-meh ah oon PEE-soh mahss AHL-toh (mahss BAH-hoh).

Floor show
When does the floor show start?
¿A qué hora empieza el espectaculo?
ah keh OH-rah ehm-PYEH-sah ehl ehss-pehk-TAH-koo-loh?

Food – see Meals

Forget
I forgot my money (key, passport).
He olvidado mi dinero (llave, pasaporte).
eh ohl-bee-THAH-thoh mee dee-NEH-roh (YAH-beh, pah-sah-POHR-teh).

I am sorry, I have forgotten your name.
Lo siento, me he olvidado de su nombre.
loh SYEHN-toh, meh eh ohl-bee-THAH-thoh deh soo NOHM-breh.

Fork
Please bring me another fork.
Por favor, tráigame otro tenedor.
pohr fah-BOHR, TRAH-ee-gah-meh OH-troh teh-neh-THOHR.

Forward
Please forward all mail to this address.
Por favor, expidame todo el correo a esta dirección.
pohr fah-BOHR, ehss-PEE-thah-meh TOH-thoh ehl koh-RREH-oh ah EHSS-tah dee-rehk-SYOHN.

Fragile
Handle this carefully, please; it is fragile.
Trate esto con cuidado, por favor; es fragil.
TRAH-teh EHSS-toh kohn kwee-THAH-thoh, pohr fah-BOHR; ehss FRAH-heel.

Free
Are you free now?
¿Está usted libre ahora?
ehss-TAH oo-STEHTH LEE-breh ah-OH-rah?

Will you be free this afternoon (tonight, tomorrow)?
¿Estará usted libre esta tarde (esta noche, mañana)?
*ehss-tah-*RAH *oo-*STEHTH *lee-breh* EHSS*-tah* TAHR*-theh*
(EHSS*-tah* NOH*-cheh, mah-*NYAH*-nah)?*

Is the admission free?
¿Es gratuita la entrada?
*ehss grah-*TWEE*-tah lah ehn-*TRAH*-thah?*

Is that table free?
¿Está libre esa mesa?
*ehss-*TAH LEE*-breh* EH*-sah* MEH*-sah?*

Fresh
Is this fresh?
¿Está fresco?
*ehss-*TAH FREHSS*-koh?*

Friend(s)
Have you seen my friends?
¿Ha visto usted a mis amigos?
ah BEESS*-toh oo-*STEHTH *ah meess ah-*MEE*-gohss?*

I am with a friend.
Estoy con un amigo.
*ehss-*TOY *kohn oon ah-*MEE*-goh.*

Front
I want to sit in front (farther front).
Quiero sentarme delante (más adelante).
KYEH*-roh sehn-*TAHR*-meh deh-*LAHN*-teh (mahss ah-theh-*LAHN*-teh).*

Furnished
I want a furnished apartment.
Deseo un apartamento amueblado.
*deh-*SEH*-oh oon ah-pahr-tah-*MEHN*-toh ah-mweh-*BLAH*-thoh.*

I want an unfurnished apartment.
Deseo un apartamento desamueblado.
*deh-*SEH*-oh oon ah-pahr-tah-*MEHN*-toh dehss-ah-mweh-*BLAH*-thoh.*

Is the linen furnished?

¿Se incluye la ropa de cama?

seh een-KLOO-yeh lah RROH-*pah deh* KAH-*mah?*

Gamble – see Casino

Game

Will you have a game with me?

¿Quiere jugar una partida conmigo?

KYEH-*reh hoo-*GAHR OO-*nah pahr-*TEE-*thah kohn-*MEE-*goh?*

Garage

Where is the nearest garage?

¿Dónde está el garage más próximo?

DOHN-*deh ehss-*TAH *ehl gah-*RAH-*heh mahss* PROHK-*see-moh?*

Does the hotel have a garage?

¿Tiene el hotel un garaje?

TYEH-*neh ehl oh-*TEHL *oon gah-*RAH-*heh?*

Garbage

Where do I dispose of the garbage?

¿Dónde se echa la basura?

DOHN-*deh seh* EH-*chah lah bah-*SOO-*rah?*

Will you please take care of the garbage?

¿Quiere hacer el favor de ocuparse de la basura?

KYEH-*reh ah-*SEHR *ehl fah-*BOHR *deh oh-koo-*PAHR-*seh deh lah bah-*SOO-*rah?*

Gardens

I would like to see the gardens.

Me gustaría ver los jardines.

*meh gooss-tah-*REE-*ah behr lohss hahr-*THEE-*nehss.*

Gas, Gasoline – see Automobile

Gate – see also Platform

What gate does it leave from?

¿De qué andén sale?

*deh keh ahn-*DEHN SAH-*leh?*

Where is gate number _____?

¿Dónde está el andén número _____?

DOHN-*deh ehss-*TAH *ehl ahn-*DEHN NOO-*meh-roh* _____?

Get

How do I get to _____?
¿Cómo se llega a _____?
KOH-*moh seh* YEH-*gah ah* _____?

Will you tell me where to get off?
¿Me puede indicar dónde debo bajarme?
meh PWEH-*theh een-dee*-KAHR DOHN-*deh* DEH-*boh bah-*
HAHR-*meh?*

Where can I get _____?
¿Dónde puedo conseguir _____?
DOHN-*deh* PWEH-*thoh kohn-seh*-GHEER _____?

Glass

Please bring me a glass of water (milk, wine).
Por favor, tráigame un vaso de agua (leche, vino).
pohr fah-BOHR, TRAH-*ee-gah-meh oon* BAH-*soh deh* AH-
*gwah (*LEH-*cheh,* BEE-*noh).*

Please bring me another glass.
Por favor, tráigame otro vaso.
pohr fah-BOHR, TRAH-*ee-gah-meh* OH-*troh* BAH-*soh.*

Glasses

I have lost my glasses.
He perdido los anteojos.
eh pehr-THEE-*thoh lohss ahn-teh*-OH-*hohss.*

Can you repair my glasses?
¿Puede arreglarme los anteojos?
PWEH-*theh ah-rreh*-GLAHR-*meh lohss ahn-teh*-OH-*hohss?*

Here is my prescription for eyeglasses.
Aquí tiene la receta para mis anteojos.
ah-KEE TYEH-*neh lah rreh*-SEH-*tah pah-rah meess ahn-*
teh-OH-*hohss.*

I do not have my eyeglasses prescription.
No tengo receta para mis anteojos.
noh TEHN-*goh rreh*-SEH-*tah pah-rah meess ahn-teh*-OH-
hohss.

Go

I want to go to _____.
Quiero ir a _____.
KYEH-*roh eer ah* _____.

How do I go to _____?
¿Cómo voy a _____?
KOH-*moh boy ah* _____?

I am going to _____.
Voy a _____.
boy ah _____.

Golf

Do you play golf?
¿Juega usted al golf?
HWEH-*gah oo*-STEHTH *ahl* GOHLF?

Where is the nearest golf course?
¿Dónde está el campo de golf más próximo?
DOHN-*deh ehss*-TAH *ehl* KAHM-*poh deh* GOHLF *mahss*
PROHK-*see-moh*?

Which is the best golf course?
¿Cuál es el mejor campo de golf?
kwahl ehss ehl meh-HOHR KAHM-*poh deh* GOHLF?

Good

It is (not) very good.
(No) es muy bueno.
(noh) ehss mwee BWEH-*noh*.

Goodbye

Goodbye.
Adiós.
ah-THYOHSS.

Good Evening

Good evening.
Buenas tardes.
BWEH-*nahss* TAHR-*thehss*.

Good Morning

Good Morning.
Buenos días.
BWEH-*nohss* DEE-*ahss*.

Good Night

Good night.
Buenas noches.
BWEH-*nahss* NOH-*chehss*.

Grateful

I am very grateful to you.
Se lo agradezco mucho.
*seh loh ah-grah-*THEHSS*-koh* MOO*-choh.*

Grocery Store

Where is a grocery store?
¿Dónde hay una tienda de comestibles?
DOHN*-deh ahy* OO*-nah* TYEHN*-dah deh koh-mehss-*TEE*-blehss?*

Guest

This lady (this gentleman) is my guest.
Esta señora (este caballero) es mi invitada (invitado).
EHSS*-tah seh-*NYOH*-rah* (EHSS*-teh kah-bah-*YEH*-roh) ehss mee een-bee-*TAH*-thah (een-bee-*TAH*-thoh).*

Will you be my guest?
¿Le gustaría ser mi invitado?
*leh gooss-tah-*REE*-ah sehr mee een-bee-*TAH*-thoh?*

Guide

Where can we get a guide?
¿Dónde podemos conseguir un guía?
DOHN*-deh poh-*THEH*-mohss kohn-seh-*GHEER *oon* GHEE*-ah?*

I want an English-speaking guide.
Quisiera un guía de habla inglesa.
*kee-*SYEH*-rah oon* GHEE*-ah deh* AH*-blah een-*GLEH*-sah.*

Guidebook

Do you sell guidebooks?
¿Vende usted guías?
BEHN*-deh oo-*STEHTH GHEE*-ahss?*

Hair – see also Barber, Beauty Parlor

Where can I get my hair cut?
¿Dónde me pueden cortar el pelo?
DOHN*-deh meh* PWEH*-thehn kohr-*TAHR *ehl* PEH*-loh?*

Hanger

Please bring me some hangers.
Por favor, tráigame algunas perchas.
*pohr fah-*BOHR, TRAH*-ee-gah-meh ahl-*GOO*-nahss* PEHR*-chahss.*

Happy
I am happy to meet you.
Tengo mucho gusto en conocerle.
TEHN-*goh* MOO-*choh* GOOSS-*toh ehn* koh-noh-SEHR-*leh.*

Harbor
Is swimming permitted in the harbor?
¿Se permite nadar en el puerto?
seh pehr-MEE-*teh* nah-THAHR *ehn ehl* PWEHR-*toh?*

Hat
Is this your hat?
¿Es suyo este sombrero?
ehss SOO-*yoh* EHSS-*teh* sohm-BREH-*roh?*

Have you seen my hat?
¿Ha visto usted mi sombrero?
ah BEESS-*toh* oo-STEHTH *mee* sohm-BREH-*roh?*

Have
Have you any _____?
¿Tiene usted algún(a) _____?
TYEH-*neh* oo-STEHTH *ahl-*GOON*(-ah)* _____?

Headwaiter
Please ask the headwaiter to come over here.
Por favor, diga al maitre que venga aquí.
*pohr fah-*BOHR, DEE-*gah ahl* MEH-*treh keh* BEHN-*gah ah-*KEE.

Health
My health has been poor.
He estado mal de salud.
eh ehss-TAH-*thoh mahl deh* sah-LOOTH.

How is your health?
¿Cómo está usted de salud?
KOH-*moh* ehss-TAH oo-STEHTH *deh* sah-LOOTH?

To your health!
¡Salud!
sah-LOOTH!

Hear
I did not hear you. Please repeat.
No le oí. Por favor, repita.
noh leh oh-EE. *pohr fah-*BOHR, *rreh-*PEE-*tah.*

Heater

Please show me how to operate the heater.

Por favor, enséñeme cómo poner la calefacción.

pohr fah-BOHR, ehn-SEH-nyeh-meh KOH-*moh poh-*NEHR *lah kah-leh-fahk-*SYOHN.

Heavy

It is very (too) heavy.

Es muy (demasiado) pesado.

*ehss mwee (deh-mah-*SYAH-*thoh) peh-*SAH-*thoh.*

Heel

Please replace the heels.

Por favor, ponga nuevos tacones.

*pohr fah-*BOHR, POHN-*gah* NWEH-*bohss tah-*KOH-*nehss.*

Help — see also Accident

Help!

¡Socorro!

*soh-*KOH-*rroh!*

Can you help me?

¿Puede ayudarme?

PWEH-*theh ah-yoo-*THAHR-*meh?*

Here

Come here, please.

Venga aquí, por favor.

BEHN-*gah ah-*KEE, *pohr fah-*BOHR.

When will it be here?

¿Cuándo estará aquí?

KWAHN-*doh ehss-tah-*RAH *ah-*KEE?

Here is my _____.

Aquí está mi _____.

*ah-*KEE *ehss-*TAH *mee* _____.

High

The price is too high.

El precio es demasiado elevado.

ehl PREH-*syoh ehss deh-mah-*SYAH-*thoh eh-leh-*BAH-*thoh.*

Hire

How much would it cost to hire _____?

¿Cuánto costaría alquilar _____?

KWAHN-*toh kohss-tah*-REE-*ah ahl-kee*-LAHR _____?

Hitchhiking

Is hitchhiking allowed?

¿Se permite el autostop?

seh pehr-MEE-*teh ehl ow-toh*-STOHP?

Holiday

When is the next holiday?

¿Cuándo será la próxima vacación?

KWAHN-*doh seh*-RAH *lah* PROHK-*see-mah bah-kah*-SYOHN?

Is today a holiday?

¿Es hoy día feriado?

ehss oy DEE-*ah feh*-RYAH-*thoh?*

Home

May I take you home?

¿Puedo acompañarle a casa?

PWEH-*thoh ah-kohm-pah*-NYAHR-*leh ah* KAH-*sah?*

Honeymoon

We are on our honeymoon.

Estamos en luna de miel.

ehss-TAH-*mohss ehn* LOO-*nah deh* MYEHL.

Horse

Where can I get a horse?

¿Dónde puedo conseguir un caballo?

DOHN-*deh* PWEH-*thoh kohn-seh*-GHEER *oon kah*-BAH-*yoh?*

Will there be any horse races here?

¿Habrá alguna carrera de caballos aquí?

ah-BRAH *ahl*-GOO-*nah kah*-RREH-*rah deh kah*-BAH-*yohss ah*-KEE?

Horseback Riding

Would you like to go horseback riding with me?

¿Le gustaría montar a caballo conmigo?

leh gooss-tah-REE-*ah mohn*-TAHR *ah kah*-BAH-*yoh kohn*-MEE-*goh?*

Hospital – see also Accident, Medical

Where is the hospital?
¿Dónde está el hospital?
DOHN-*deh ehss*-TAH *ehl ohss-pee*-TAHL?

Please take me (direct me) to the hospital.
Por favor, lléveme (diríjame) al hospital.
pohr fah-BOHR, YEH-*beh-meh* (*dee*-REE-*hah-meh*) *ahl
ohss-pee*-TAHL.

Hostel

Is there a youth hostel nearby?
¿Hay un albergue de juventud cerca?
ahy oon ahl-BEHR-*gheh deh hoo-behn*-TOOTH SEHR-*kah*?

May I have a list of the member hostels?
¿Me podría dar una lista de los albergues asociados?
meh poh-THREE-*ah dahr* OO-*nah* LEESS-*tah deh lohss
ahl*-BEHR-*ghehss ah-soh*-SYAH-*thohss?*

I am staying at the hostel.
Me estoy alojando en el hostal.
meh ehss-TOY *ah-loh*-HAHN-*doh ehn ehl ohss*-TAHL.

Hot

May I have some hot water?
¿Me podría dar agua caliente?
meh poh-THREE-*ah dahr* AH-*gwah kah*-YEHN-*teh?*

This is not hot enough. (Please take it back.)
No está bastante caliente. (Por favor, lléveselo.)
noh ehss-TAH *bahss*-TAHN-*teh kah*-YEHN-*teh. (pohr fah*-
BOHR, YEH-*beh-seh-loh.)*

There is no hot water.
No hay agua caliente.
noh ahy AH-*gwah kah*-YEHN-*teh.*

Hotel

Can you recommend a good hotel?
¿Puede recomendarme un buen hotel?
PWEH-*theh rreh-koh-mehn*-DAHR-*meh oon bwehn oh*-
TEHL?

Where is the _____ hotel?

¿Dónde está el hotel _____?

DOHN-*deh ehss*-TAH *ehl oh*-TEHL _____ ?

Please send it to my hotel.

Por favor, envíelo a mi hotel.

pohr fah-BOHR, *ehn*-BEE-*eh-loh ah mee oh*-TEHL.

Hour

What is the charge per hour?

¿Cuánto cuesta por hora?

KWAHN-*toh* KWEHSS-*tah pohr* OH-*rah?*

At what hour shall we meet?

¿A qué hora nos veremos?

ah keh OH-*rah nohss beh*-REH-*mohss?*

At what hour should I come?

¿A qué hora debo venir?

ah keh OH-*rah* DEH-*boh beh*-NEER?

How

How do you do?

¿Cómo está usted?

KOH-*moh ehss*-TAH *oo*-STEHTH?

How long?

¿Cuánto tiempo?

KWAHN-*toh* TYEHM-*poh?*

How far?

¿A qué distancia?

ah keh deess-TAHN-*syah?*

How many?

¿Cuántos?

KWAHN-*tohss?*

How much?

¿Cuánto?

KWAHN-*toh?*

How long (will it take)?

¿Cuánto tiempo (tardará)?

KWAHN-*toh* TYEHM-*poh (tahr-thah*-RAH*)?*

How do you say "_____" in _____?

¿Cómo se dice "_____" en _____?

KOH-*moh seh* DEE-*seh* "_____" *ehn* _____?

Hungry

I am (not) hungry.

(No) tengo hambre.

(noh) TEHN-*goh* AHM-*breh.*

Hurry

Please hurry.

Por favor, dese prisa.

pohr fah-BOHR, DEH-*seh* PREE-*sah.*

Hurt

Does it hurt?

¿Le duele?

leh DWEH-*leh?*

Are you hurt?

¿Está herido (herida)?

ehss-TAH *eh*-REE-*thoh (eh*-REE-*thah)?*

Ice

Please bring me some ice.

Por favor, tráigame hielo.

pohr fah-BOHR, TRAH-*ee-gah-meh* YEH-*loh.*

Icebag

Do you have an icebag?

¿Tiene usted una bolsa para hielo?

TYEH-*neh oo*-STEHTH OO-*nah* BOHL-*sah pah-rah* YEH-*loh?*

Identification

Here is my identification.

Aquí está mi identificación.

ah-KEE *ehss*-TAH *mee ee-dehn-tee-fee-kah*-SYOHN.

Ill – see also Medical, Accident

I am ill.

Estoy enfermo (enferma).

ehss-TOY *ehn*-FEHR-*moh (ehn*-FEHR-*mah).*

Immediately

Call a doctor immediately.
Llame a un médico inmediatamente.
YAH-*meh ah oon* MEH-*thee-koh een-meh-thyah-tah-*
MEHN-*teh.*

Please do it immediately.
Por favor, hágalo inmediatamente.
*pohr fah-*BOHR, AH-*gah-loh een-meh-thyah-tah-*MEHN-
teh.

I want to leave immediately.
Quiero salir inmediatamente.
KYEH-*roh sah-*LEER *een-meh-thyah-tah-*MEHN-*teh.*

I need it immediately.
Lo necesito inmediatamente.
*loh neh-seh-*SEE-*toh een-meh-thyah-tah-*MEHN-*teh.*

Important

It is very important.
Es muy importante.
*ehss mwee eem-pohr-*TAHN-*teh.*

Include

Are all meals included?
¿Se incluyen todas las comidas?
*seh een-*KLOO-*yehn* TOH-*thahss lahss koh-*MEE-*thahss?*

Is breakfast (lunch, supper) included?
¿Se incluye el desayuno (el almuerzo, la cena)?
*seh een-*KLOO-*yeh ehl deh-sah-*YOO-*noh (ehl ahl-*MWEHR-
soh, lah SEH-*nah)?*

Is the tip included?
Se incluye la propina?
*seh een-*KLOO-*yeh lah proh-*PEE-*nah?*

Is coffee (dessert) included?
¿Se incluye el café (el postre)?
*seh een-*KLOO-*yeh ehl kah-*FEH *(ehl* POHSS-*treh)?*

Incorrect

This is incorrect.
Esto es incorrecto.
EHSS-*toh ehss een-koh-*RREHK-*toh.*

Indigestion

I have indigestion. (Please bring me a _____).

Tengo indigestion (Por favor, tráigame un (una)
　　_____).

TEHN-*goh een-dee-hehss*-TYOHN *(pohr fah*-BOHR, TRAH-
　　ee-gah-meh oon (OO-*nah*) _____).

Indoors

I will stay indoors today (this morning, this afternoon,
　　this evening).

Me quedaré en casa hoy (esta mañana, esta tarde,
　　esta noche).

meh keh-thah-REH *ehn* KAH-*sah oy* (EHSS-*tah mah*-
　　NYAH-*nah,* EHSS-*tah* TAHR-*theh,* EHSS-*tah* NOH-*cheh*).

Inexpensive

Can you recommend an inexpensive restaurant?

¿Puede recomendarme un restaurante económico?

PWEH-*theh rreh-koh-mehn*-DAHR-*meh* oon *rrehss-tah-oo*-
　　RAHN-*teh eh-koh*-NOH-*mee-koh?*

I want something inexpensive.

Quisiera algo barato.

kee-SYEH-*rah* AHL-*goh bah*-RAH-*toh.*

Informal

Can I dress informally?

¿Puedo vestirme sin etiqueta?

PWEH-*thoh behss*-TEER-*meh seen eh-tee*-KEH-*tah?*

Information

I would like some information (about _____).

Quisiera algunos informes (sobre _____).

kee-SYEH-*rah* ahl-GOO-*nohss een*-FOHR-*mehss (*SOH-*breh*
　　_____).

Where is the information desk (the information
　　window)?

¿Dónde está la mesa de información (la ventanilla de
　　información)?

DOHN-*deh ehss*-TAH *lah* MEH-*sah deh een-fohr-mah*-
　　SYOHN *(lah behn-tah*-NEE-*yah deh een-fohr-mah*-
　　SYOHN*)?*

Please direct me to the information bureau.
Por favor, diríjame a la oficina de información.
pohr fah-BOHR, dee-REE-hah-meh ah lah oh-fee-SEE-nah deh een-fohr-mah-SYOHN.

Inland

What is the best route inland?
¿Cuál es el mejor camino hacia el interior?
kwahl ehss ehl meh-HOHR kah-MEE-noh AH-syah ehl een-teh-RYOHR?

Inn

Can you recommend a good inn?
¿Puede recomendarme una buena posada?
PWEH-theh rreh-koh-mehn-DAHR-meh OO-nah BWEH-nah poh-SAH-thah?

Insect

Have you any insect spray?
¿Tiene usted algún insecticida?
TYEH-neh oo-STEHTH ahl-GOON een-sehk-tee-SEE-thah?

Interpreter

I want to hire an interpreter.
Quisiera contratar un intérprete.
kee-SYEH-rah kohn-trah-TAHR oon een-TEHR-preh-teh.

Where can I find an interpreter?
¿Dónde puedo encontrar un intérprete?
DOHN-deh PWEH-thoh ehn-kohn-TRAHR oon een-TEHR-preh-teh?

Introduce

May I introduce _____.
Permítame presentar a _____.
pehr-MEE-tah-meh preh-sehn-TAHR ah _____.

Invite

Thank you for the invitation.
Muchas gracias por la invitacion.
MOO-chahss GRAH-syahss pohr lah een-bee-tah-SYOHN.

I invite you to come with me (to be my guest).
Le invito a venir conmigo (a ser mi invitado).
leh een-BEE-toh ah beh-NEER kohn-MEE-goh (ah sehr mee een-bee-TAH-thoh).

Itemize

I would like to have this itemized.

¿Quiero que me apunten esto artículo por artículo.

KYEH-*roh keh meh ah-*POON-*tehn* EHSS-*toh ahr-*TEE-*koo-loh pohr ahr-*TEE-*koo-loh.*

Jacket

Do I need to wear a jacket?

¿Debo ponerme la chaqueta?

DEH-*boh poh-*NEHR-*meh lah chah-*KEH-*tah?*

Jewelry

I would like to leave my jewelry in your safe.

Quisiera dejar mis joyas en su caja fuerte.

kee-SYEH-*rah deh-*HAHR *mees* HOH-*yahss ehn soo* KAH-*hah* FWEHR-*teh.*

Jewish

I am Jewish.

Soy judío (judía).

*soy hoo-*THEE-*oh (hoo-*THEE-*ah).*

Are you Jewish?

¿Es usted judío (judía)?

*ehss oo-*STEHTH *hoo-*THEE-*oh (hoo-*THEE-*ah)?*

Job (employment)

What kind of job do you have?

¿Qué tipo de empleo tiene usted?

keh TEE-*poh deh ehm-*PLEH-*oh* TYEH-*neh oo-*STEHTH?

Key

I have lost my key.

He perdido la llave.

*eh pehr-*THEE-*thoh lah* YAH-*beh.*

May I have another key?

¿Puede darme otra llave?

PWEH-*theh* DAHR-*meh* OH-*trah* YAH-*beh?*

Kilogram

How much per kilogram for excess baggage?

¿Cuánto por kilógramo por el exceso?

KWAHN-*toh pohr kee-*LOH-*grah-moh pohr ehl ehss-*SEH-*soh?*

Kilometer

How many kilometers to _____?

¿Cuántos kilómetros hay hasta _____?

KWAHN-*tohss kee*-LOH-*meh-trohss ahy* AHSS-*tah* _____?

How many kilometers from _____ to _____?

¿Cuántos kilómetros hay desde _____ a _____?

KWAHN-*tohss kee*-LOH-*meh-trohss ahy* DEHZ-*deh* _____ *ah* _____?

Knife

Please bring me another knife.

Por favor, tráigame otro cuchillo.

pohr fah-BOHR, TRAH-*ee-gah-meh* OH-*troh koo*-CHEE-*yoh.*

Know

Do you know where _____ is?

¿Sabe usted dónde está _____?

SAH-*beh oo*-STEHTH DOHN-*deh ehss*-TAH _____?

I (don't) know how.

(No) sé cómo.

(noh) seh KOH-*moh.*

Please let me know when we get to _____.

Por favor, avíseme cuando lleguemos a _____.

pohr fah-BOHR, *ah*-BEE-*seh-meh* KWAHN-*doh yeh*-GHEH-*mohss ah* _____.

Kosher

Do you serve (sell) kosher food?

Se sirve (vende) comida kosher?

seh SEER-*beh (*BEHN-*deh) koh*-MEE-*thah* KOH-*shehr?*

Laundry and Dry Cleaning

Do you have (overnight) laundry service?

¿Tienen ustedes servicio de lavandería (por la noche)?

TYEH-*nehn oo*-STEH-*thehss sehr*-BEE-*syoh deh lah-bahn-deh*-REE-*ah (pohr lah* NOH-*cheh)?*

I want this (these) washed (cleaned, pressed).

Quiero que me laven (limpien, planchen) esto (estos).

KYEH-*roh keh meh* LAH-*behn (*LEEM-*pyehn,* PLAHN-*chehn)* EHSS-*toh (*EHSS-*tohss).*

Can you remove this spot (stain)?
¿Puede quitar esta mancha?
PWEH-*theh kee*-TAHR EHSS-*tah* MAHN-*chah?*

Don't wash this in hot water.
No lave esto con aqua caliente.
noh LAH-*beh* EHSS-*toh kohn* AH-*gwah kah*-YEHN-*teh.*

No starch, please.
Sin almidón, por favor.
seen ahl-mee-THOHN, *pohr fah*-BOHR.

I would like this button sewn on.
Quisiera que me cosieran este botón.
kee-SYEH-*rah keh meh koh*-SYEH-*rahn* EHSS-*teh boh*-
TOHN.

I would like this mended.
Quisiera que me arreglase esto.
kee-SYEH-*rah keh meh ah-rreh*-GLAH-*seh* EHSS-*toh.*

When can I have it (them) back?
¿Cuándo me lo podría devolver?
KWAHN-*doh meh loh poh*-THREE-*ah deh-bohl*-BEHR?

Will it be ready today (tonight, tomorrow)?
¿Estará listo hoy (esta noche, mañana)?
ehss-tah-RAH LEESS-*toh oy* (EHSS-*tah* NOH-*cheh, mah*-
NYAH-*nah)?*

A button (the belt) is missing.
Falta un botón (el cinturón).
FAHL-*tah oon boh*-TOHN *(ehl seen-too*-ROHN).

Less – see also Shopping
Do you have anything less expensive?
¿Tiene usted algo menos caro?
TYEH-*neh oo*-STEHTH AHL-*goh* MEH-*nohss* KAH-*roh?*

Let
Let me know when we get to _____.
Avíseme cuando lleguemos a _____.
ah-BEE-*seh-meh* KWAHN-*doh yeh*-GHEH-*mohss ah* _____.

Letters – see also Post Office

Is there any letter for me?
¿Hay alguna carta para mí?
ahy ahl-GOO-*nah* KAHR-*tah pah-rah* MEE?

Where can I mail these letters?
¿Dónde puedo echar estas cartas al correo?
DOHN-*deh* PWEH-*thoh eh*-CHAHR EHSS-*tahss* KAHR-*tahss*
   ahl koh-RREH-*oh?*

Please mail these letters.
Por favor, eche estas cartas al correo.
pohr fah-BOHR, EH-*cheh* EHSS-*tahss* KAHR-*tahss ahl koh*-
   RREH-*oh.*

Library

Please take me (direct me) to the library.
Por favor, lléveme (diríjame) a la biblioteca.
pohr fah-BOHR, YEH-*beh-meh (dee*-REE-*hah-meh) ah lah
   bee-blyoh-TEH-*kah.*

License – see Driver's License

Lifeboats

Where are the lifeboats?
¿Dónde están las lanchas de salvavidas?
DOHN-*deh ehss*-TAHN *lahss* LAHN-*chahss deh sahl-bah*-
   BEE-*thahss?*

Life Preservers

Where are the life preservers?
¿Dónde están los salvavidas?
DOHN-*deh ehss*-TAHN *lohss sahl-bah*-BEE-*thahss?*

How do you use the life preservers?
¿Cómo se utilizan los salvavidas?
KOH-*moh seh oo-tee*-LEE-*sahn lohss sahl-bah*-BEE-
   thahss?

Light

May I have a light?
¿Puede darme fuego?
PWEH-*theh* DAHR-*meh* FWEH-*goh?*

Like – see also Shopping
I (don't) like _____.
(No) me gusta _____.
(noh) meh GOOSS-*tah* _____.

Limit
What is the speed limit?
¿Cuál es la velocidad máxima?
*kwahl ehss lah beh-loh-see-*THAHTH MAHK-*see-mah?*

What is the weight limit?
¿Cuál es el peso máximo?
kwahl ehss ehl PEH-*soh* MAHK-*see-moh?*

Limousine
Is there limousine service to the airport?
¿Hay servicio de coche al aeropuerto?
*ahy sehr-*BEE-*syoh deh* KOH-*cheh ahl ah-eh-roh-*PWEHR-*toh?*

When does the limousine leave for the airport?
¿Cuándo sale el coche para el aeropuerto?
KWAHN-*doh* SAH-*leh ehl* KOH-*cheh pah-rah ehl ah-eh-roh-*PWEHR-*toh?*

I want to hire a limousine.
Quiero alquilar un coche con chófer.
KYEH-*roh ahl-kee-*LAHR *oon* KOH-*cheh kohn* CHOH-*fehr.*

Liquor
Where can I buy some liquor?
¿Dónde puedo comprar licor?
DOHN-*deh* PWEH-*thoh kohm-*PRAHR *lee-*KOHR?

How much liquor can I take out?
¿Qué cantidad de bebidas alcoholicas puedo sacar?
*keh kahn-tee-*THAHTH *deh beh-*BEE-*thahss ahl-koh-*OH-*lee-kahss* PWEH-*thoh sah-*KAHR?

Little
I want just a little, please.
Sólo quiero un poco, por favor.
SOH-*loh* KYEH-*roh oon* POH-*koh, pohr fah-*BOHR.

A little more (less), please.
Un poco más (menos), por favor.
oon POH-*koh* MAHSS *(*MEH-*nohss), pohr fah-*BOHR.

Live

Where do you live?
¿Dónde vive usted?
DOHN-*deh* BEE-*beh* oo-STEHTH?

Lobby

I'll meet you in the lobby.
Le veré en el vestibulo.
*leh beh-*REH *ehn ehl behss-*TEE-*boo-loh.*

Local

Where do I get the local train?
¿Dónde puedo tomar el tren local?
DOHN-*deh* PWEH-*thoh toh-*MAHR *ehl* TREHN *loh-*KAHL?

Is this the local?
¿Es éste el tren local?
ehss EHSS-*teh ehl* TREHN *loh-*KAHL?

Lock

Please lock my door.
Por favor, cierre la puerta con llave.
*pohr fah-*BOHR, SYEH-*rreh lah* PWEHR-*tah kohn* YAH-*beh.*

The lock does not work.
La cerradura no funciona.
*lah seh-rrah-*THOO-*rah noh foon-*SYOH-*nah.*

How does the lock work?
¿Cómo funciona la cerradura?
KOH-*moh foon-*SYOH-*nah lah seh-rrah-*THOO-*rah?*

I have lost the key (for the lock).
He perdido la llave (para la cerradura).
*eh pehr-*THEE-*thoh lah* YAH-BEH *(pah-rah lah seh-rrah-*THOO-*rah).*

Locker

Where can I rent a locker?

¿Dónde puedo alquilar una taquilla?

DOHN-*deh* PWEH-*thoh ahl-kee-*LAHR OO-*nah tah-*KEE-*yah?*

Long

How long will it take (last)?

¿Cuánto tiempo tardará (durará)?

KWAHN-*toh* TYEHM-*poh tahr-thah-*RAH (*doo-rah-*RAH)?

How long is the stop at _____?

¿Cuánto tiempo parará en _____?

KWAHN-*toh* TYEHM-*poh pah-rah-*RAH *ehn* _____?

How long must I wait?

¿Cuánto tiempo debo esperar?

KWAHN-*toh* TYEHM-*poh* DEH-*boh ehss-peh-*RAHR?

How long will it be open?

¿Cuánto tiempo estará abierto?

KWAHN-*toh* TYEHM-*poh ehss-tah-*RAH *ah-*BYEHR-*toh?*

Lost

I am lost. Where is _____?

Estoy perdido (perdida). ¿Dónde está _____?

*ehss-*TOY *pehr-*THEE-*thoh* (*pehr-*THEE-*thah*). DOHN-*deh ehss-*TAH _____?

I have lost my key (passport, wallet).

He perdido mi llave (pasaporte, cartera).

*eh pehr-*THEE-*thoh mee* YAH-*beh* (*pah-sah-*POHR-*teh, kahr-*TEH-*rah*).

Where is lost and found?

¿Dónde está la oficina de objetos perdidos?

DOHN-*deh ehss-*TAH *lah oh-fee-*SEE-*nah deh ohb-*HEH-*tohss pehr-*THEE-*thohss?*

Love

I love you.

Te quiero.

teh KYEH-*roh.*

I love my wife (husband).
Quiero a mi mujer (marido).
KYEH-*roh ah mee moo*-HEHR *(mah*-REE-*thoh)*.

I love _____.
Me gusta mucho _____.
meh GOOSS-*tah* MOO-*choh* _____.

Lower

I want a lower berth.
Quisiera una litera baja.
kee-SYEH-*rah* OO-*nah lee*-TEH-*rah* BAH-*hah*.

I want a room on a lower floor.
Quisiera una habitación en un piso más bajo.
kee-SYEH-*rah* OO-*nah ah-bee-tah*-SYOHN *ehn oon* PEE-*soh mahss* BAH-*hoh*.

Lunch

Can we have lunch now?
¿Podemos tomar el almuerzo ahora?
poh-THEH-*mohss toh*-MAHR *ehl ahl*-MWEHR-*soh ah*-OH-*rah*?

When is lunch served?
¿Cuándo se sirve el almuerzo?
KWAHN-*doh seh* SEER-*beh ehl ahl*-MWEHR-*soh*?

How late (how early) do you serve lunch?
¿Hasta cuándo (desde cuándo) sirven el almuerzo?
AHSS-*tah* KWAHN-*doh (*DEHZ-*deh* KWAHN-*doh)* SEER-*behn ehl ahl*-MWEHR-*soh*?

Will you have lunch with me?
¿Quiere almorzar conmigo?
KYEH-*reh ahl-mohr*-SAHR *kohn*-MEE-*goh*?

Does that include lunch?
¿Incluye eso el almuerzo?
een-KLOO-*yeh* EH-*soh ehl ahl*-MWEHR-*soh*?

Magazine

Where are (English-language) magazines sold?
¿Dónde se venden revistas (en inglés)?
DOHN-*deh seh* BEHN-*dehn rreh*-BEESS-*tahss (ehn een*-GLEHSS*)*?

Maid

Please send the maid to my room.

Por favor, diga a la criada que suba a mi habitación.

*pohr fah-*BOHR*, DEE-gah ah lah kree-*AH*-thah keh* SOO-*
bah ah mee ah-bee-tah-*SYOHN.

Mail – see also Post Office

Is there any mail for me?

¿Hay correo para mí?

*ahy koh-*RREH*-oh pah-rah* MEE*?*

When is the mail delivered?

¿Cuándo se entrega el correo?

KWAHN*-doh seh ehn-*TREH*-gah ehl koh-*RREH*-oh?*

Please send this (these) by mail.

Por favor, envíe esto (estas) por correo.

*pohr fah-*BOHR*, ehn-*BEE*-eh* EHSS*-toh (*EHSS*-tahss) pohr
koh-*RREH*-oh.*

Mailbox

Where is there a mailbox, please?

¿Dónde hay un buzón, por favor?

DOHN*-deh ahy oon boo-*SOHN*, pohr fah-*BOHR*?*

Make

Please make the bed.

Por favor, haga la cama.

*pohr fah-*BOHR*, AH-gah lah* KAH*-mah.*

Man – see also Men's Room

Who is that man?

¿Quién es ese hombre?

KYEHN *ehss* EH*-seh* OHM*-breh?*

Manager

I want to see the manager.

Quiero hablar con el gerente.

KYEH*-roh ah-*BLAHR *kohn ehl heh-*REHN*-teh.*

Are you the manager?

¿Es usted el gerente?

*ehss oo-*STEHTH *ehl heh-*REHN*-teh?*

Manicure – see Beauty Parlor

Map

Do you have a map of _____?

¿Tiene usted un mapa de _____?

TYEH-*neh* oo-STEHTH *oon* MAH-*pah deh* _____?

I need a map of _____, please.

Necesito un mapa de _____, por favor.

*neh-seh-*SEE-*toh oon* MAH-*pah deh* _____, *pohr fah-*BOHR.

Married

I am (not) married.

(No) estoy casado (casada).

(noh) ehss-TOY *kah-*SAH-*thoh (kah-*SAH-*thah).*

Are you married?

¿Está usted casado (casada)?

ehss-TAH oo-STEHTH *kah-*SAH-*thoh (kah-*SAH-*thah)?*

Mass

What time is mass?

¿A qué hora se celebra la misa?

ah keh OH-*rah seh seh-*LEH-*brah lah* MEE-*sah?*

Massage

I would like to have a massage.

Quisiera que me dieran un masaje.

*kee-*SYEH-*rah keh meh* DYEH-*rahn oon mah-*SAH-*heh.*

Match

Excuse me, do you have a match?

Perdone, ¿tiene usted un fosforo?

*pehr-*THOH-*neh,* TYEH-*neh* oo-STEHTH *oon* FOHS-*foh-roh?*

Matinee

Is there a matinee today?

¿Hay matinée hoy?

*ahy mah-tee-*NEH *oy?*

Matter

What is the matter?

¿Qué pasa? (or: ¿Qué ocurre?).

keh PAH-*sah? (keh oh-*KOO-*rreh?).*

Mattress

I would like another mattress.
Quisiera otro colchón.
kee-SYEH-*rah* OH-*troh kohl*-CHOHN.

This mattress is too hard (soft, uncomfortable).
Este colchón es demasiado duro (blando, incómodo).
EHSS-*teh kohl*-CHOHN *ehss deh-mah*-SYAH-*thoh* DOO-*roh*
   (BLAHN-*doh, een*-KOH-*moh-thoh*).

Meals

When are meals served?
¿Cuándo se sirven las comidas?
KWAHN-*doh seh* SEER-*behn lahss koh*-MEE-*thahss?*

Does that include meals?
¿Incluye eso las comidas?
een-KLOO-*yeh* EH-*soh lahss koh*-MEE-*thahss?*

What meals are included?
¿Qué comidas se incluyen?
keh koh-MEE-*thahss seh een*-KLOO-*yehn?*

Mean

What is it you mean?
¿Qué es lo que usted quiere decir?
keh ehss loh keh oo-STEHTH KYEH-*reh deh*-SEER?

That is (not) what I mean.
Eso (no) es lo que quiero decir.
EH-*soh (noh) ehss loh keh* KYEH-*roh deh*-SEER.

What does _____ mean?
¿Qué quiere decir _____?
keh KYEH-*reh deh*-SEER _____?

Medical – see also Accident

Is there a (an English-speaking) doctor near here (in
   the hotel)?
¿Hay un médico (de habla inglesa) cerca de aquí (en el
   hotel)?
ahy oon MEH-*thee-koh (deh* AH-*blah een*-GLEH-*sah)*
   SEHR-*kah deh ah*-KEE *(ehn ehl oh*-TEHL)?

Can you recommend a good (English-speaking) doctor?
¿Puede recomendarme un buen médico (de habla
  inglesa)?
PWEH-*theh rreh-koh-mehn*-DAHR-*meh oon bwehn* MEH-
  thee-koh (deh AH-*blah een-*GLEH-*sah)?*

Can you give me an appointment as soon as possible?
¿Podría usted darme cita lo más pronto posible?
*poh-*THREE-*ah oo-*STEHTH DAHR-*meh* SEE-*tah loh mahss*
  PROHN-*toh poh-*SEE-*bleh?*

Could I see you right away?
¿Podría verle ahora mismo?
*poh-*THREE-*ah* BEHR-*leh ah-*OH-*rah* MEEZ-*moh?*

I (don't) have an appointment.
(No) tengo cita.
(noh) TEHN-*goh* SEE-*tah.*

I am having trouble breathing (sleeping).
Me cuesta trabajo respirar (dormir).
meh KWEHSS-*tah trah-*BAH-*hoh rreh-spee-*RAHR *(dohr-*
  MEER*).*

I have a stomach ache.
Me duele el estómago.
meh DWEH-*leh ehl ehss-*TOH-*mah-goh.*

I have diarrhea (dysentery, food poisoning, nausea,
  cramps).
Tengo diarrea (disentería, descomposición de
  estómago, náuseas, entumecimiento).
TEHN-*goh dee-ah-*RREH-*ah (dee-sehn-tehr-*EE-*ah, dehss-
  kohm-poh-see-*SYOHN *deh ehss-*TOH-*mah-goh,* NAH-*oo-
  seh-ahss, ehn-too-meh-see-*MYEHN-*toh).*

I am constipated.
Estoy estreñido (estreñida).
*ehss-*TOY *ehss-treh-*NYEE-*thoh (ehss-treh-*NYEE-*thah).*

I have a pain in my chest (my back, my arm, my leg,
  my hand, my foot).
Me duele el pecho (la espalda, el brazo, la pierna, la
  mano, el pie).
meh DWEH-*leh ehl* PEH-*choh (lah ehss-*PAHL-*dah, ehl*
  BRAH-*soh, lah* PYEHR-*nah, lah* MAH-*noh, ehl* PYEH*).*

I have an earache.
Me duele el oído.
meh DWEH-*leh ehl* oh-EE-*thoh.*

I have a bad cough.
Estoy tosiendo mucho.
ehss-TOY *toh*-SYEHN-*doh* MOO-*choh.*

I have a sore throat.
Tengo dolor de garganta.
TEHN-*goh doh*-LOHR *deh gahr*-GAHN-*tah.*

I have a splitting headache.
Me duele mucho la cabeza.
meh DWEH-*leh* MOO-*choh lah kah*-BEH-*sah.*

I have a bad sunburn.
Estoy quemado (quemada) del sol.
ehss-TOY *keh*-MAH-*thoh (keh*-MAH-*thah) dehl* SOHL.

I have sunstroke.
Tengo insolación.
TEHN-*goh een-soh-lah*-SYOHN.

I have a fever (chills).
Tengo fiebre (escalofríos).
TEHN-*goh* FYEH-*breh (ehss-kah-loh*-FREE-*ohss).*

I have sprained my wrist (my ankle).
Me he torcido la muñeca (el tobillo).
meh eh tohr-SEE-*thoh lah moo*-NYEH-*kah (ehl toh*-BEE-*yoh).*

I have something in my eye.
Tengo algo en el ojo.
TEHN-*goh* AHL-*goh ehn ehl* OH-*hoh.*

Are you going to take X-rays?
¿Piensa hacerse una radiografía?
PYEHN-*sah ah*-SEHR-*seh* OO-*nah rah-thee-oh-grah*-FEE-*ah?*

Do I have to go to the hospital?
¿Tengo que ir al hospital?
TEHN-*goh keh eer ahl ohss-pee*-TAHL?

I am allergic to _____.
Soy alérgico (alérgica) a _____.
soy ah-LEHR-hee-koh (al-LEHR-hee-kah) ah _____.

Please (don't) use anesthesia.
Por favor, (no) use anestesia.
pohr fah-BOHR, (noh) OO-seh ah-nehss-TEH-syah.

Can I have a tranquilizer (aspirin, sleeping pills)?
¿Me puede dar un tranquilizante (aspirinas, píldoras
    contra el insomnio)?
meh PWEH-theh dahr oon trahn-kee-lee-SAHN-teh (ahss-
    pee-REE-nahss, PEEL-doh-rahss KOHN-trah ehl een-
    SOHM-nee-oh)?

Do I have to stay in bed?
¿Debo quedarme en la cama?
DEH-boh keh-THAHR-meh ehn lah KAH-mah?

For how long?
¿Durante cuánto tiempo?
doo-RAHN-teh KWAHN-toh TYEHM-poh?

When do you think I will be better?
¿Cuándo cree usted que estaré mejor?
KWAHN-doh KREH-eh oo-STEHTH keh ehss-tah-REH meh-
    HOHR?

Where can I have this prescription filled?
¿Dónde me pueden hacer esta receta?
DOHN-deh meh PWEH-then ah-SEHR EHSS-tah rreh-SEH-
    tah?

When should I see you again?
¿Cuándo debo volver a verle?
KWAHN-doh DEH-boh bohl-BEHR ah BEHR-leh?

Medium
I like my meat medium (medium rare).
Me gusta la carne no muy (bien) cocida.
meh GOOSS-tah lah KAHR-neh noh mwee (byehn) koh-
    SEE-thah.

Meet

Let's meet at _____.
Nos encontremos en _____.
*nohss ehn-kohn-*TREH*-mohss ehn* _____.

I am going to meet my husband (wife, friend).
Voy a encontrar a mi esposo (esposa, amigo).
*boy ah ehn-kohn-*TRAHR *ah mee ehss-*POH*-soh (ehss-*POH*-sah, ah-*MEE*-goh).*

I am very pleased to meet you.
Tengo mucho gusto en conocerle.
TEHN*-goh* MOO*-choh* GOOSS*-toh ehn koh-noh-*SEHR*-leh.*

I would like to meet him (meet her).
Me gustaría conocerle (conocerla).
*meh goss-tah-*REE*-ah koh-noh-*SEHR*-leh (koh-noh-*SEHR*-lah).*

Mend – see Laundry

Men's Room

Where is the men's room?
¿Dónde está el cuarto de caballeros?
DOHN*-deh ehss-*TAH *ehl* KWAHR*-toh deh kah-bah-*YEH*-rohss?*

Menu

The menu, please.
El menú, por favor.
*ehl meh-*NOO*, pohr fah-*BOHR*.*

Is _____ on the menu?
¿Hay _____ en el menú?
ahy _____ *ehn ehl meh-*NOO*?*

Message

I would like to leave a message.
Quisiera dejar un recado.
*kee-*SYEH*-rah deh-*HAHR *oon rreh-*KAH*-thoh.*

Is there any message for me?
¿Hay algún recado para mí?
*ahy ahl-*GOON *rreh-*KAH*-thoh pah-rah* MEE*?*

Milk

May I have a glass of milk, please.

¿Me podría dar un vaso de leche, por favor?

*meh poh-*THREE*-ah dahr oon* BAH*-soh deh* LEH*-cheh,*
*pohr fah-*BOHR*?*

Is the milk pasteurized?

¿Está la leche pasteurizada?

*ehss-*TAH *lah* LEH*-cheh pahss-teh-oo-ree-*SAH*-thah?*

Mind

Do you mind if I smoke?

¿Le importa que fume?

*leh eem-*POHR*-tah kah* FOO*-meh?*

Mine

That is mine.

Eso es mío.

EH*-soh ehss* MEE*-oh.*

Minister – see also Priest

Where can I find a (an English-speaking) minister?

¿Dónde podría encontrar a un pastor (de habla inglesa)?

DOHN*-deh poh-*THREE*-ah ehn-kohn-*TRAHR *ah oon*
*pahss-*TOHR *(deh* AH*-blah een-*GLEH*-sah)?*

Minutes

I'll see you in _____ minutes.

Le veré dentro de _____ minutos.

*leh beh-*REH DEHN*-troh deh* _____ *mee-*NOO*-tohss.*

Miss

I missed my plane (train); when is the next one?

Perdí el avión (tren); ¿cuándo sale el próximo?

*pehr-*THEE *ehl ah-*BYOHN *(*TREHN*); *KWAHN*-doh* SAH*-leh*
ehl PROHK*-see-moh?*

Mistake

Is there a mistake ?

¿Hay algún error?

*ahy ahl-*GOON *eh-*RROHR*?*

There must be some mistake.

Tiene que haber un error.

TYEH*-neh keh ah-*BEHR *oon eh-*RROHR*.*

Moderate

Can you recommend a moderate-priced hotel (restaurant)?

¿Puede recomendarme un hotel (restaurante) de precio modico?

PWEH-theh rreh-koh-mehn-DAHR-meh oon oh-TEHL (rrehss-tah-oo-RAHN-teh) deh PREH-yoh MOH-thee-koh?

Moment

Wait a moment.

Espere un momento.

ehss-PEH-reh oon moh-MEHN-toh.

Stop here a moment, please.

Deténgase aquí un momento, por favor.

deh-TEHN-gah-seh ah-KEE oon moh-MEHN-toh, pohr fah-BOHR.

I'll see you in a moment.

Le veré en seguida.

leh beh-REH ehn seh-GHEE-thah.

Money – see also Bank

I need some local money.

Necesito dinero del país.

neh-seh-SEE-toh dee-NEH-roh dehl pah-EESS.

Will you accept American money?

¿Aceptará dinero americano?

ah-seph-tah-RAH dee-NEH-roh ah-meh-ree-KAH-noh?

I have no money with me.

No llevo dinero conmigo.

noh YEH-boh dee-NEH-roh kohn-MEE-goh.

Money Order

I wish to send a money order.

Quisiera enviar un giro postal.

kee-SYEH-rah ehn-BYAHR oon HEE-roh pohss-TAHL.

More

I would like some more, please.

Quisiera más, por favor.

kee-SYEH-rah MAHSS, pohr fah-BOHR.

Please speak more slowly.
Por favor, hable más despacio.
*pohr fah-*BOHR*, AH-*bleh *mahss dehss-*PAH*-syoh.*

Morning

We will leave tomorrow morning.
Saldremos mañana por la mañana.
*sahl-*DREH*-mohss mah-*NYAH*-nah pohr lah mah-*NYAH *nah.*

I'll see you in the morning.
Le veré por la mañana.
*leh beh-*REH *pohr lah mah-*NYAH*-nah.*

Most

What is the most I can take?
¿Qué es lo máximo que puedo llevar conmigo?
keh ehss loh MAHK*-see-moh keh* PWEH*-thoh yeh-*BAHR *kohn-*MEE*-goh?*

Motor – see also Automobile

There is something wrong with the motor.
El motor tiene algo mal.
*ehl moh-*TOHR TYEH*-neh* AHL*-goh* MAHL.

Move

I want to move to another room (to another hotel).
Quiero mudarme a otra habitación (a otro hotel).
KYEH*-roh moo-*THAHR*-meh ah* OH*-trah ah-bee-tah-*SYOHN *(ah* OH*-troh oh-*TEHL*).*

Movie

What movie is being shown?
¿Qué película se está dando?
*keh peh-*LEE*-koo-lah seh ehss-*TAH DAHN*-doh?*

Would you like to go to the movies with me?
¿Quiere ir al cine conmigo?
KYEH*-reh eer ahl* SEE*-neh kohn-*MEE*-goh?*

Much

How much is it?
¿Cuánto es?
KWAHN*-toh* EHSS?

That is too much.
Eso es demasiado.
EH-*soh ehss deh-mah*-SYAH-*thoh.*

I like it very much.
Me gusta mucho.
meh GOOSS-*tah* MOO-*choh.*

Museum
Where is the Museum (of _____), please?
¿Dónde está el museo (de _____), por favor?
DOHN-*deh ehss*-TAH *ehl moo*-SEH-*oh (deh* _____*), pohr*
fah-BOHR?

Music
Where can we hear some good music?
¿Dónde podemos oír buena musica?
DOHN-*deh poh*-THEH-*mohss oh*-EER BWEH-*nah* MOO-*see-*
kah?

Must
I must leave now.
Debo irme ahora.
DEH-*boh* EER-*meh ah*-OH-*rah.*

Name – see also Call
What is your name?
¿Cómo se llama usted?
KOH-*moh seh* YAH-*mah oo*-STEHTH?

My name is _____.
Me llamo _____.
meh YAH-*moh* _____.

Napkin
May I have a (another) napkin, please.
¿Me puede dar una (otra) servilleta, por favor?
meh PWEH-*theh dahr* OO-*nah (*OH-*trah) sehr-bee-*YEH-
tah, pohr fah-BOHR?

National
What is the national dish?
¿Cuál es el plato nacional?
KWAHL *ehss ehl* PLAH-*toh nah-syoh*-NAHL?

Near

Are we near it?

¿Estamos cerca?

*ehss-*TAH*-mohss* SEHR*-kah?*

How near are we?

¿A qué distancia estamos?

*ah keh deess-*TAHN*-syah ehss-*TAH*-mohss?*

How near is _____?

¿A qué distancia está _____?

*ah keh deess-*TAHN*-syah ehss-*TAH _____?

Necessary

It is (not) necessary.

(No) es necesario.

*(noh) ehss neh-seh-*SAH*-ryoh.*

Need

I need _____.

Necesito _____.

*neh-seh-*SEE*-toh* _____.

Do I need tokens (reservations)?

¿Necesito fichas (reservas)?

*neh-seh-*SEE*-toh* FEE*-chahss (rreh-*SEHR*-bahss)?*

How much (how many) do you need?

¿Cuánto (Cuántos) necesita?

KWAHN*-toh (*KWAHN*-tohss) neh-seh-*SEE*-tah?*

Needle

I would like to buy some needles and thread.

Quisiera comprar unas agujas e hilo.

*kee-*SYEH*-rah kohm-*PRAHR *ah-*GOO*-hahss eh* EE*-loh.*

New

This is something new to me.

Esto es algo nuevo para mí.

EHSS*-toh ehss* AHL*-goh* NWEH*-boh pah-rah* MEE.

Newspaper

Where can I buy a (an American, English) newspaper?

¿Dónde puedo comprar un periódico (americano, inglés)?

DOHN*-deh* PWEH*-thoh kohm-*PRAHR *oon peh-*RYOH*-thee-koh (ah-meh-ree-*KAH*-noh, een-*GLEHSS*)?*

May I look at your newspaper for a moment?
¿Podría echar una mirada a su periódico por un
 momento?
*poh-*THREE-*ah* eh-CHAHR OO-*nah* mee-RAH-*thah ah soo*
 peh-RYOH-*thee-koh* pohr oon moh-MEHN-*toh?*

Next

What is the next town (stop)?
¿Cuál es la próxima población (parada)?
KWAHL *ehss lah* PROHK-*see-mah* pohb-lah-SYOHN *(pah-*
 RAH-*thah)?*

When is the next boat (train, plane)?
¿Cuándo sale el próximo barco (tren, avión)?
KWAHN-*doh* SAH-*leh ehl* PROHK-*see-moh* BAHR-*koh*
 (TREHN, *ah-*BYOHN)?

I want to get off at the next stop, please.
Quiero bajarme en la próxima parada, por favor.
KYEH-*roh bah-*HAHR-*meh ehn lah* PROHK-*see-mah* pah-
 RAH-*thah, pohr fah-*BOHR.

Nice

It is nice to meet you.
Me agrada mucho verle.
*meh ah-*GRAH-*thah* MOO-*choh* BEHR-*leh.*

That is very nice of you.
Es usted muy amable.
ehss oo-STEHTH *mwee ah-*MAH-*bleh.*

She (he) is very nice.
Ella (el) es muy amable.
EH-*yah* (EHL) *ehss mwee ah-*MAH-*bleh.*

Nightclub

Can you recommend a good nightclub?
¿Puede recomendarme un buen cabaret?
PWEH-*theh* rreh-koh-mehn-DAHR-*meh* oon bwehn kah-
 bah-REH?

Let's go to a nightclub.
Vámonos a un cabaret.
BAH-*moh-nohss ah* oon kah-bah-REH.

Noise

There is too much noise in my room; I want to change it.

Hay mucho ruido en mi habitación; quiero mudarme.

ahy MOO-*choh* RWEE-*thoh ehn mee ah-bee-tah-*SYOHN; KYEH-*roh moo-*THAHR-*meh.*

Noon

We are leaving at noon.

Salimos al mediodía.

*sah-*LEE-*mohss ahl meh-thyoh-*THEE-*ah.*

Nothing

I have nothing to declare.

No tengo nada que declarar.

noh TEHN-*goh* NAH-*thah keh deh-klah-*RAHR.

Nothing, thank you.

Nada, gracias.

NAH-*thah,* GRAH-*syahss.*

Think nothing of it.

De nada.

deh NAH-*thah.*

Number

What is your telephone (room) number?

¿Cuál es su número de teléfono (de habitación)?

KWAHL *ehss soo* NOO-*meh-roh deh teh-*LEH-*foh-noh (deh ah-bee-tah-*SYOHN)?

What is my room number?

¿Cuál es el número de mi habitación?

KWAHL *ehss ehl* NOO-*meh-roh deh mee ah-bee-tah-*SYOHN?

What number bus do I take to _____?

¿Qué número de autobús debo tomar para _____?

keh NOO-*meh-roh deh ow-toh-*BOOSS DEH-*boh toh-*MAHR *pah-rah* _____?

I am in number _____.

Estoy en el número _____.

*ehss-*TOY *ehn ehl* NOO-*meh-roh* _____.

Nurse

Is there a doctor or nurse aboard?

¿Hay algún médico o enfermera a bordo?

*ahy ahl-*GOON MEH-*thee-koh oh ehn-fehr-*MEH-*rah ah*
   BOHR-*thoh?*

Obtain

Where can I obtain _____?

¿Dónde podría conseguir _____?

DOHN-*deh poh-*THREE-*ah kohn-seh-*GHEER _____?

Occupation

What is your occupation?

¿Cuál es su profesión?

KWAHL *ehss soo proh-feh-*SYOHN?

Occupy

Is this occupied?

¿Está esto ocupado?

*ehss-*TAH EHSS-*toh oh-koo-*PAH-*thoh?*

Off

How do you turn it off?

¿Cómo se puede cerrar?

KOH-*moh seh* PWEH-*theh seh-*RRAHR?

Please tell me when (where) to get off.

Por favor, dígame cuándo (dónde) debo bajarme.

*pohr fah-*BOHR, DEE-*gah-meh* KWAHN-*doh (*DOHN-*deh,*
   DEH-*boh bah-*HAHR-*meh.*

Get off at the next stop, please.

Bájese en la próxima parada, por favor.

BAH-*heh-seh ehn lah* PROHK-*see-mah pah-*RAH-*thah,*
   *pohr fah-*BOHR.

Often

How often do you come here?

¿Con qué frecuencia viene usted por aquí?

*kohn keh freh-*KWEHN-*syah* BYEH-*neh oo-*STEHTH *pohr*
   *ah-*KEE?

How often do the buses (trains, planes, boats) run?
¿Con qué frecuencia van los autobuses (trenes,
  aviones, barcos)?
*kohn keh freh-KWEHN-syah BAHN lohss ow-toh-BOO-
  sehss (TREH-nehss, ah-BYOH-nehss, BAHR-kohss)?*

Do you come here often?
¿Viene usted aquí a menudo?
BYEH-neh oo-STEHTH ah-KEE ah meh-NOO-thoh?

I (don't) come here often.
(No) vengo aquí a menudo.
(noh) BEHN-goh ah-KEE ah meh-NOO-thoh.

Old

How old are you?
¿Qué edad tiene?
keh eh-THAHTH TYEH-neh?

I am _____ years old.
Tengo _____ años (de edad).
TEHN-goh _____ AH-nyohss (deh eh-THAHTH).

How old is this building?
¿En qué año se construyó este edificio?
*ehn keh AH-nyoh seh kohn-stroo-YOH EHSS-teh eh-thee-
  FEE-syoh?*

It is (not) old.
(No) es antiguo.
(noh) ehss ahn-TEE-gwoh.

On

How do you turn it on?
¿Cómo se pone en marcha?
KOH-moh seh POH-neh ehn MAHR-chah?

What flight are you on?
¿Qué vuelo ha reservado?
keh BWEH-loh ah rreh-sehr-BAH-thoh?

One Way

A one-way ticket to _____, please.
Un billete de ida a _____, por favor.
oon bee-YEH-teh deh EE-thah ah _____, pohr fah-BOHR.

Is this street one way?

¿Es esta calle de sentido unico?

ehss EHSS-*tah* KAH-*yeh deh sehn*-TEE-*thoh* OO-*nee-koh?*

Only

I speak only English.

Hablo inglés solamente.

AH-*bloh een*-GLEHSS *soh-lah*-MEHN-*teh.*

Open

May I open the door (window)?

¿Me permite abrir la puerta (ventana)?

meh pehr-MEE-*teh ah*-BREER *lah* PWEHR-*tah (behn*-TAH-*nah)?*

Please (don't) open the door (window).

Por favor, (no) abra la puerta (ventana).

pohr fah-BOHR, *(noh)* AH-*brah lah* PWEHR-*tah (behn*-TAH-*nah).*

Is it still open?

¿Está todavía abierta?

ehss-TAH *toh-thah*-BEE-*ah ah*-BYEHR-*tah?*

When do you open?

¿Cuándo abre usted?

KWAHN-*doh* AH-*breh oo*-STEHTH*?*

How long does it stay open?

¿Hasta cuándo está abierta?

AHSS-*tah* KWAHN-*doh ehss*-TAH *ah*-BYEHR-*tah?*

Opener

Excuse me, but have you a can opener (bottle opener)?

Discúlpeme, ¿tiene usted un abrelatas (sacacorchos)?

dees-KOOL-*peh-meh,* TYEH-*neh oo*-STEHTH *oon ah-breh*-LAH-*tahss (sah-kah*-KOHR-*chohss)?*

Opera

Where is the opera house?

¿Dónde está la ópera?

DOHN-*deh ehss*-TAH *lah* OH-*peh-rah?*

What opera is being given tonight?

¿Qué ópera se da esta noche?

keh OH-*peh-rah seh dah* EHSS-*tah* NOH-*cheh?*

Would you like to go to the opera with me?

¿Le gustaría ir a la ópera conmigo?

leh gooss-tah-REE-ah eer ah lah OH-peh-rah kohn-MEE-goh?

Operator — see Telephone

Opposite

What is that building opposite?

¿Qué es ese edificio de enfrente?

keh ehss EH-seh eh-thee-FEE-syoh deh ehn-FREHN-teh?

Orchestra

Is the orchestra playing tonight?

¿Toca la orquesta esta noche?

TOH-kah lah ohr-KEHSS-tah EHSS-tah NOH-cheh?

Order

May I order, please?

¿Puedo pedir, por favor?

PWEH-thoh peh-THEER, pohr fah-BOHR?

Where can I cash a money order?

¿Dónde puedo cobrar un giro postal?

DOHN-deh PWEH-thoh koh-BRAHR oon HEE-roh pohss-TAHL?

I did not order this service.

No encargué este servicio.

noh ehn-kahr-GHEH EHSS-teh sehr-BEE-syoh.

This is (not) what I ordered.

Esto (no) es lo que pedí.

EHSS-toh (noh) ehss loh keh peh-THEE.

Outlet

Where is the electrical outlet?

¿Dónde está el enchufe eléctrico?

DOHN-deh ehss-TAH ehl ehn-CHOO-feh eh-LEHK-tree-koh?

Overcooked

This is overcooked; please take it back.

Esto está demasiado hecho; por favor, lléveselo.

EHSS-toh ehss-TAH deh-mah-SYAH-thoh EH-choh; pohr fah-BOHR, YEH-beh-seh-loh.

Overnight

We will be staying overnight.
Pasaremos la noche.
*pah-sah-*REH*-mohss lah* NOH*-cheh.*

May I leave the car here overnight?
¿Puedo dejar el coche aquí durante la noche?
PWEH*-thoh deh-*HAHR *ehl* KOH*-cheh ah-*KEE *doo-*RAHN*-teh lah* NOH*-cheh?*

Overtime

What is the charge for overtime?
¿Cuánto se cobra por las horas extraordinarias?
KWAHN*-toh seh* KOH*-brah pohr lahss* OH*-rahss ehss-trah-ohr-thee-*NAH*-ree-ahss?*

Is there a charge for overtime?
¿Están las horas extraordinarias sujetas a sobrecargo?
*ehss-*TAHN *lahss* OH*-rahss ehss-trah-ohr-thee-*NAH*-ree-ahss soo-*HEH*-tahss ah soh-breh-*KAHR*-goh?*

Owe

How much do I owe?
¿Cuánto le debo?
KWAHN*-toh leh* DEH*-boh?*

Owner

May I speak to the owner, please?
¿Podría hablar con el propietario, por favor?
*poh-*THREE*-ah ah-*BLAHR *kohn ehl proh-pree-eh-*TAH*-ryoh, pohr fah-*BOHR*?*

Are you the owner?
¿Es usted el propietario?
*ehss oo-*STEHTH *ehl proh-pree-eh-*TAH*-ryoh?*

Pack

Please, pack this carefully.
Haga el favor de empaquetar esto con cuidado.
AH*-gah ehl fah-*BOHR *deh ehm-pah-keh-*TAHR EHSS*-toh kohn kwee-*THAH*-thoh.*

Package

Has a package arrived for me?
¿Ha llegado un paquete para mí?
*ah yeh-*GAH*-thoh oon pah-*KEH*-teh pah-rah* MEE*?*

Page

Please page _____.

Por favor, haga llamar a _____.

pohr fah-BOHR, AH-gah yah-MAHR ah _____.

Pain

Do you feel any pain?

¿Siente usted algún dolor?

SYEHN-teh oo-STEHTH ahl-GOON doh-LOHR?

Paper

Where can I buy a paper?

¿Dónde puedo comprar un periódico?

DOHN-deh PWEH-thoh kohm-PRAHR oon peh-RYOH-thee-koh?

May I have some writing paper?

Me puede dar papel de escribir?

meh PWEH-theh dahr pah-PEHL deh ehss-kree-BEER?

Parcel

What will it cost to send this parcel?

¿Cuánto costará enviar este paquete?

KWAHN-toh kohss-tah-RAH ehn-BYAHR EHSS-teh pah-KEH-teh?

Parcel Post – see Post Office

Pardon

Pardon me!

¡Perdóneme!

pehr-THOH-neh-meh!

Park

May I park here for a while?

¿Puedo estacionar (aparcar) aquí un rato?

PWEH-thoh ehss-tah-syoh-NAHR (ah-pahr-KAHR) ah-KEE oon RRAH-toh?

Where can I park?

¿Dónde puedo aparcar?

DOHN-deh PWEH-thoh ah-pahr-KAHR?

Pass

Do I need a pass?

¿Necesito un pase?

neh-seh-SEE-toh oon PAH-seh?

May I have a pass?
¿Puede darme un pase?
PWEH-*theh* DAHR-*meh oon* PAH-*seh?*

Passport
Here is my passport.
Aquí está mi pasaporte.
ah-KEE *ehss*-TAH *mee pah-sah*-POHR-*teh.*

I don't have my passport with me.
No llevo mi pasaporte.
noh YEH-*boh mee pah-sah*-POHR-*teh.*

I have lost my passport.
He perdido mi pasaporte.
eh pehr-THEE-*thoh mee pah-sah*-POHR-*teh.*

Pastry
What kind of pastry do you have?
¿Qué tippo de pasteles tiene usted?
keh TEE-*poh deh pahss*-TEH-*lehss* TYEH-*neh oo*-STEHTH?

Pawn; Pawnshop
I would like to pawn this.
Quisiera empeñar esto.
kee-SYEH-*rah ehm-peh*-NYAHR EHSS-*toh.*

Could you direct me to a pawnshop?
¿Puede indicarme una casa de empeño?
PWEH-*theh een-dee*-KAHR-*meh* OO-*nah* KAH-*sah deh* ehm-PEH-*nyoh?*

Pay
Where (whom) do I pay?
¿Dónde (a quién) pago?
DOHN-*deh (ah* KYEHN*)* PAH-*goh?*

How much must I pay?
¿Cuánto tengo que pagar?
KWAHN-*toh* TEHN-*goh keh pah*-GAHR?

Do I pay now or later?
¿Pago ahora o luego?
PAH-*goh ah*-OH-*rah oh* LWEH-*goh?*

I have already paid.
Ya he pagado.
*yah eh pah-*GAH-*thoh.*

I have not paid yet.
Todavía no he pagado.
*toh-thah-*BEE-*ah noh eh pah-*GAH-*thoh.*

Have you paid?
¿Ha pagado usted?
*ah pah-*GAH-*thoh oo-*STEHTH?

Pen (Pencil)

Have you a pen (a pencil) I could borrow?
¿Puede prestarme usted una pluma (un lápiz)?
PWEH-*theh prehss-*TAHR-*meh oo-*STEHTH OO-*nah* PLOO-
mah (oon LAH-*peess)?*

Pepper -

May I have the pepper, please?
¿Me da la pimienta, por favor?
*meh dah lah pee-*MYEHN-*tah, pohr fah-*BOHR?

Performance

When does the (evening) performance begin?
¿Cuándo comienza la sesión (de la tarde)?
KWAHN-*doh koh-*MYEHN-*sah lah seh-*SYOHN *(deh lah*
TAHR-*theh)?*

Permit

Do I need a permit?
¿Necesito un permiso?
*neh-seh-*SEE-*toh oon pehr-*MEE-*soh?*

Personal

This is for my personal use.
Esto es para mi uso personal.
EHSS-*toh ehss pah-rah mee* OO-*soh pehr-soh-*NAHL.

Will you accept (cash) a personal check?
¿Aceptaría (cambiaría) usted an cheque personal?
*ah-sehp-tah-*REE-*ah (kahm-byah-*REE-*ah) oo-*STEHTH
oon CHEH-*keh pehr-soh-*NAHL?

Phone – see also Telephone
I would like to make a phone call to _____.
Quisiera llamar por teléfono a _____.
*kee-*SYEH*-rah yah-*MAHR *pohr teh-*LEH*-foh-noh ah*

_____.

Photograph
Excuse me, but I would like you to take a photograph
of me (us).
Perdone, quisiera que me (nos) tomara usted una foto.
*pehr-*THOH*-neh, kee-*SYEH*-rah keh meh (nohss) toh-*MAH*-
rah oo-*STEHTH OO*-nah* FOH*-toh.*

Am I allowed to take photographs here?
¿Está permitido sacar fotografías aquí?
*ehss-*TAH *pehr-mee-*TEE*-thoh sah-*KAHR *foh-toh-grah-*
FEE*-ahss ah-*KEE?

Piano
I play the piano.
Yo toco el piano.
yoh TOH*-koh ehl pee-*AH*-noh.*

Do you play the piano?
¿Toca usted el piano?
TOH*-kah oo-*STEHTH *ehl pee-*AH*-noh?*

Picnic
Let's have a picnic.
Vamos a hacer un picnic.
BAH*-mohss ah ah-*SEHR *oon* PEEK*-neek.*

Pillow
Please bring me a (another) pillow.
Por favor, tráigame una (otra) almohada.
*pohr fah-*BOHR, TRAH*-ee-gah-meh* OO-NAH (*oh-*TRAH)
*ahl-moh-*AH*-thah.*

Plane – see Flight

Plate
May I have a (another) (clean) plate, please.
¿Me da un (otro) plato (limpio), por favor?
*meh dah oon (*OH*-troh)* PLAH*-toh (*LEEM*-pyoh), pohr fah-*
BOHR?

Platform – see also Gate

At which platform is the train for _____?
¿En qué andén está el tren a _____?
ehn keh ahn-DEHN ehss-TAH ehl TREHN ah _____?

Play

I want to see a play tonight.
Quiero ver una obra (de teatro) esta noche.
KYEH-roh BEHR OO-nah OH-brah (deh teh-AH-troh) EHSS-tah NOH-cheh.

Which play would you recommend?
¿Qué obra recomienda usted?
keh OH-brah rreh-koh-MYEHN-dah oo-STEHTH?

Will you attend the play with me?
¿Me acompañaría a una obra de teatro?
meh ah-kohm-pah-nyah-REE-ah ah OO-nah OH-brah deh teh-AH-troh?

When does the play begin?
¿Cuándo comienza la obra?
KWAHN-doh koh-MYEHN-sah lah OH-brah?

Do you play golf (tennis, bridge, chess)?
¿Juega usted al golf (tenis, bridge, ajedrez)?
HWEH-gah oo-STEHTH ahl GOHLF (TEH-neess, BREEDJ, ah-heh-DREHSS)?

Would you like to play golf (tennis, bridge, chess)?
¿Quiere usted jugar al golf (tenis, bridge, ajedrez)?
KYEH-reh oo-STEHTH hoo-GAHR ahl GOHLF (TEH-neess, BREEDJ, ah-heh-DREHSS)?

I don't play (very well).
No juego (muy bien).
noh HWEH-goh (mwee BYEHN).

Please

Please don't do that.
Por favor, no haga eso.
pohr fah-BOHR, noh AH-gah EH-soh.

Please pass the _____.
¿Me da el (la) _____, por favor?
meh dah ehl (lah) _____, pohr fah-BOHR?

Plenty

I have plenty, thanks.
Tengo de sobra, gracias.
TEHN-*goh deh* SOH-*brah,* GRAH-*syahss.*

Point

Please point the way to _____.
Por favor, indíqueme el camino a _____.
*pohr fah-*BOHR, *een-*DEE-*keh-meh ehl kah-*MEE-*noh ah*

_____.

Point to the phrase in this book.
Indique la frase en este libro.
*een-*DEE-*keh lah* FRAH-*seh ehn* EHSS-*teh* LEE -*broh.*

Police

Call the police!
¡Llame a la policía!
YAH-*meh ah lah poh-lee-*SEE-*ah!*

Where is the police station?
¿Dónde está la comisaría de policía?
DOHN-*deh ehss-*TAH *lah koh-mee-sah-*REE-*ah deh poh-*
*lee-*SEE-*ah?*

Policeman

Call a policeman!
¡Llame a un policía!
YAH-*meh ah oon poh-lee-*SEE-*ah!*

Polish

Could you polish my shoes, please?
¿Puede usted limpiar mis zapatos, por favor?
PWEH-*theh oo-*STEHTH *leem-*PYAHR *meess sah-*PAH-
*tohss, pohr fah-*BOHR?

Pool

Where is the pool?
¿Dónde está la piscina?
DOHN-*deh ehss-*TAH *lah peess-*SEE-*nah?*

Is there a charge for the pool?
¿Se cobra algo para la piscina?
seh KOH-*brah* AHL-*goh pah-rah lah peess-*SEE-*nah?*

Port

What is the next port?
¿Cuál es el próximo puerto?
KWAHL *ehss ehl* PROHK-*see-moh* PWEHR-*toh?*

When do we reach port?
¿Cuándo llegamos al puerto?
KWAHN-*doh yeh*-GAH-*mohss ahl* PWEHR-*toh?*

Porter

I need a porter.
Necesito un mozo.
neh-seh-SEE-*toh oon* MOH-*soh.*

Possible

As soon as possible.
Lo más pronto posible.
loh mahss PROHN-*toh poh*-SEE-*bleh.*

Postage – see also Post Office

What is the postage on this?
¿Cuál es el franqueo de esto?
KWAHL *ehss ehl frah*-KEH-*oh deh* EHSS-*toh?*

Postcards

Do you sell postcards?
¿Vende usted tarjetas postales?
BEHN-*deh oo*-STEHTH *tahr*-HEH-*tahss pohss*-TAH-*lehss?*

Do you have postcards of _____?
¿Tiene usted tarjetas postales de _____?
TYEH-*neh oo*-STEHTH *tahr*-HEH-*tahss pohss*-TAH-*lehss
deh _____?*

Please mail these postcards for me.
Haga el favor de echar estas tarjetas postales al
correo.
AH-*gah ehl fah*-BOHR *deh eh*-CHAHR EHSS-*tahss tahr*-
HEH-*tahss pohss*-TAH-*lehss ahl koh*-RREH-*oh.*

Postman

At what time does the postman arrive?
¿A qué hora llega el cartero?
ah keh OH-*rah* YEH-*gah ehl kahr*-TEH-*roh?*

Please give this to the postman.
Por favor, dé esto al cartero.
pohr fah-BOHR, DEH EHSS-toh ahl kahr-TEH-roh.

Post Office

Where is the post office?
¿Dónde está el correo?
DOHN-*deh ehss-TAH ehl koh-RREH-oh?*

Where can I buy air mail stamps (for the United
  States)?
¿Dónde puedo comprar estampillas de correo aéreo
  (para los Estados Unidos)?
DOHN-*deh* PWEH-*thoh kohm-*PRAHR *ehss-tahm-*PEE-*
  yahss deh koh-RREH-oh ah-EH-reh-oh (pah-rah lohss
  ehss-TAH-thohss oo-NEE-thohss)?*

How many stamps do I need for _____?
¿Cuántas estampillas necesito par _____?
KWAHN-*tahss ehss-tahm-*PEE-*yahss neh-seh-*SEE-*toh
  pah-rah* _____?

How much is the postage?
¿Cuánto cuesta el franqueo?
KWAHN-*toh* KWEHSS-*tah ehl frahn-*KEH-*oh?*

How long will it take to get to _____?
¿Cuánto tardará en llegar a _____?
KWAHN-*toh tahr-thah-*RAH *ehn yeh-*GAHR *ah* _____?

Will it arrive within _____ days (weeks)?
¿Llegará dentro de _____ días (semanas)?
*yeh-gah-*RAH DEHN-*troh deh* _____ DEE-*ahss (seh-*MAH-*
  nahss)?*

Please send this (these) by air mail (registered,
  insured, special delivery).
Por favor, envíe esto (estos) por correo aéreo
  (certificado, asegurado, entrega inmediata).
*pohr fah-*BOHR, *ehn-*BEE-*eh* EHSS-*toh (*EHSS-*tohss) pohr
  koh-RREH-oh ah-EH-reh-oh (sehr-tee-fee-*KAH-*thoh, ah-
  seh-goo-*RAH-*thoh, ehn-*TREH-*gah een-meh-thee-*AH-*
  tah).*

Could you wrap this package for me?
¿Puede usted envolver este paquete?
PWEH-*theh* oo-STEHTH *ehn-bohl*-BEHR EHSS-*teh pah*-
  KEH-*teh?*

Will the receiver have to pay duty?
¿Tendrá que pagar impuesto el destinatario?
tehn-DRAH *keh pah*-GAHR *eem*-PWEHSS-*toh ehl dehss-
tee-nah*-TAH-*ryoh?*

Pounds

How many pounds of baggage per person?
¿Cuántas libras de equipaje por persona?
KWAHN-*tahss* LEE-*brahss deh eh-kee*-PAH-*heh pohr pehr*-
  SOH-*nah?*

How many pounds of overweight baggage do I have?
¿Cuántas libras tengo de exceso?
KWAHN-*tahss* LEE-*brahss* TEHN-*goh deh ehss*-SEH-*soh?*

Prefer – see also Rather

I prefer something better (cheaper).
Prefiero algo mejor (más barato).
preh-FYEH-*roh* AHL-*goh meh*-HOHR *(mahss bah*-RAH-
  toh).

I prefer (to do) this.
Prefiero (hacer) esto.
preh-FYEH-*roh (ah*-SEHR*)* EHSS-*toh.*

Pregnant

I am pregnant.
Estoy embarazada.
ehss-TOY *ehm-bah-rah*-SAH-*thah.*

Prescription – see also Medical

Can you fill this prescription?
¿Puede usted preparar esta receta?
PWEH-*theh* oo-STEHTH *preh-pah*-RAHR EHSS-*tah rreh*-
  SEH-*tah?*

When will my prescription be ready?
¿Cuándo estará lista mi receta?
KWAHN-*doh ehss-tah*-RAH LEESS-*tah mee rreh*-SEH-*tah?*

Press – see Laundry

Priest — see also Minister

Where can I find a (an English-speaking) priest?

¿Dónde puedo encontrara un sacerdote (que hable inglés)?

DOHN-*deh* PWEH-*thoh ehn-kohn-*TRAHR *ah oon sah-sehr-*DOH-*teh (keh-*AH-*bleh een-*GLEHSS*)?*

Private

I want a private room (a private bathroom, a private compartment).

Quiero una habitación privada (un cuarto de baño privado, un compartimiento privado).

KYEH-*roh* OO-*nah ah-bee-tah-*SYOHN *pree-*BAH-*thah (oon KWAHR-*toh deh* BAH-*nyoh pree-*BAH-*thoh, oon kohm-pahr-tee-*MYEHN-*toh pree-*BAH-*thoh).*

Profession

What is your profession?

¿Cuál es su profesión?

KWAHL *ehss soo proh-feh-*SYOHN?

Program

Where can I get a program?

¿Dónde puedo conseguir un programa?

DOHN-*deh* PWEH-*thoh kohn-seh-*GHEER *oon proh-*GRAH-*mah?*

Is there a charge for the program?

¿Se cobra para el programa?

seh KOH-*brah pah-rah ehl proh-*GRAH-*mah?*

When does the program begin?

¿Cuándo comienza el programa?

KWAHN-*doh koh-*MYEHN-*sah ehl proh-*GRAH-*mah?*

Pronounce

How do you pronounce this?

¿Cómo se pronuncia esto?

KOH-*moh seh proh-*NOON-*syah* EHSS-*toh?*

Protestant

I am a Protestant.

Soy protestante.

*soy proh-tehss-*TAHN-*teh.*

Can you direct me to the nearest protestant church?

¿Puede usted dirigirme a la iglesia protestante más próxima?

PWEH-*theh* oo-STEHTH *dee-ree-*HEER-*meh ah-lah ee-*GLEH-*syah proh-tess-*TAHN-*teh mahss* PROHK-*see-mah?*

Public

Is this open to the public?

¿Está esto abierto al publico? (¿Se admite aquí al publico?)

ehss-TAH EHSS-*toh ah-*BYEHR-*toh ahl* POO-*blee-koh?(seh ahd-*MEE-*teh ah-*KEE *ahl* POO-*blee-koh?*)

Push

Can you push my car?

¿Puede empujarme el auto?

PWEH-*theh ehm-poo-*HAHR-*meh ehl* OW-*toh?*

Put

Please put this in the safe (in my room).

Por favor, ponga esto en la caja fuerte (en mi habitación).

*pohr fah-*BOHR, POHN-*gah* EHSS-*toh ehn soo* KAH-*hah* FWEHR-*teh (ehn mee ah-bee-tah-*SYOHN*).

Quality

I want the best quality.

Quiero la major calidad.

KYEH-*roh lah meh-*HOHR *kah-lee-*THAHTH.

Quantity

What quantity may I take (can you give me)?

¿Qué cantidad puedo llevar (me puede dar)?

*keh kahn-tee-*THAHTH PWEH-*thoh yeh-*BAHR *(meh* PWEH-*theh* DAHR*)?*

Question

I have a question.

Tengo una pregunta.

TEHN-*goh* OO-*nah preh-*GOON-*tah.*

Quickly

Call a doctor quickly!
¡Llame a un médico en seguida!
YAH-*meh ah oon* MEH-*thee-koh ehn seh*-GHEE-*thah!*

Call the police quickly!
¡Llame a la policía en seguida!
YAH-*meh ah lah poh-lee*-SEE-*ah ehn seh*-GHEE-*thah!*

Come here quickly!
¡Venga aquí en seguida!
BEHN-*gah ah*-KEE *ehn seh*-GHEE-*thah!*

Quiet

Can you recommend a nice, quiet restaurant (hotel)?
¿Puede recomendarme un restaurante (hotel)
   agradable y tranquilo?
PWEH-*theh rreh-koh-mehn*-DAHR-*meh oon rrehss-tah-oo-*
   RAHN-*teh (oh*-TEHL*) ah-grah*-THAH-*bleh ee trahn*-KEE-
   loh?

Quiet, please!
¡Silencio, por favor!
see-LEHN-*syoh, pohr fah*-BOHR!

Rabbi

Where can I find a (an English-speaking) rabbi?
¿Dónde puedo encontrar a un rabino (que hable
   inglés)?
DOHN-*deh* PWEH-*thoh ehn-kohn*-TRAHR *ah oon rrah*-BEE-
   noh (keh AH-*bleh een*-GLEHSS*)?*

Radio

May I have a radio for my room, please?
¿Me da un aparato de radio para mi habitación, por
   favor?
meh DAH *oon ah-pah*-RAH-*toh deh* RRAH-*thyoh pah-rah*
   mee ah-bee-tah-SYOHN, *pohr fah*-BOHR?

The radio in my room does not work.
El aparato de radio de mi habitación no funciona.
ehl ah-pah-RAH-*toh deh* RRAH-*thyoh deh mee ah-bee-tah*-
   SYOHN *noh foon*-SYOH-*nah.*

Railroad

Can you direct me (take me) to the railroad station?

¿Puede dirigirme (llevarme) usted a la estación del ferrocarril?

PWEH-*theh* dee-ree-HEER-*meh* (*yeh*-BAHR-*meh*) oo-STEHTH *ah lah ehss-tah-*SYOHN *deh feh-rroh-kah-*RREEL?

Rain

There will be rain this morning (afternoon, evening).

Llovera esta mañana (tarde, noche).

*yoh-beh-*RAH EHSS-*tah mah-*NYAH-*nah (*TAHR-*theh*, NOH-*cheh).

Is it raining?

¿Llueve ahora?

YWEH-*beh ah-*OH-*rah?*

Rare

I want my meat rare (medium rare), please.

Quiero la carne poco asada, por favor.

KYEH-*roh lah* KAHR-*neh* POH-*koh ah-*SAH-*thah, pohr fah-*BOHR.

I ordered this rare; please take it back.

Pedí esto poco asado; haga el favor de llevárselo.

*peh-*THEE EHSS-*toh* POH-*koh ah-*SAH-*thoh;* AH-*gah ehl fah-*BOHR *deh yeh-*BAHR-*seh-loh.*

This is too rare; please take it back.

Esto está muy poco asado; haga el favor de llevárselo.

EHSS-*toh ehss-*TAH *mwee* POH-*koh ah-*SAH-*thoh;* AH-*gah ehl fah-*BOHR *deh yeh-*BAHR-*seh-loh.*

Rate — see also Bank

What is the rate per kilometer (per minute, per hour, per day, per week, per month, per word)?

¿Cuál es la tarifa por kilómetro (minuto, hora, día, semana, mes, palabra)?

KWAHL *ehss lah tah-*REE-*fah pohr kee-*LOH-*meh-troh (mee-*NOO-*toh,* OH-*rah,* DEE-*ah, seh-*MAH-*nah,* MEHSS, *pah-*LAH-*brah)?*

What is your rate to _____?
¿Cuál es su tarifa hasta _____?
KWAHL *ehss soo tah*-REE-*fah* AHSS-*tah* _____?

What is the rate of exchange?
¿Cuál es el tipo de cambio?
KWAHL *ehss ehl* TEE-*poh deh* KAHM-*byoh?*

Rather – see also Prefer

I would rather go to _____ than _____.
Preferiría ir a _____ en vez de _____.
*preh-feh-ree-*REE-*ah eer ah* _____ *ehn behss deh* _____.

I would rather not.
Preferiría que no.
*preh-feh-ree-*REE-*ah keh noh.*

It is rather hot today.
Hace bastante calor hoy.
AH-*seh bahss-*TAHN-*teh kah-*LOHR *oy.*

Raw

I like my meat nearly raw.
Me gusta la carne casi cruda.
meh GOOSS-*tah lah* KAHR-*neh kah-see* KROO-*thah.*

This is raw; please take it back.
Esto está crudo; por favor, lléveselo.
EHSS-*toh ehss-*TAH KROO-*thoh; pohr fah-*BOHR, YEH-*beh-
seh-loh.*

Razor

Where is the electrical outlet for the razor?
¿Dónde está el enchufe eléctrico para la máquina de
afeitar?
DOHN-*deh ehss-*TAH *ehl ehn-*CHOO-*feh eh-*LEHK-*tree-koh
pah-rah lah* MAH-*kee-nah deh ah-fey-*TAHR?

Where can I buy razor blades?
¿Dónde puedo comprar hojas de afeitar?
DOHN-*deh* PWEH-*thoh kohm-*PRAHR OH-*hahss deh ah-
fey-*TAHR?

Ready

When will it (you) be ready?
¿Cuándo estará listo?
KWAHN-*doh ehss-tah-rah* LEESS-*toh?*

Are they ready?

¿Están (ellos) listos?

*ehss-*TAHN *(EH-yohss)* LEESS-*tohss?*

I am (not) ready.

(No) estoy listo (lista).

*(noh) ehss-*TOY LEESS-*toh (*LEESS-*tah).*

Reasonable

Can you recommend a hotel with reasonable rates?

¿Puede usted recomendar un hotel con precios
   módicos?

PWEH-*theh oo-*STEHTH *rreh-koh-mehn-*DAHR *oon oh-*
   TEHL *kohn* PREH-*syohss* MOH-*thee-kohss?*

Receipt

Give me a receipt, please.

Deme un recibo, por favor.

DEH-*meh oon rreh-*SEE-*boh, pohr fah-*BOHR.

Recipe

Would you (the chef) give me the recipe for this dish?

¿Puede usted (el cocinero) darme la receta para este
   plato?

PWEH-*theh oo-*STEHTH *(ehl koh-see-*NEH-*roh)* DAHR-*meh
   lah rreh-*SEH-*tah pah-rah* EHSS-*teh* PLAH-*toh?*

Recommend

Can you recommend a good restaurant (hotel)?

¿Puede recomendar un buen restaurante (hotel)?

PWEH-*theh rreh-koh-mehn-*DAHR *oon bwehn rrehss-tah-*
   *oo-*RAHN-*teh (oh-*TEHL*)?*

What do you recommend?

¿Qué recomienda usted?

*keh rreh-koh-*MYEHN-*dah oo-*STEHTH?

Record

Can you tell me where records are sold?

¿Puede decirme usted dónde se venden discos?

PWEH-*theh deh-*SEER-*meh oo-*STEHTH DOHN-*deh seh*
   BEHN-*dehn* DEESS-*kohss?*

Reduce

I am trying to reduce.

Estoy tratando de adelgazar.

ehss-TOY *trah*-TAHN-*doh deh ah-dehl-gah*-SAHR.

Refrigerator

I would like a room with a refrigerator.

Quisiera una habitación con refrigerador.

kee-SYEH-*rah* OO-*nah ah-bee-tah*-SYOHN *kohn rreh-free-heh-rah*-THOHR.

Refund

Will you give me a refund?

¿Me reembolsara usted?

meh rreh-ehm-bohl-sah-RAH *oo*-STEHTH?

Refuse (garbage)

Where does one dispose of refuse?

¿Dónde se echa la basura?

DOHN-*deh seh* EH-*chah lah bah*-SOO-*rah?*

Register

Where do I register?

¿Dónde me inscribo?

DOHN-*deh meh een*-SKREE-*boh?*

Remember

I do not remember your name (the address).

No recuerdo su nombre (la dirección).

noh rreh-KWEHR-*thoh soo* NOHM-*breh (lah dee-rehk*-SYOHN*).*

Rent

Where can I rent _____?

¿Dónde puedo alquilar _____?

DOHN-*deh* PWEH-*thoh ahl-kee*-LAHR _____?

How much does it cost to rent _____?

¿Cuánto cuesta alquilar _____?

KWAHN-*toh* KWEHSS-*tah ahl-kee*-LAHR _____?

Repair

Can you repair this? Do you know who can?

¿Puede usted arreglar esto? ¿Sabe usted quién puede hacerlo?

PWEH-*theh* oo-STEHTH ah-rreh-GLAHR EHSS-*toh*? SAH-*beh* oo-STEHTH KYEHN PWEH-*theh* ah-SEHR-*loh*?

Repeat

Repeat it, please.

Repita, por favor.

rreh-PEE-*tah, pohr fah*-BOHR.

Request

I have a request.

Tengo un pedido.

TEHN-*goh oon peh*-THEE-*thoh*.

Reservation

I want to confirm (cancel) my reservation to _____.

Quiero confirmar (anular) mi reserva a _____.

KYEH-*roh kohn-feer*-MAHR (*ah-noo*-LAHR) mee rreh-SEHR-*bah ah* _____.

Do I need a reservation?

¿Necesito una reserva?

neh-seh-SEE-*toh* OO-*nah* rreh-SEHR-*bah?*

I (don't) have a reservation.

(No) tengo una reserva.

(*noh*) TEHN-*goh* OO-*nah* rreh-SEHR-*bah.*

Should we make the reservation well in advance?

¿Debemos hacer la reserva con mucha anticipación?

deh-BEH-*mohss ah*-SEHR *lah* rreh-SEHR-*bah kohn* MOO-*chah ahn-tee-see-pah*-SYOHN?

Could I make a reservation on the flight to _____?

¿Puedo hacer una reserva en el vuelo a _____?

PWEH-*thoh ah*-SEHR OO-*nah* rreh-SEHR-*bah ehn ehl* BWEH-*loh ah* _____?

Reserve

Can I reserve a (front, window) seat?

¿Puedo reservar un asiento (delantero, de ventanilla)?

PWEH-*thoh rreh-sehr*-BAHR *oon ah*-SYEHN-*toh* (*deh-lahn*-TEH-*roh, deh behn-tah*-NEE-*yah*)?

Is this reserved?

¿Está (esto) reservado?

ehss-TAH (EHSS-toh) rreh-sehr-BAH-thoh?

Resident

Are you a resident of _____?

¿Es usted residente de _____?

ehss oo-STEHTH rreh-see-THEHN-teh deh _____?

Resort

Can you recommend a good summer resort?

¿Puede recomendarme usted un buen lugar de veraneo?

PWEH-theh rreh-koh-mehn-DAHR-meh oo-STEHTH oon bwehn loo-GAHR-deh beh-rah-NEH-oh?

Restaurant

Can you recommend a good restaurant (that isn't expensive)?

¿Puede recomendarme un buen restaurante (que no sea caro)?

PWEH-theh rreh-koh-mehn-DAHR-meh oon bwehn rrehss-tah-oo-RAHN-teh (keh noh SEH-ah KAH-roh)?

Return

I want to return (on Saturday).

Quiero regresar (el sábado).

KYEH-roh rreh-greh-SAHR (ehl SAH-bah-thoh).

When will he (she) return?

¿Cuándo regresará él (ella)?

KWAHN-doh rreh-greh-sah-RAH EHL (EH-yah)?

Reverse

I would like to reverse the charges.

Quisiera que el pago lo hiciera el destinatario.

kee-SYEH-rah keh ehl PAH-goh loh ee-SYEH-rah ehl dehss-tee-nah-TAH-ryoh.

How do you get it into reverse?

¿Cómo se mete la marcha atrás?

KOH-moh seh MEH-teh lah MAHR-chah ah-TRAHSS?

Reward

I am offering a reward of _____.

Ofrezco una recompensa de _____.

oh-FREHSS-koh OO-nah rreh-kohm-PEHN-sah deh _____.

Ride

May I have a ride (to _____)?

¿Puede llevarme (a _____)?

PWEH-theh yeh-BAHR-meh (ah _____)?

Let's go for a bicycle (automobile) ride.

Vamos a dar una vuelta en bicicleta (en coche).

BAH-mohss ah dahr OO-nah BWEHL-tah ehn bee-see-KLEH-tah (ehn KOH-cheh).

River

What river is this?

¿Qué río es éste?

keh RREE-oh ehss EHSS-teh?

Road

Is this the road to _____?

¿Es ésta la carretera a _____?

ehss EHSS-tah lah kah-rreh-TEH-rah ah _____?

Which is the road to _____?

¿Cuál es la carretera a _____?

KWAHL ehss lah kah-rreh-TEH-rah ah _____?

Which road should I take?

¿Qué carretera debo tomar?

keh kah-rreh-TEH-rah DEH-boh toh-MAHR?

Where does this road go?

¿Adónde va esta carretera?

ah-DOHN-deh BAH EHSS-tah kah-rreh-TEH-rah?

Is the road paved (bumpy)?

¿Está asfaltada (llena de baches) la carretera?

ehss-TAH ahss-fahl-TAH-thah (YEH-nah deh BAH-chehss) lah kah-rreh-TEH-rah?

Robbed

I have been robbed! Call the police (the manager)!

¡Me han robado! ¡Llame a la policía (al gerente)!

meh ahn rroh-BAH-thoh! YAH-meh ah lah poh-lee-SEE-ah (ahl heh-REHN-teh)!

Room

I want a room with a double bed (single bed, twin beds) and bath.

Quiero una habitación con una cama doble (cama individual, dos camas) y baño.

KYEH-*roh* OO-*nah ah-bee-tah*-SYOHN *kohn* OO-*nah* KAH-*mah* DOH-*bleh (*KAH-*mah een-dee-bee*-THWAHL, *dohss* KAH-*mahss) ee* BAH-*nyoh.*

Do you have a room?

¿Tiene usted una habitación?

TYEH-*neh oo*-STEHTH OO-*nah ah-bee-tah*-SYOHN?

Is there a room for us?

¿Tiene usted una habitación para nosotros?

TYEH-*neh oo*-STEHTH OO-*nah ah-bee-tah*-SYOHN *pah-rah noh*-SOH-*trohss?*

I am in room number _____.

Estoy en la habitación número _____.

ehss-TOY *ehn lah ah-bee-tah*-SYOHN NOO-*meh-roh* _____.

Room service, please.

El servicio de habitación, por favor.

ehl sehr-BEE-*syoh deh ah-bee-tah*-SYOHN, *pohr fah*-BOHR.

Round Trip

A round-trip ticket to _____, please.

Un billete para un viaje de ida y vuelta, a _____, por favor.

oon bee-YEH-*teh pah-rah oon* BYAH-*heh deh* EE-*thah ee* BWEHL-*tah, ah* _____, *pohr fah*-BOHR.

How much is a round-trip ticket?

¿Cuánto cuesta un billete para un viaje de ida y vuelta?

KWAHN-*toh* KWEHSS-*tah oon bee*-YEH-*teh pah-rah oon* BYAH-*heh deh* EE-*thah ee* BWEHL-*tah?*

Route

Which is the best route to _____?

¿Cuál es la mejor ruta a _____?

KWAHL *ehss lah meh*-HOHR RROO-*tah ah* _____?

Rubbish

Please take care of this rubbish.

Por favor, encárguese de esta basura.

pohr fah-BOHR, ehn-KAHR-gheh-seh deh EHSS-tah bah-SOO-rah.

Ruins

Is there a tour of the ruins?

¿Hay alguna excursión a las ruinas?

ahy ahl-GOO-nah ehss-koor-SYOHN ah lahss RWEE-nahss?

Which way are the ruins?

¿En qué dirección están las ruinas?

ehn keh dee-rehk-SYOHN ehss-TAHN lahss RWEE-nahss?

Safe

Is it safe?

¿Es seguro?

ehss seh-GOO-roh?

Please keep these in the safe for me.

Por favor, guárdeme éstos (éstas) en la caja fuerte.

pohr fah-BOHR, GWAHR-theh-meh EHSS-tohss (EHSS-tahss) ehn lah KAH-hah FWEHR-teh.

Sale

Is this for sale?

¿Se vende esto?

seh BEHN-deh EHSS-toh?

Salt

May I have the salt, please.

¿Me da la sal, por favor?

meh DAH lah SAHL, pohr fah-BOHR?

Please cook it without salt.

Por favor, concínelo sin sal.

pohr fah-BOHR, koh-SEE-neh-loh seen SAHL.

Sandwiches

Do you have sandwiches?

¿Tiene usted sandwiches?

TYEH-neh oo-STEHTH SAHN-wee-chehss?

Say

How do you say _____ in _____?

¿Cómo se dice _____ en _____?

KOH-*moh seh* DEE-*seh* _____ *ehn* _____?

What did you (he, she) say?

¿Qué dijo usted (él, ella)?

keh DEE-*hoh oo*-STEHTH (EHL, EH-*yah*)?

Schedule

May I have a copy of the schedule?

¿Puede darme una copia de la lista?

PWEH-*theh* DAHR-*meh* OO-*nah* KOH-*pyah deh lah* LEESS-*tah*?

School

Are you in school?

¿Es usted estudiante?

ehss oo-STEHTH *ehss-too*-THYAHN-*teh*?

Where do you go to school?

¿Dónde estudia usted?

DOHN-*deh ehss*-TOO-*thyah oo*-STEHTH?

Seasick

I am seasick.

Estoy mareado (mareada).

ehss-TOY *mah-reh*-AH-*thoh* (*mah-reh*-AH-*thah*).

Seat

Is this seat taken?

¿Está ocupado este asiento?

ehss-TAH *oh-koo*-PAH-*thoh* EHSS-*teh ah*-SYEHN-*toh*?

I want a window seat, please.

Quisiera un asiento de ventana, por favor.

kee-SYEH-*rah oon ah*-SYEHN-*toh deh behn*-TAH-*nah*, *pohr fah*-BOHR.

Is there a seat available?

¿Hay algún asiento disponible?

ahy ahl-GOON *ah*-SYEHN-*toh deess-poh*-NEE-*bleh*?

See

May I see you tonight?

¿Puedo verle a usted esta noche?

PWEH-*thoh* BEHR-*leh ah oo*-STEHTH EHSS-*tah* NOH-*cheh*?

Have you seen my _____?
¿Ha visto usted mi _____?
ah BEESS-toh oo-STEHTH mee _____ ?

I want to see _____.
Quiero ver _____.
KYEH-*roh* BEHR _____.

Sell
Would you sell me this?
¿Me vendería usted esto?
meh behn-deh-REE-ah oo-STEHTH EHSS-toh?

Separate
We want separate rooms.
Queremos habitaciones separadas.
keh-REH-mohss ah-bee-tah-SYOH-nehss seh-pah-RAH-thahss.

Servant
I would like to hire (advertise for) a servant.
Quisiera contratar (poner un anuncio para) una
   sirvienta.
kee-SYEH-rah kohn-trah-TAHR (poh-NEHR oon ah-NOON-syoh pah-rah) OO-*nah seer-BYEHN-tah.*

Service
Is the service charge included?
¿Está incluido el porcentaje de servicio?
*ehss-TAH een-kloo-EE-thoh ehl pohr-sehn-TAH-heh deh
   sehr-BEE-syoh?*

Room service, please.
Por favor, el servicio de habitación.
pohr fah-BOHR, ehl sehr-BEE-syoh deh ah-bee-tah-SYOHN.

Is there bus (limousine) service to the airport (hotel)?
Hay servicio de autobús (automóvil) al aeropuerto
   (hotel)?
*ahy sehr-BEE-syoh deh ow-toh-BOOSS (ow-toh-MOH-beel)
   ahl ah-eh-roh-PWEHR-toh (oh-TEHL)?*

When is the church service?
¿Cuándo se celebra el servicio religioso?
KWAHN-*doh seh seh-LEH-brah ehl sehr-BEE-syoh rreh-lee-HYOH-soh?*

Sew – see Laundry

Share

I do not want to share a bath.

No quiero compartir un baño.

noh KYEH-*roh kohm-pahr*-TEER *oon* BAH-*nyoh.*

Sharp

This knife is not very sharp.

Este cuchillo no está bien afilado.

EHSS-*teh koo*-CHEE-*yoh noh ehss*-TAH BYEHN *ah-fee*-LAH-*thoh.*

Shave – see Barber

Shaver

Where can I plug in an electric shaver?

¿Dónde puedo enchufar una máquina de afeitar eléctrica?

DOHN-*deh* PWEH-*thoh ehn-choo*-FAHR OO-*nah* MAH-*kee-nah deh ah-fey*-TAHR *eh*-LEHK-*tree-kah?*

Sheet

Please change the sheets.

Por favor, cambie las sábanas.

pohr fah-BOHR, KAHM-*byeh lahss* SAH-*bah-nahss.*

Shine

Please shine my shoes.

Por favor, limpie mis zapatos.

pohr fah-BOHR, LEEM-*pyeh meess sah*-PAH-*tohss.*

Ship

When does the ship arrive (leave)?

¿Cuándo llega (sale) el barco?

KWAHN-*doh* YEH-*gah* (SAH-*leh) ehl* BAHR-*koh?*

Shoe

Where can I get my shoes repaired?

¿Dónde pueden arreglarme mis zapatos?

DOHN-*deh* PWEH-*thehn ah-rreh*-GLAHR-*meh meess sah*-PAH-*tohss?*

Shopping

Where is the shopping center?
¿Dónde está el centro?
DOHN-*deh* ehss-TAH *ehl* SEHN-*troh?*

Is there a salesman (a salesgirl) who speaks English?
¿Hay un dependiente (una dependienta) que hable
  inglés?
ahy oon deh-pehn-DYEHN-*teh (*OO-*nah deh-pehn*-DYEHN-
  tah) keh AH-*bleh een*-GLEHSS*?*

Do you speak English?
¿Habla usted inglés?
AH-*blah oo*-STEHTH *een*-GLEHSS*?*

May I help you?
¿Puedo ayudarle?
PWEH-*thoh ah-yoo*-THAHR-*leh?*

Can you help me?
¿Puede ayudarme?
PWEH-*theh ah-yoo*-THAHR-MEH*?*

I am just looking, thank you.
No, gracias, estoy mirando solamente.
noh, GRAH-*syahss, ehss*-TOY *mee*-RAHN-*doh soh-lah-*
  MEHN-*teh.*

I want to buy _____.
Quiero comprar _____.
KYEH-*roh kohm*-PRAHR _____.

Do you sell _____?
¿Vende usted _____?
BEHN-*deh oo*-STEHTH _____?

Can I see _____?
¿Puedo ver _____?
PWEH-*thoh* BEHR _____?

I want to spend about _____.
Quiero gastar alrededor de _____.
KYEH-*roh gahss*-TAHR *ahl-reh-theh-thohr* DEH _____.

What else do you have?
¿Qué otras cosas tiene usted?
keh OH-*trahss* KOH-*sahss* TYEH-*neh* oo-STEHTH?

How much is it?
¿Cuánto cuesta?
KWAHN-*toh* KWEHSS-*tah*?

It is too expensive.
Es demasiado caro.
*ehss deh-mah-*SYAH-*thoh* KAH-*roh*.

Can I see something else?
¿Puedo ver alguna otra cosa?
PWEH-*thoh* BEHR *ahl-*GOO-*nah* OH-*trah* KOH-*sah*?

Something better (less expensive)?
¿Algo mejor (menos caro)?
AHL-*goh* meh-HOHR (MEH-*nohss* KAH-*roh*)?

I prefer this one.
Prefiero éste.
*preh-*FYEH-*roh* EHSS-*teh*.

I'll take this one.
Me llevaré éste.
*meh yeh-bah-*REH EHSS-*teh*.

May I try it on?
¿Puedo probármelo?
PWEH-*thoh proh-*BAHR-*meh-loh*?

It does not fit.
No me queda bien.
noh meh KEH-*thah* BYEHN.

Do you make alterations here?
¿Hacen ustedes alteraciones aquí?
AH-*sehn* oo-STEH-*thehss ahl-teh-rah-*SYOH-*nehss*
*ah-*KEE?

Can you take it in (let it out, shorten it, lengthen it)?
¿Puede usted estrecharlo (ensancharlo, acortarlo,
alargarlo)?
PWEH-*theh* oo-STEHTH *ehss-treh-*CHAHR-*loh* (*ehn-sahn-*
CHAHR-*loh, ah-kohr-*TAHR-*loh, ah-lahr-*GAHR-*loh*)?

Will you take my measurements?

¿Quiere usted tomar mis medidas?

KYEH-*reh* oo-STEHTH *toh*-MAHR *meess meh*-THEE-
thahss?

My size in the United States is _____.

Mi número en los Estados Unidos es _____.

mee NOO-*meh-roh ehn lohss* ehss-TAH-*thohss* oo-NEE-
thohss ehss _____ .

Does it come in other colors?

¿Lo tienen ustedes en otros colores?

loh TYEH-*nehn* oo-STEH-*thehss ehn* OH-*trohss* koh-LOH-
rehss?

Do you accept this credit card (American money,
travelers checks, personal checks)?

¿Aceptan ustedes esta tarjeta de crédito (dinero de los
Estados Unidos, cheques de viajero, un cheque
personal)?

ah-SEHP-*tahn* oo-STEH-*thehss* EHSS-*tah tahr*-HEH-*tah
deh* KREH-*thee-toh (dee*-NEH-*roh deh lohss* ehss-TAH-
thohss oo-NEE-*thohss,* CHEH-*kehss deh byah*-HEH-*roh,
oon* CHEH-*keh pehr-soh*-NAHL*)?*

Do you accept returns?

¿Aceptan ustedes las devoluciones?

ah-SEHP-*tahn* oo-STEH-*thehss lahss deh-boh-loo*-SYOH-
nehss?

I bought it here.

Lo compré aquí.

lah kohm-PREH *ah*-KEE.

I would like to exchange it for a larger size.

Quisiera cambiarlo por un número más grande.

kee-SYEH-*rah kahm*-BYAHR-*loh pohr oon* NOO-*meh-roh
mahss* GRAHN-*deh.*

Will you wrap this, please?

Haga el favor de envolver ésto.

AH-*gah ehl fah*-BOHR *deh ehn-bohl*-BEHR EHSS-*toh.*

Do you deliver?
¿Entregan ustedes a domicilio (al hotel)?
*ehn-*TREH*-gahn oo-*STEH*-thehss ah doh-mee-*SEE*-lyoh
(ahl oh-*TEHL*)?*

Please deliver it to my hotel.
Por favor, llévenlo a mi hotel.
*pohr fah-*BOHR, YEH*-behn-loh ah mee oh-*TEHL.

Please sent it to _____.
Por favor, envíenlo a _____.
*pohr fah-*BOHR, *ehn-*BEE*-ehn-loh ah _____.*

How much will it cost to insure it?
¿Cuánto costará asegurarlo?
KWAHN*-toh kohss-tah-*RAH *ah-seh-goo-*RAHR*-loh?*

I want to send it as a gift?
Quiero enviarlo como un regalo.
KYEH*-roh ehn-*BYAHR*-loh koh-moh oon rreh-*GAH*-loh.*

Will the receiver have to pay duty?
¿Tendrá que pagar derechos el destinatario?
*tehn-*DRAH *keh pah-*GAHR *deh-*REH*-chohss ehl dehss-tee-
nah-*TAH*-ryoh?*

Give me a receipt, please.
Déme un recibo, por favor.
DEH*-meh oon rreh-*SEE*-boh, pohr fah-*BOHR.

Show

Please show me the way to _____.
Por favor, muéstreme el camino para _____.
*pohr fah-*BOHR, MWEHSS*-treh-meh ehl kah-*MEE*-noh pah-
rah _____.*

When is the next show?
¿Cuándo es la próxima representación?
KWAHN*-doh ehss lah* PROHK*-see-mah rreh-preh-sehn-
tah-*SYOHN*?*

Shower

I want a room with a shower, please.
Quiero una habitación con ducha, por favor.
KYEH*-roh* OO*-nah ah-bee-tah-*SYOHN *kohn* DOO*-chah,
pohr fah-*BOHR.

Shut

Please shut the door (window).

Por favor, cierre la puerta (ventana).

pohr fah-BOHR, SYEH-rreh lah PWEHR-tah (behn-TAH-nah).

Sick

I am sick.

Estoy enfermo (enferma).

ehss-TOY ehn-FEHR-moh (ehn-FEHR-mah).

Side Dish

May I have a side dish of _____, please.

¿Puede darme un platillo de _____, por favor?

PWEH-theh DAHR-meh oon plah-TEE-yoh deh _____, pohr fah-BOHR?

Sightseeing

I want to go sightseeing.

Quiero ver los lugares más interesantes.

KYEH-roh BEHR lohss loo-GAH-rehss mahss een-teh-reh-SAHN-tehss.

What tours can you arrange?

¿Qué excursiones puede usted preparar?

keh ehss-koor-SYOH-nehss PWEH-theh oo-STEHTH preh-pah-RAHR?

Sign

What does that sign mean?

¿Qué significa el letrero?

keh seeg-nee-FEE-kah ehl leh-TREH-roh?

Single

I want a room with single bed and bath.

Quiero una habitación con cama individual y baño.

KYEH-roh OO-nah ah-bee-tah-SYOHN kohn KAH-mah een-dee-bee-THWAHL ee BAH-nyoh.

I am single.

Soy soltero (soltera).

soy sohl-TEH-roh (sohl-TEH-rah).

Are you single?

¿Es usted soltero (soltera)?

ehss oo-STEHTH sohl-TEH-roh (sohl-TEH-rah)?

Sit

I would like to sit down for awhile.

Quisiera sentarme un instante (un rato).

*kee-*SYEH-*rah sehn-*TAHR-*meh oon een-*STAHN-*teh (oon*
RRAH-*toh).*

Size

What size is it?

¿Qué tamaño tiene?

*keh tah-*MAH-*nyoh* TYEH-*neh?*

It is (not) the right size.

(No) es el tamaño apropiado.

*(noh) ehss ehl tah-*MAH-*nyoh ah-proh-pee-*AH-*thoh.*

Skate

Do you like to skate?

¿Le gusta patinar?

leh GOOSS-*tah pah-tee-*NAHR?

I cannot skate.

No sé patinar.

*noh seh pah-tee-*NAHR.

Where can I find a skating rink?

¿Dónde hay una pista de patinaje?

DOHN-*deh ahy* OO-*nah* PEESS-*tah deh pah-tee-*NAH-*heh?*

Ski

Do you like to ski?

¿Le gusta esquiar?

leh GOOSS-*tah ehss-kee-*AHR?

Where is the best place to ski?

¿Dónde está el mejor lugar para esquiar?

DOHN-*deh ehss-*TAH *ehl meh-*HOHR *loo-*GAHR *pah-rah*
*ehss-kee-*AHR?

Skin Dive

Do you like to skin dive?

¿Le gusta bucear?

leh GOOSS-*tah boo-seh-*AHR?

I don't know how to skin dive.

No sé bucear.

*noh seh boo-seh-*AHR.

Where is the best place for skin diving?

¿Cuál es el mejor lugar para el buceo?

KWAHL *ehss ehl meh*-HOHR *loo*-GAHR *pah-rah ehl boo*-SEH-*oh?*

Sleep

I am going to sleep.

Voy a dormir.

boy ah dohr-MEER.

Sleeping

My wife (husband) is sleeping.

Mi esposa (esposo) está durmiendo.

mee ehss-POH-*sah (ehss*-POH-*soh) ehss*-TAH *door*-MYEHN-*doh.*

Does the train have sleeping accommodations?

¿Lleva el tren coches-cama?

YEH-*bah ehl* TREHN KOH-*chehss* KAH-*mah?*

Slope

Where are the best slopes (for skiing)?

¿Dónde están las mejores pendientes (para esquiar)?

DOHN-*deh ehss*-TAHN *lohss meh*-HOH-*rehss pehn*-DYEHN-*tehss (pah-rah ehss-kee*-AHR)?

Slow

Slow down!

¡Más despacio!

MAHSS *dehss*-PAH-*syoh!*

Slower

Drive slower, please.

Maneje más despacio, por favor.

mah-NEH-*heh* MAHSS *dehss*-PAH-*syoh, pohr fah*-BOHR.

Slowly

Please speak (drive) more slowly.

Por favor, hable (maneje) más despacio.

pohr fah-BOHR, AH-*bleh (mah*-NEH-*heh)* MAHSS *dehss*-PAH-*syoh.*

Small

This is too small.

Esto es demasiado pequeño.

EHSS-*toh ehss deh-mah*-SYAH-*thoh peh*-KEH-*nyoh.*

This is not small enough.
Esto no es bastante pequeño.
EHSS-*toh noh ehss bahss*-TAHN-*teh peh*-KEH-*nyoh.*

Smoke
Do you smoke?
¿Fuma usted?
FOO-*mah oo*-STEHTH?

Do you mind if I smoke?
¿Le importa que fume?
leh eem-POHR-*tah keh* FOO-*meh?*

Smoking
Where is the smoking car?
¿Dónde está el coche de fumar?
DOHN-*deh ehss*-TAH *ehl* KOH-*cheh deh foo*-MAHR?

Snack
Where can I get a snack?
¿Dónde puedo tomar un bocado?
DOHN-*deh* PWEH-*thoh toh*-MAHR *oon boh*-KAH-*thoh?*

Soap
Please bring me some soap.
Por favor, tráigame jabón.
pohr fah-BOHR, TRAH-*ee-gah-meh hah*-BOHN.

Soil
My _____ is soiled.
Mi _____ está sucio.
mee _____ *ehss*-TAH SOO-*syoh.*

Sole
A new pair of soles, please.
Por favor, un nuevo par de suelas.
pohr fah-BOHR, *oon* NWEH-*boh* PAHR *deh* SWEH-*lahss.*

Something
Can we get something to eat (drink)?
¿Puede darnos algo para comer (beber)?
PWEH-*theh* DAHR-*nohss* AHL-*goh pah-rah koh*-MEHR
(*beh*-BEHR)?

Soon

I'll see you soon.
Le veré a usted pronto.
leh beh-REH ah oo-STEHTH PROHN-toh.

How soon does the bus (plane, boat, train) leave (arrive)?
¿Cuánto tardará en salir (llegar) el autobús (ómnibus, avión, barco, tren)?
KWAHN-*toh tahr-thah-RAH ehn sah-*LEER *(yeh-*GAHR*)*
*ehl ow-toh-*BOOSS *(*OHM-*nee-booss, ah-*BYOHN, BAHR-*koh,* TREHN*)?*

Sorry

I am sorry about that.
Lo siento mucho.
loh SYEHN-*toh* MOO-*choh.*

Sorry!
¡Perdone!
*pehr-*THOH-*neh!*

Sound

What is that sound?
¿Qué ruido es ese?
keh RWEE-*thoh ehss* EH-*seh?*

Souvenir

Where can I find a souvenir shop?
¿Dónde puedo encontrar una tienda de recuerdos?
DOHN-*deh* PWEH-*thoh ehn-kohn-*TRAHR OO-*nah* TYEHN-*dah deh rreh-*KWEHR-*thohss?*

Speak

Do you speak English?
¿Habla usted inglés?
AH-*blah oo-*STEHT *een-*GLEHSS*?*

I speak only English.
No hablo más que inglés.
noh AH-*bloh* MAHSS *keh een-*GLEHSS.

Please speak more slowly.
Por favor, hable más lentamente.
*pohr fah-*BOHR, AH-*bleh* MAHSS *lehn-tah-*MEHN-*teh.*

May I please speak with _____.
Quisiera hablar con _____.
*kee-*SYEH-*rah ah-*BLAHR *kohn* _____.

I don't speak _____ (very well).
No hablo _____ (muy bien).
noh AH-*bloh* _____ *(mwee* BYEHN*).*

I want a guide (driver) who speaks English.
Quiero un guía (chófer) que hable inglés.
KYEH-*roh oon* GHEE-*ah (*CHOH-*fehr) keh* AH-*bleh een-*
    GLEHSS.

Special Delivery — see Post Office

Spectacles — see Glasses

Speed
What is the speed limit?
¿Cuál es la velocidad máxima?
KWAHL *ehss lah beh-loh-see-*THAHTH MAHK-*see-mah?*

Spoon
Please bring me a (another) spoon.
Por favor, tráigame una (otra) cuchara.
*pohr fah-*BOHR, TRAH-*ee-gah-meh* OO-*nah (*OH-*trah)*
    *koo-*CHAH-*rah.*

Stables
Where are the stables?
¿Dónde están los establos?
DOHN-*deh ehss-*TAHN *lohss ehss-*TAH-*blohss?*

Stamps — see Post Office

Standby
Please put me on standby.
Por favor, póngame en la lista de espera.
*pohr fah-*BOHR, POHN-*gah-meh ehn lah* LEESS-*tah deh*
    *ehss-*PEH-*rah.*

Stateroom
Where is stateroom _____?
¿Dónde está el camarote _____?
DOHN-*deh ehss-*TAH *ehl kah-mah-*ROH-*teh* _____?

I am in stateroom _____.
Estoy en el camarote _____.
ehss-TOY *ehn ehl kah-mah*-ROH-*teh* _____.

Which stateroom are you in?
¿En qué camarote está usted?
ehn keh kah-mah-ROH-*teh ehss*-TAH *oo*-STEHTH?

Station

Can you direct me (take me) to the railroad (bus)
   station?
¿Puede usted dirigirme (llevarme) a la estación de
   ferrocarril (ómnibus)?
PWEH-*theh oo*-STEHTH *dee-ree*-HEER-*meh (yeh*-BAHR-
   meh) ah lah ehss-tah-SYOHN *deh feh-rroh-kah*-RREEL
   (OHM-*nee-booss)*?

Stay

I am going to stay for _____ days (weeks).
Voy a quedarme _____ días (semanas).
boy ah keh-THAHR-*meh* _____ DEE-*ahss (seh*-MAH-
   nahss).

How long are you planning to stay?
¿Cuánto tiempo piensa usted quedarse?
KWAHN-*toh* TYEHM-*poh* PYEHN-*sah oo*-STEHTH *keh*-
   THAHR-*seh*?

Where are you staying?
¿Dónde se aloja usted?
DOHN-*deh seh ah*-LOH-*hah oo*-STEHTH?

I am staying at _____.
Estoy alojado en _____.
ehss-TOY *ah-loh*-HAH-*thoh ehn* _____.

Stolen

My _____ has been stolen!
¡Me han robado mi _____!
meh ahn rroh-BAH-*thoh mee* _____!

Call the police (the manager)!
¡Llame a la policía (al gerente)!
YAH-*meh ah lah poh-lee*-SEE-*ah (ahl heh*-REHN-*teh)*!

Stop

Stop here, please.
Pare aquí, por favor.
PAH-reh ah-KEE, pohr fah-BOHR.

Next stop, please.
En la próxima parada, por favor.
ehn lah PROHK-see-mah pah-RAH-thah, pohr fah-BOHR.

Do we stop at _____?
¿Paramos en _____?
pah-RAH-mohss ehn _____?

When (What) is the next stop?
¿Cuándo (Cuál) es la próxima parada?
KWAHN-doh (KWAHL) ehss lah PROHK-see-mah pah-RAH-thah?

Stop!
¡Pare!
PAH-reh!

Stranger

I am a stranger here.
Aquí soy extranjero.
ah-KEE soy ehss-trahn-HEH-roh.

Street

What street is this?
¿Qué calle es ésta?
keh KAH-yeh ehss EHSS-tah?

What street comes after _____?
¿Qué calle viene después de _____?
keh KAH-yeh BYEH-neh dehss-PWEHSS deh _____?

It is on _____ street.
Está en la calle _____.
ehss-TAH ehn lah KAH-yeh _____.

Student

I am a student.
Soy estudiante.
soy ehss-too-THYAHN-teh.

Are you a student?

¿Es usted estudiante?

*ehss oo-*STEHTH *ehss-too-*THYAHN*-teh?*

Do you give student rates?

¿Ofrece usted tarifas para estudiantes?

*oh-*FREH*-seh oo-*STEHTH *tah-*REE*-fahss pah-rah ehss-too-*
THYAHN*-tehss?*

Subtitles

Does the movie have English subtitles?

¿Tiene la película subtítulos en inglés?

TYEH*-neh lah peh-*LEE*-koo-lah soob-*TEE*-too-lohss ehn*
*een-*GLEHSS*?*

Subway

What subway do I take to _____?

¿Qué metro tomo para _____?

keh MEH*-troh* TOH*-moh pah-rah* _____?

Where can I find the subway for _____?

¿Dónde puedo tomar el metro para _____?

DOHN*-deh* PWEH*-thoh toh-*MAHR *ehl* MEH*-troh pah-rah*
_____?

Sugar

May I have some sugar, please?

¿Me da el azúcar, por favor?

*meh dah ehl ah-*SOO*-kahr, pohr fah-*BOHR*?*

Suit

Where can I have a suit made (cleaned, pressed)?

¿Dónde pueden hacerme (limpiarme, plancharme) un traje?

DOHN*-deh* PWEH*-thehn ah-*SEHR*-meh (leem-*PYAHR*-meh,*
*plahn-*CHAHR*-meh) oon* TRAH*-heh?*

Please clean (press) this suit.

Por favor, límpieme (pláncheme) este traje.

*pohr fah-*BOHR, LEEM*-pyeh-meh (*PLAHN*-cheh-meh)*
EHSS*-teh* TRAH*-heh.*

Suitcase
This is my suitcase.
Esta es mi maleta.
EHSS-*tah ehss mee* mah-LEH-*tah.*

Would you carry my suitcase, please?
¿Puede usted llevar mi maleta, por favor?
PWEH-*theh* oo-STEHTH *yeh*-BAHR *mee* mah-LEH-*tah,
pohr fah*-BOHR?

Sunburn
What do you have for sunburn?
¿Qué tiene usted para curar las quemaduras de sol?
keh TYEH-*neh* oo-STEHTH *pah-rah koo*-RAHR *lahss keh-
mah*-THOO-*rahss deh* SOHL?

Sweet
This is too sweet.
Esto es demasiado dulce.
EHSS-*toh ehss deh-mah*-SYAH-*thoh* DOOL-*seh.*

This is not sweet enough.
Esto no es bastante dulce.
EHSS-*toh noh ehss bahss*-TAHN-*teh* DOOL-*seh.*

Swim
Where can I go swimming?
¿Dónde se puede nadar?
DOHN-*deh seh* PWEH-*theh nah*-THAHR?

I don't know how to swim.
No sé nadar.
noh SEH *nah*-THAHR.

Synagogue
Can you direct me (take me) to the nearest synagogue,
  please?
¿Puede usted dirigirme (llevarme) a la sinagoga más
  cercana, por favor?
PWEH-*theh* oo-STEHTH *dee-ree*-HEER-*meh* (*yeh*-BAHR-
  meh) *ah lah see-nah*-GOH-*gah mahss sehr*-KAH-*nah,
  pohr fah*-BOHR?

Table

A table by the window (at the side, in the corner).
Una mesa junto a la ventana (a un lado, en un rincón).
OO-*nah* MEH-*sah* HOON-*toh ah lah behn*-TAH-*nah (ah oon*
    LAH-*thoh, ehn oon reen*-KOHN*)*.

A table for two (three, four, just myself) please.
Una mesa para dos (tres, cuatro, mí sólo) por favor.
OO-*nah* MEH-*sah pah-rah* DOHSS (TREHSS, KWAH-*troh*,
    MEE SOH-*loh*), *pohr fah*-BOHR.

Take

How long will it take?
¿Cuánto tardará?
KWAHN-*toh tahr-thah*-RAH?

Take me to the _____.
Lléveme al (a la) _____.
YEH-*beh-meh ahl (ah lah)* _____.

Please take my bags.
Por favor, tome mis maletas.
pohr fah-BOHR, TOH-*meh meess mah*-LEH-*tahss*.

Take it away, please.
Lléveselo, por favor.
YEH-*beh-seh-loh, pohr fah*-BOHR.

Is this taken?
¿Está reservado?
ehss-TAH *rreh-sehr*-BAH-*thoh?*

Taste

This has a strange taste.
Esto tiene un sabor extraño.
EHSS-*toh* TYEH-*neh oon sah*-BOHR *ehss*-TRAH-*nyoh*.

It does not taste right.
No me sabe bien.
noh meh SAH-*beh* BYEHN.

May I taste it?
¿Puedo probarlo?
PWEH-*thoh proh*-BAHR-*loh?*

Tax

Is the tax included?

¿Se incluye el impuesto?

*seh een-*KLOO*-yeh ehl eem-*PWEHSS*-toh?*

How much is the tax?

¿Cuánto es el impuesto?

KWAHN*-toh ehss ehl eem-*PWEHSS*-toh?*

Taxi

Please get me a taxi.

Por favor, consígame un taxi.

*pohr fah-*BOHR*, kohn-*SEE*-gah-meh oon* TAHK*-see.*

Where can I get a taxi?

¿Dónde puedo conseguir un taxi?

DOHN*-deh* PWEH*-thoh kohn-seh-*GHEER *oon* TAHK*-see?*

Tea

May I please have some (more) tea.

¿Puede darme (más) té, por favor?

PWEH*-theh* DAHR*-meh (mahss)* TEH*, pohr fah-*BOHR*?*

With lemon, with milk, iced.

Con limón, con leche, helado.

*kohn lee-*MOHN*, kohn* LEH*-cheh, eh-*LAH*-thoh.*

Teach

Will you teach me how to _____?

¿Me enseñará como se _____?

*meh ehn-seh-nyah-*RAH KOH*-moh seh* _____*?*

Telegram

Where can I send a telegram?

¿Dónde puedo enviar un telegrama?

DOHN*-deh* PWEH*-thoh ehn-*BYAHR *oon teh-leh-*GRAH*-mah?*

I want to send a telegram to _____ at _____.

Quiero enviar un telegrama a _____ en _____.

KYEH*-roh ehn-*BYAHR *oon teh-leh-*GRAH*-mah ah* _____ *ehn* _____*.*

What is the cost per word?

¿Cuánto cuesta cada palabra?

KWAHN*-toh* KWEHSS*-tah* KAH*-thah pah-*LAH*-brah?*

What is the night rate to _____?
¿Cuál es la tarifa nocturna para _____?
KWAHL *ehss lah tah-*REE-*fah nohk-*TOOR-*nah pah-rah*
_____?

It is urgent; when will it be delivered to _____?
Es urgente; ¿cuándo se entregará a _____?
*ehss oor-*HEHN-*teh;* KWAHN-*doh seh ehn-treh-gah-*RAH
ah _____?

I want to pay for the answer.
Quiero pagar la respuesta.
KYEH-*roh pah-*GAHR *lah rrehss-*PWEHSS-*tah.*

Please read it back to me.
Por favor, léamelo.
*pohr fah-*BOHR, LEH-*ah-meh-loh.*

Telephone
Where can I make a telephone call?
¿Dónde puedo hacer una llamada telefónica?
DOHN-*deh* PWEH-*thoh ah-*SEHR OO-*nah yah-*MAH-*thah*
*teh-leh-*FOH-*nee-kah?*

Do I need tokens?
¿Necesito fichas?
*neh-seh-*SEE-*toh* FEE-*chahss?*

Where can I get some tokens?
¿Dónde puedo conseguir las fichas?
DOHN-*deh* PWEH-*thoh kohn-seh-*GHEER *lahss* FEE-
chahss?

Will you telephone for me?
¿Puede usted telefonear por mí?
PWEH-*theh oo-*STEHTH *teh-leh-foh-neh-*AHR *pohr* MEE?

A local call, number _____.
Una llamada local, número _____.
OO-*nah yah-*MAH-*thah loh-*KAHL, NOO-*meh-roh* _____.

Long distance operator, please.
Por favor, la operadora de larga distancia.
*pohr fah-*BOHR, *lah oh-peh-rah-*THOH-*rah deh* LAHR-*gah*
*deess-*TAHN-*syah.*

Overseas operator, please.
Por favor, la operadora internacional.
*pohr fah-*BOHR, *lah oh-peh-rah-*THOH-*rah een-tehr-nah-syoh-*NAHL.

How much is a call to _____?
¿Cuánto cuesta una llamada a _____?
KWAHN-*toh* KWEHSS-*tah* OO-*nah yah-*MAH-*thah ah* _____?

I want number _____ in _____.
Quiero el número _____ en _____.
KYEH-*roh ehl* NOO-*meh-roh* _____ *ehn* _____.

Information, please.
Información, por favor.
*een-fohr-mah-*SYOHN, *pohr fah-*BOHR.

Operator, that's the wrong number.
Telefonista, ese número está equivocado.
*teh-leh-foh-*NEESS-*tah,* EH-*seh* NOO-*meh-roh ehss-*TAH *eh-kee-boh-*KAH-*thoh.*

There is no answer.
No contestan.
*noh kohn-*TEHSS-*tahn.*

The line is busy.
La línea está ocupada.
lah LEE-*neh-ah ehss-*TAH *oh-koo-*PAH-*thah.*

Hold the line, please.
No cuelgue, por favor.
noh KWEHL-*gheh, pohr fah-*BOHR.

I would like to speak with _____.
Quisiera hablar con _____.
*kee-*SYEH-*rah ah-*BLAHR *kohn* _____.

When (where) can I reach him?
¿Cuándo (dónde) puedo hablar con él?
KWAHN-*doh (*DOHN-*deh)* PWEH-*thoh ah-*BLAHR *kohn* EHL?

This is _____ speaking.
Aquí habla _____.
*ah-*KEE AH-*blah* _____.

Please take a message for _____.
Por favor, ¿puede tomar un recado para _____?
pohr fah-BOHR, PWEH-theh toh-MAHR oon rreh-KAH-thoh
    pah-rah _____?

Have him call _____, at number _____.
Por favor, dígale que llame a _____, número _____.
pohr fah-BOHR, DEE-gah-leh keh YAH-meh ah _____,
    NOO-meh-roh _____.

I'll call back later.
Llamaré más tarde.
yah-mah-REH mahss TAHR-theh.

Television

Is there a television in the room (lobby)?
¿Hay un aparato de televisión en la habitación (sala)?
ahy oon ah-pah-RAH-toh deh teh-leh-bee-SYOHN ehn lah
    ah-bee-tah-SYOHN (SAH-lah)?

Can I have a television in my room?
¿Puede poner un aparato de televisión en mi
    habitación?
PWEH-theh poh-NEHR oon ah-pah-RAH-toh deh teh-leh-
    bee-SYOHN ehn mee ah-bee-tah-SYOHN?

The television in my room does not work.
La televisión en mi habitación no funciona.
lah teh-leh-bee-SYOHN ehn mee ah-bee-tah-SYOHN noh
    foon-SYOH-nah.

Tell

Please tell me when (where) to get off.
Por favor, dígame cuándo (dónde) debo bajarme.
pohr fah-BOHR, DEE-gah-meh KWAHN-doh (DOHN-deh)
    DEH-boh bah-HAHR-meh.

Temple – see Synogogue

Tennis

Let's play tennis.
Vamos a jugar al tenis.
BAH-mohss ah hoo-GAHR ahl TEH-neess.

Where can we play tennis?
¿Dónde puedo jugar al tenis?
DOHN-deh PWEH-thoh hoo-GAHR ahl TEH-neess?

Thank You

Thank you very much.
Muchísimas gracias.
*moo-*CHEE*-see-mahss* GRAH*-syahss.*

No, thank you.
No, gracias.
NOH, GRAH*-syahss.*

That

What is that?
¿Qué es eso?
KEH*-ehss* EH*-soh?*

What is that in _____?
¿Qué es eso en _____?
KEH *ehss* EH*-soh ehn* _____?

That will be all.
Eso es todo.
EH*-soh ehss* TOH*-thoh.*

Theater

I want to go to the theater tonight, what do you
  recommend?
Quisiera ir al teatro esta noche, ¿qué me recomienda
  usted?
*kee-*SYEH*-rah eer ahl teh-*AH*-troh* EHSS*-tah* NOH*-cheh,*
  KEH *meh rreh-koh-*MYEHN*-dah oo-*STEHTH?

Can you direct me (take me) to the theater, please?
¿Puede usted dirigirme (llevarme) al teatro, por favor?
PWEH*-theh oo-*STEHTH *dee-ree-*HEER*-meh (yeh-*BAHR*-
  meh) ahl teh-*AH*-troh, pohr fah-*BOHR?

Would you like to go to the theater with me?
¿Le gustaría ir al teatro conmigo?
*leh gooss-tah-*REE*-ah eer ahl teh-*AH*-troh kohn-*MEE*-goh?*

Thermometer

Where is the thermometer?
¿Dónde está el termómetro?
DOHN*-deh ehss-*TAH *ehl tehr-*MOH*-meh-troh?*

Things
Where are your things?
¿Dónde están sus cosas?
DOHN-*deh ehss*-TAHN *sooss* KOH-*sahss?*

Those things are mine.
Estas cosas son mías.
EHSS-*tahss* KOH-*sahss sohn* MEE-*ahss.*

Thirsty
I am (not) thirsty.
(No) tengo sed.
(noh) TEHN-*goh* SEHTH.

This
What is this in _____?
¿Qué es esto en _____?
KEH *ehss* EHSS-*toh ehn* _____?

What street (town) is this?
¿Qué calle (ciudad) es esta?
KEH KAH-*yeh (syoo*-THAHTH*)* *ehss* EHSS-*tah?*

Is this the way?
¿Es éste el camino?
ehss EHSS-*teh ehl* kah-MEE-*noh?*

Through
I want to check this through to _____.
Quiero mandar esto directamente a _____.
KYEH-*roh mahn*-DAHR EHSS-*toh dee-rehk-tah*-MEHN-*teh*
ah _____.

What city are we passing through?
¿Por qué ciudad estamos pasando ahora?
pohr KEH *syoo*-THAHTH *ehss*-TAH-*mohss pah*-SAHN-*doh*
ah-OH-*rah?*

I want to pass through _____.
Quiero pasar por _____.
KYEH-*roh pah*-SAHR *pohr* _____.

Ticket

A one-way (round-trip) ticket to _____, please.
Por favor, un billete de ida (de ida y vuelta) a _____.
pohr fah-BOHR, oon bee-YEH-teh deh EE-thah (deh EE-thah ee BWEHL-tah) ah _____.

How much is a ticket to _____?
¿Cuánto cuesta un billete a _____?
KWAHN-*toh* KWEHSS-*tah oon bee-*YEH-*teh ah _____?*

Do you have any tickets for tonight?
¿Tiene usted algunas entradas para esta noche?
TYEH-*neh oo-*STEHTH *ahl-*GOO-*nahss ehn-*TRAH-*thahss pah-rah* EHSS-*tah* NOH-*cheh?*

Where is the (ticket) window?
¿Dónde está la ventanilla (de billetes)?
DOHN-*deh ehss-*TAH *lah behn-tah-*NEE-*yah (deh bee-*YEH-*tehss)?*

Tide

What time is high (low) tide?
¿A qué hora hay marea alta (baja)?
ah keh OH-*rah ahy mah-*REH-*ah* AHL-*tah (*BAH-*hah)?*

Time

What time is it?
¿Qué hora es?
KEH OH-*rah* EHSS?

What time is breakfast (lunch, dinner) served?
¿A qué hora se sirve el desayuno (el almuerzo, la cena)?
ah keh OH-*rah seh* SEER-*beh ehl deh-sah-*YOO-*noh (ehl ahl-*MWEHR-*soh, lah* SEH-*nah)?*

Timetable

Please give me a timetable.
Por favor, deme un horario.
*pohr fah-*BOHR, DEH-*meh oon oh-*RAH-*ree-oh.*

Tip

Is the tip included?
¿Se incluye la propina?
*seh een-*KLOO-*yeh lah proh-*PEE-*nah?*

How much tip should I leave?
¿Cuánto debo dejar de propina?
KWAHN-*toh* DEH-*boh* deh-HAHR *deh* proh-PEE-*nah?*

Tired
I am (not) tired.
(No) estoy cansado (cansada).
(noh) ehss-TOY *kahn*-SAH-*thoh* (*kahn*-SAH-*thah*).

Tissues
Please bring me some tissues.
Por favor, tráigame algunos kleenex.
pohr fah-BOHR, TRAH-*ee-gah-meh* ahl-GOO-*nohss* KLEE-
nehks.

Tobacco
Where can I buy some tobacco?
¿Dónde puedo comprar tabaco?
DOHN-*deh* PWEH-*thoh kohm*-PRAHR *tah*-BAH-*koh?*

Today
We are leaving today.
Salimos hoy.
sah-LEE-*mohss* OY.

I need it today.
Lo necesito hoy.
loh neh-seh-SEE-*toh* OY.

Toilet Paper
Please give me some toilet paper.
Por favor, deme papel higienico.
pohr fah-BOHR, DEH-*meh pah*-PEHL *ee*-HYEH-*nee-koh.*

Token
Do I need a token?
¿Necesito una ficha?
neh-seh-SEE-*toh* OO-*nah* FEE-*chah?*

Where can I buy some tokens?
¿Dónde puedo comprar algunas fichas?
DOHN-*deh* PWEH-*thoh kohm*-PRAHR *ahl*-GOO-*nahss* FEE-
chahss?

Tomorrow

We are leaving tomorrow.
Salimos mañana.
*sah-*LEE-*mohss mah-*NYAH-*nah.*

I would like a reservation for tomorrow.
Quisiera una reserva para mañana.
*kee-*SYEH-*rah* OO-*nah rreh-*SEHR-*bah pah-rah mah-*NYAH-*nah.*

May I see you tomorrow.
¿Puedo verle mañana?
PWEH-*thoh* BEHR-*leh mah-*NYAH-*nah?*

I need it tomorrow.
Lo necesito mañana.
*loh neh-seh-*SEE-*toh mah-*NYAH-*nah.*

Tonight

A room for tonight only, please.
Una habitación para esta noche solamente, por favor.
OO-*nah ah-bee-tah-*SYOHN *pah-rah* EHSS-*tah* NOH-*cheh
soh-lah-*MEHN-*teh, pohr fah-*BOHR.

May I see you tonight?
¿Puedo verle esta noche?
PWEH-*thoh* BEHR-*leh* EHSS-*tah* NOH-*cheh?*

Toothache — see also Dentist

I have a toothache.
Tengo dolor de muelas.
TEHN-*goh doh-*LOHR *deh* MWEH-*lahss.*

Tough

This meat is too tough; please take it back.
Esta carne es demasiado dura; por favor, llévesela.
EHSS-*tah* KAHR-*neh ess deh-mah-*SYAH-*thoh* DOO-*rah;
pohr fah-*BOHR, YEH-*beh-seh-lah.*

Tour

We would like a tour of the city.
Quisiéramos hacer una excursión por la ciudad.
*kee-*SYEH-*rah-mohss ah-*SEHR OO-*nah ehss-koor-*SYOHN
*pohr lah syoo-*THAHTH.

Can you arrange a tour for this morning (this afternoon, this evening)?

¿Puede usted prepararnos una excursión para esta mañana (esta tarde, esta noche)?

PWEH-*theh* oo-STEHTH *preh-pah*-RAHR-*nohss* OO-*nah ehss-koor*-SYOHN *pah-rah* EHSS-*tah mah*-NYAH-*nah* (EHSS-*tah* TAHR-*theh,* EHSS-*tah* NOH-*cheh)?*

Where can we get a tour to _____?

¿Dónde podemos tomar una excursión a _____?

DOHN-*deh poh*-THEH-*mohss* toh-MAHR OO-*nah ehss-koor*-SYOHN *ah* _____ ?

Do any tours leave from this hotel?

¿Hay alguna excursión que salga de este hotel?

ahy ahl-GOO-*nah ehss-koor*-SYOHN *keh* SAHL-*gah deh* EHSS-*teh* oh-TEHL?

When do they leave?

¿Cuándo salen?

KWAHN-*doh* SAH-*lehn?*

Tourist

A ticket in tourist class, please.

Un billete de clase turista, por favor.

oon bee-YEH-*teh deh* KLAH-*seh* too-REESS-*tah, pohr fah-*BOHR.

Towels

Please bring me some towels.

Por favor, tráigame toallas.

pohr fah-BOHR, TRAH-*ee-gah-meh* toh-AH-*yahss.*

Town

What town is this?

¿Qué ciudad es ésta?

keh syoo-THAHTH *ehss* EHSS-*tah?*

What is the next town?

¿Cuál es la próxima ciudad?

KWAHL *ehss lah* PROHK-*see-mah* syoo-THAHTH?

May I have a ride to town?

¿Puede llevarme hasta la ciudad?

PWEH-*theh* yeh-BAHR-*meh* AHSS-*tah lah* syoo-THAHTH?

Track – see also Platform

What track does it leave from?
¿De qué vía sale?
deh keh BEE-*ah* SAH-*leh?*

Where is track number _____?
¿Dónde está la vía número _____?
DOHN-*deh* ehss-TAH *lah* BEE-*ah* NOO-*meh-roh* _____?

Trade

Will you trade me that for this?
¿Me cambia eso por esto?
meh KAHM-*byah* EH-*soh pohr* EHSS-*toh?*

Train

When does the train arrive (leave)?
¿Cuándo llega (sale) el tren?
KWAHN-*doh* YEH-*gah* (SAH-*leh*) *ehl* TREHN?

Does this train stop at _____?
¿Para este tren en _____?
PAH-*rah* EHSS-*teh* TREHN *ehn* _____?

Is this the train for _____?
¿Va este tren a _____?
BAH EHSS-*teh* TREHN *ah* _____?

Does the train have sleeping accommodations (a dining car)?
¿Lleva el tren coches-cama (vagón restaurante)?
YEH-*bah ehl* TREHN KOH-*chehss*-KAH-*mah (bah*-GOHN *rrehss-tah-oo*-RAHN-*teh)?*

Transfer

Where do I transfer?
¿Dónde hago el trasbordo?
DOHN-*deh* AH-*goh ehl trahss*-BOHR-*thoh?*

Transportation

What kind of transportation is there to _____?
¿Qué tipo de trasporte hay a _____?
keh TEE-*poh deh trahss*-POHR-*teh ahy ah* _____?

Travel Agency

Where is the nearest travel agency?

¿Dónde está la agencia de viajes más próxima?

DOHN-*deh ehss*-TAH *lah* ah-HEHN-*syah deh* BYAH-*hehss
mahss* PROHK-*see-mah?*

Travelers Checks — see also Bank

I have travelers checks.

Tengo cheques de viajero.

TEHN-*goh* CHEH-*kehss deh byah*-HEH-*roh.*

Do you accept travelers checks?

¿Acepta usted cheques de viajero?

ah-SEHP-*tah oo*-STEHTH CHEH-*kehss deh byah*-HEH-*roh?*

Trip

How long does the trip take?

¿Cuánto tarda el viaje?

KWAHN-*toh* TAHR-*thah ehl* BYAH-*heh?*

This is my (our) first (second, third) trip.

Este es mi (nuestro) primer (segundo, tercer) viaje.

EHSS-*teh ehss mee* (NWEHSS-*troh*) *pree*-MEHR (*seh*-GOON-*doh, tehr*-SEHR) BYAH-*heh.*

Trouble

What is the trouble with you?

¿Qué le ocurre?

KEH *leh oh*-KOO-*rreh?*

True

That is (not) true.

Eso (no) es verdad.

EH-*soh (noh) ehss behr*-THAHTH.

Trunk

That is my trunk.

Ese es mi baúl.

EH-*seh ehss mee bah*-OOL.

Please take my trunk to the hotel (to the airport, to
  my room, to the railroad station).
Por favor, lleve mi baúl al hotel (al aeropuerto, a mi
  habitación, a la estación de ferrocarril).
*pohr fah-*BOHR, YEH-*beh mee bah-*OOL *ahl oh-*TEHL *(ahl
  ah-eh-roh-*PWEHR-*toh, ah mee ah-bee-tah-*SYOHN, *ah
  lah ehss-tah-*SYOHN *deh feh-rroh-kah-*RREEL*).*

Try
May I try this on?
¿Puedo probármelo?
PWEH-*thoh proh-*BAHR-*meh-loh?*

Tub
I would like a bath with a tub.
Quisiera un cuarto de baño con bañera.
*kee-*SYEH-*rah oon* KWAHR-*toh deh* BAH-*nyoh kohn bah-*
  NYEH-*rah.*

Turn
Where should I turn?
¿Dónde debo doblar?
DOHN-*deh* DEH-*boh doh-*BLAHR?

Typewriter
Where can I rent a typewriter?
¿Dónde puedo alquilar una máquina de escribir?
DOHN-*deh* PWEH-*thoh ahl-kee-*LAHR OO-*nah* MAH-*kee-*
  *nah deh ehss-kree-*BEER?

Umbrella
Where can I buy an umbrella?
¿Dónde puedo comprar un paraguas?
DOHN-*deh* PWEH-*thoh kohm-*PRAHR *oon pah-*RAH-*
  gwahss?*

Undercooked
This is undercooked; please take it back.
Esto está poco cocido; por favor, lléveselo.
EHSS-*toh ehss-*TAH POH-*koh koh-*SEE-*thoh; pohr fah-*
  BOHR, YEH-*beh-seh-loh.*

Understand

I (don't) understand.
(No) comprendo.
(noh) kohm-PREHN-doh.

Do you understand?
¿Comprende usted?
kohm-PREHN-deh oo-STEHTH?

Undertow

Is there an undertow?
¿Hay resaca?
ahy rreh-SAH-kah?

United States

I am from the United States.
Soy de los Estados Unidos.
soy deh lohss ehss-TAH-thohss oo-NEE-thohss.

Have you ever been to the United States?
¿Ha estado usted alguna vez en los Estados Unidos?
*ah-ehss-TAH-thoh oo-STEHTH ahl-GOO-nah BEHSS ehn
lohss ehss-TAH-thohss oo-NEE-thohss?*

University

Which is the best way to the university?
¿Cuál es el mejor camino hacia la universidad?
*KWAHL ehss ehl meh-HOHR kah-MEE-noh AH-syah lah
oo-nee-behr-see-THAHTH?*

Do you study (teach) at the university?
¿Estudia (Enseña) usted en la universidad?
*ehss-TOO-thyah (ehn-SEH-nyah) oo-STEHTH ehn lah oo-
nee-behr-see-THAHTH?*

Upper

I want an upper berth.
Quiero una litera alta.
KYEH-roh OO-nah lee-TEH-rah AHL-tah.

Urgent

It is urgent.
Es urgente.
ehss oor-HEHN-teh.

Use

I don't know how to use this.

No sé cómo se usa esto.

noh SEH KOH-*moh seh* OO-*sah* EHSS-*toh.*

That is for my own use.

Eso es para mi uso personal.

EH-*soh ehss pah-rah mee* OO-*soh pehr-soh-*NAHL.

Vacancies

Have you any vacancies?

¿Tiene alguna habitación disponible?

TYEH-*neh ahl-*GOO-*nah ah-bee-tah-*SYOHN *deess-poh-*NEE-*bleh?*

Vacation

I am on my vacation.

Estoy de vacaciones.

*ehss-*TOY *deh bah-kah-*SYOH-*nehss.*

Vaccinate

I have been vaccinated against _____.

Me han vacunado contra _____.

*meh ahn bah-koo-*NAH-*thoh* KOHN-*trah* _____.

Vaccum

Please vacuum the rug.

Por favor, limpie la alfombra con aspirador.

*pohr fah-*BOHR, LEEM-*pyeh lah ahl-*FOHM-*brah kohn ahss-pee-rah-*THOHR.

Valid

For how long is the ticket valid?

¿Qué vigencia tiene este billete?

*keh bee-*HEHN-*syah* TYEH-*neh* EHSS-*teh bee-*YEH-*teh?*

Valuables

Please, place these valuables in your safe.

Por favor, ponga estos objetos de valor en su caja fuerte.

*pohr fah-*BOHR, POHN-*gah* EHSS-*tohss ohb-*HEH-*tohss deh bah-*LOHR *ehn soo* KAH-*hah* FWEHR-*teh.*

Vegetarian

I am a vegetarian.

Soy vegetariano.

*soy beh-heh-tah-*RYAH*-noh.*

Vicinity

Are we in the vicinity of _____?

¿Estamos cerca de _____?

*ehss-*TAH*-mohss* SEHR*-kah deh* _____?

View

I want a room (table) with a good view.

Quiero una habitación (mesa) con una buena vista.

KYEH*-roh* OO*-nah ah-bee-tah-*SYOHN *(*MEH*-sah) kohn* OO-
nah BWEH*-nah* BEESS*-tah.*

Village

What village is this?

¿Qué pueblo es éste?

keh PWEH*-bloh ehss* EHSS*-teh?*

How far is it to the (next) village?

¿A qué distancia está el (próximo) pueblo?

*ah keh deess-*TAHN*-syah ehss-*TAH *ehl (*PROHK*-see-moh)*
PWEH*-bloh?*

What is the next village?

¿Cuál es el próximo pueblo?

KWAHL *ehss ehl* PROHK*-see-moh* PWEH*-bloh?*

Visa

Do I need a visa for _____?

¿Necesito una visa para _____?

*neh-seh-*SEE*-toh* OO*-nah* BEE*-sah pah-rah* _____?

Here is my visa.

Aquí está mi visa.

*ah-*KEE *ehss-*TAH *mee* BEE*-sah.*

I don't have a visa.

No tengo visa.

noh TEHN*-goh* BEE*-sah.*

Where do I apply for a visa?

¿Dónde puedo solicitar una visa?

DOHN*-deh* PWEH*-thoh soh-lee-see-*TAHR OO*-nah* BEE-
sah?

Visit

Come visit us when you are in the United States.

Venga a visitarnos cuando esté en los Estados Unidos.

BEHN-*gah ah bee-see-*TAHR-*nohss kwahn-doh ehss-*TEH
*ehn lohss ehss-*TAH-*thohss oo-*NEE-*thohss.*

This is our first visit.

Esta es nuestra primera visita.

EHSS-*tah ehss* NWEHSS-*trah pree-*MEH-*rah bee-*SEE-*tah.*

We are visiting.

Estamos de visita.

*ehss-*TAH-*mohss deh bee-*SEE-*tah.*

Visitors

Can visitors come on board?

¿Pueden subir a bordo los visitantes?

PWEH-*thehn soo-*BEER *ah* BOHR-*thoh lohss bee-see-*
TAHN-*tehss?*

Voltage

What is the voltage?

¿Cuál es el voltaje?

KWAHL *ehss ehl bohl-*TAH-*heh?*

Wait

Wait a moment!

¡Espere un momento!

*ehss-*PEH-*reh oon moh-*MEHN-*toh!*

How long must I wait?

¿Cuánto tiempo tengo que esperar?

KWAHN-*toh* TYEHM-*poh* TEHN-*goh keh ehss-peh-*RAHR?

Please (don't) wait for me.

Por favor, espéreme (no me espere).

*pohr fah-*BOHR, *ehss-*PEH-*reh-meh (noh meh ehss-*PEH-
reh).

Waiter (Waitress)

Are you our waiter (our waitress)?

¿Es usted nuestro mozo (nuestra moza)?

*ehss oo-*STEHTH NWEHSS-*troh* MOH-*soh (*NWEHSS-*trah*
MOH-*sah)?*

Please send over our waiter (our waitress).
Por favor, haga venir a nuestro mozo (nuestra moza).
pohr fah-BOHR, AH-*gah beh*-NEER *ah* NWEHSS-*troh* MOH-
soh (NWEHSS-*trah* MOH-*sah*).

Waiting
Where is the waiting room?
¿Dónde está la sala de espera?
DOHN-*deh ehss*-TAH *lah* SAH-*lah deh ehss*-PEH-*rah*?

Are you waiting for someone?
¿Está usted esperando a alguien?
ehss-TAH *oo*-STEHTH *ehss-peh*-RAHN-*doh ah* AHL-
ghyehn?

Wake
Please wake me at _____.
Por favor, despiérteme a las _____.
pohr fah-BOHR, *deess*-PYEHR-*teh-meh ah lahss* _____.

Walk
Let's walk to _____.
Vamos a dar un paseo hasta _____.
BAH-*mohss ah dahr oon pah*-SEH-*oh* AHSS-*tah* _____.

Is it easy to walk to _____?
¿Es fácil ir andando hasta _____?
ehss FAH-*seel eer ahn*-DAHN-*doh* AHSS-*tah* _____?

Want
I want to _____.
Quisiera _____.
kee-SYEH-*rah* _____.

Warm
It is not warm enough.
No está bastante caliente.
noh ehss-TAH *bahss*-TAHN-*teh kah*-YEHN-*teh*.

I am (not) warm.
(No) tengo calor.
(noh) TEHN-*goh kah*-LOHR.

Wash – see Laundry and/or Automobile

Watch

Watch out!
¡Cuidado!
*kwee-*THAH*-thoh!*

Where is a watch repair shop?
¿Dónde hay un relojero?
DOHN*-deh ahy oon rreh-loh-*HEH*-roh?*

What do you charge to clean and regulate a watch?
¿Cuánto se cobra para limpiar y regular un reloj?
KWAHN*-toh seh* KOH*-brah pah-rah leem-*PYAHR *ee rreh-goo-*LAHR *oon rreh-*LOH*?*

My watch is running fast (slow).
Mi reloj está adelantado (atrasado).
*mee rreh-*LOH *ehss-*TAH *ah-deh-lahn-*TAH*-thoh (ah-trah-*SAH*-thoh).*

My watch is broken.
Mi reloj está roto.
*mee rreh-*LOH *ehss-*TAH RROH*-toh.*

Water

Please bring some (more) water.
Por favor, tráigame (más) agua.
*pohr fah-*BOHR, TRAH*-ee-gah-meh (mahss)* AH*-gwah.*

Mineral, plain, hot, cold water.
Agua mineral, corriente, caliente, fría.
AH*-gwah mee-neh-*RAHL, *koh-*RRYEHN*-teh, kah-*YEHN*-teh,* FREE*-ah.*

There is no hot water.
No hay agua caliente.
noh ahy AH*-gwah kah-*YEHN*-teh.*

Water Ski

I don't know how to water ski.
No sé hacer el esqui acuatico.
noh SEH *ah-*SEHR *ehl ehss-*KEE *ah-*KWAH*-tee-koh.*

Where can I go water skiing?
¿Dónde puedo practicar el esqui acuatico?
DOHN*-deh* PWEH*-thoh prahk-tee-*KAHR *ehl ehss-*KEE *ah-*KWAH*-tee-koh?*

Way

Which way is _____?
¿En qué dirección está _____?
*ehn keh dee-rehk-*SYOHN *ehss-*TAH _____?

Is this the way to _____?
¿Es éste el camino a _____?
ehss EHSS-*teh ehl kah-*MEE-*noh ah* _____?

Which is the best way to _____?
¿Cuál es el mejor camino a _____?
KWAHL *ehss ehl meh-*HOHR *kah-*MEE-*noh ah* _____?

Can I go by way of _____?
¿Puedo pasar por _____?
PWEH-*thoh pah-*SAHR *pohr* _____?

Wear

What should I wear?
¿Qué debo ponerme?
keh DEH-*boh poh-*NEHR-*meh?*

Weather

What is the weather like in _____?
¿Qué tiempo hace en _____?
keh TYEHM-*poh* AH-*seh ehn* _____?

Week

I want it for one week (two weeks).
Lo quiero para una semana (dos semanas).
loh KYEH-*roh pah-rah* OO-*nah seh-*MAH-*nah (*DOHSS *seh-*MAH-*nahss).*

Weight

How much weight is allowed?
¿Cuánto peso se permite?
KWAHN-*toh* PEH-*soh seh pehr-*MEE-*teh?*

Is my baggage over weight?
¿Tengo exceso de peso?
TEHN-*goh ehk-*SEH-*soh deh* PEH-*soh?*

What is the rate for excess weight?
¿Cuánto cuesta el exceso de peso?
KWAHN-*toh* KWEHSS-*tah ehl ehk-*SEH-*soh deh* PEH-*soh?*

Well

I want my meat well done.
Quiero que mi carne esté bien cocida.
KYEH-*roh keh mee* KAHR-*neh ehss*-TEH BYEHN *koh*-SEE-*thah.*

This is too well done; please take it back.
Esto está demasiado cocido; por favor, lléveselo.
EHSS-*toh ehss*-TAH *deh-mah*-SYAH-*thoh koh*-SEE-*thoh;
pohr fah*-BOHR, YEH-*beh-seh-loh.*

I don't feel well.
No me siento bien.
noh meh SYEHN-*toh* BYEHN.

What

What do you want?
¿Que quiere usted?
keh KYEH-*reh oo*-STEHTH*?*

What is it?
¿Que ocurre? (¿Qué pasa? ¿qué hay?)
keh oh-KOO-*rreh? (keh* PAH-*sah? keh ahy?)*

What did you (he, she) say?
¿Que dijo usted (él, ella)?
keh DEE-*hoh oo*-STEHTH *(EHL, EH-yah)?*

What is this (that) in _____?
¿Que es esto (eso) en _____?
keh ehss EHSS-*toh (EH-soh) ehn* _____?

When

When will we arrive?
¿Cuándo llegaremos?
KWAHN-*doh yeh-gah*-REH-*mohss?*

When do you open (close)?
¿Cuándo abren (cierran)?
KWAHN-*doh* AH-*brehn (*SYEH-*rrahn)?*

When is breakfast (lunch, dinner) served?
¿Cuándo se sirve el desayuno (el almuerzo, la cena)?
KWAHN-*doh seh* SEER-*beh ehl deh-sah*-YOO-*noh (ehl ahl*-MWEHR-*soh, lah* SEH-*nah)?*

Please tell me when to get off.
Por favor, dígame cuándo tengo que bajarme.
pohr fah-BOHR, DEE-gah-meh KWAHN-*doh* TEHN-*goh keh*
bah-HAHR-meh.

Where

Where is _____?
¿Dónde está _____?
DOHN-*deh ehss-*TAH _____?

Where can I find (buy) _____?
¿Dónde puedo encontrar (comprar) _____?
DOHN-*deh* PWEH-*thoh ehn-kohn-*TRAHR (*kohm-*PRAHR)
_____?

Where are we?
¿Dónde estamos?
DOHN-*deh ehss-*TAH-*mohss?*

Please tell me where to get off.
Por favor, dígame dónde bajarme.
pohr fah-BOHR, DEE-*gah-meh* DOHN-*deh bah-*HAHR-*meh.*

Widow (Widower)

I am a widow (widower).
Soy viuda (viudo).
soy BYOO-*thah (*BYOO-*thoh).*

Window

Where is the ticket window?
¿Dónde está la ventanilla de billetes?
DOHN-*deh ehss-*TAH *lah behn-tah-*NEE-*yah deh bee-*YEH-
tehss?

A seat (a table) by the window, please.
Por favor, un asiento (una mesa) junto a la ventana.
*pohr fah-BOHR, oon ah-*SYEHN-*toh (*OO-*nah* MEH-*sah)*
HOON-*toh ah lah behn-*TAH-*nah.*

Do you mind if I open (close) the window?
¿Le importa a usted si abro (cierro) la ventana?
*leh eem-*POHR-*tah ah oo-*STEHTH *see* AH-*broh (*SYEH-
*rroh) lah behn-*TAH-*nah?*

Please (don't) open (close) the window.
Por favor, (no) abra (cierre) la ventana.
pohr fah-BOHR, (noh) AH-brah (SYEH-rreh) lah behn-
    TAH-nah.

Wine

May I have the wine list, please.
Por favor, ¿puede darme la lista de vinos?
pohr fah-BOHR, PWEH-theh DAHR-meh lah LEESS-tah
    deh BEE-nohss?

Which wine do you recommend?
¿Qué vino recomienda usted?
keh BEE-noh rreh-koh-MYEHN-dah oo-STEHTH?

A glass (a half-bottle, a bottle) of red (white) wine,
    please.
Por favor, un vaso (media botella, una botella) de vino
    tinto (blanco).
pohr fah-BOHR, oon BAH-soh (MEH-thyah boh-TEH-yah,
    OO-nah boh-TEH-yah) deh BEE-noh TEEN-toh (BLAHN-
    koh).

Woman

Who is that woman?
¿Quién es esa mujer?
KYEHN ehss EH-sah moo-HEHR?

Wood

May I have some wood for the fireplace?
¿Puede darme leña para la chimenea?
PWEH-theh DAHR-meh LEH-nyah pah-rah lah chee-meh-
    NEH-ah?

Word

What is this word?
¿Qué palabra es esa?
keh pah-LAH-brah ehss EH-sah?

Work

Where do you work?
¿Dónde trabaja usted?
DOHN-deh trah-BAH-hah oo-STEHTH?

This does not work. Can you fix it?
Esto no funciona. ¿Puede arreglarlo usted?
EHSS-*toh noh foon*-SYOH-*nah.* PWEH-*theh ah-rreh-*
GLAHR-*loh oo*-STEHTH*?*

Worth

What is it worth?
¿Cuánto vale?
KWAHN-*toh* BAH-*leh?*

It is worthless.
No tiene valor.
noh TYEH-*neh bah*-LOHR.

Wrap

Please wrap this (carefully).
Por favor, envuelva esto (con cuidado).
pohr fah-BOHR, *ehn*-BWEHL-*bah* EHSS-*toh (kohn kwee-*
THAH-*thoh).*

Write

Write it down, please.
Escríbalo, por favor.
ehss-KREE-*bah-loh, pohr fah*-BOHR.

How do you write _____ in _____?
¿Cómo se escribe _____ en _____?
KOH-*moh seh ehss*-KREE-*beh* _____ *ehn* _____?

Let's write to each other often.
Nos escribimos a menudo.
nohss ehss-kree-BEE-*mohss ah meh*-NOO-*thoh.*

Writing Paper

I need some (more) writing paper.
Necesito (más) papel de escribir.
neh-seh-SEE-*toh (mahss) pah*-PEHL *deh ehss-kree*-BEER.

Wrong

What is wrong?
¿Qué es lo que está mal?
keh ehss loh keh ehss-TAH MAHL?

Is anything wrong?
¿Pasa algo?
PAH-*sah* AHL-*goh?*

Yours

Is that yours?

¿Es eso suyo?

ehss EH-*soh* SOO-*yoh?*

That is yours.

Eso es suyo.

EH-*soh ehss* SOO-*yoh*

Youth Hostel – see Hostel

Zoo

Can you direct me (take me) to the zoo?

¿Puede dirigirme (llevarme) usted al parque zoológico?

PWEH-*theh dee-ree*-HEER-*meh (yeh*-BAHR-*meh)* oo-
STEHTH *ahl* PAHR-*keh soh-oh*-LOH-*hee-koh?*

International Road Signs

Reproduction by courtesy of
World Touring and Automobile
Organization and American
Automobile Association.

DANGER SIGNS

21

22

23

24

25

26

27

28

1 Dangerous curve	14 Beware of animals
2 Right curve	15 Animals crossing
3 Double curve	16 Road narrows
4 Intersection	17 Uneven road
5 Intersection with a non-priority road	18 Dangerous hill
	19 Slippery road
6 Draw bridge	20 Quay or river bank
7 Level-crossing with gates	21 Merging traffic
	22 Rotary ahead
8 Level-crossing without gates	23 Two-way traffic
	24 Danger
9 Low flying aircraft	25 Danger from falling rocks
10 Traffic signals ahead	26 Loose chips
11 Men working road construction ahead	27 Priority road ahead yield right of way
12 Pedestrian crossing	28 Stop at intersection
13 Children	

PROHIBITORY SIGNS

29 **Closed to all vehicles**
30 **No entry for all vehicles**
31 **No entry for all motor vehicles except motorcycles
   without sidecars**
32 **No entry for motorcycles without sidecars**

33 **No entry for all motor vehicles**
34 **No entry for pedal cyclists**
35 **No entry for commercial vehicles exceeding ...
   tons laden weight**
36 **No entry for vehicles having overall width
   exceeding ... metres**

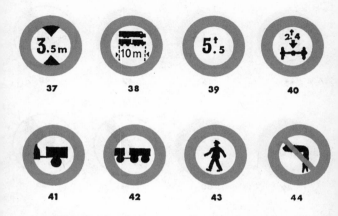

37 No entry for vehicles having overall height
     exceeding ... metres
38 No entry for vehicles having overall length
     exceeding ... metres
39 No entry for vehicles exceeding ... tons laden
     weight
40 No entry for vehicles having an axle weight
     exceeding ... tons

41 Closed to all motor vehicles drawing a trailer other
     than a semi-trailer or a single-wheel trailer
42 Closed to trucks drawing a trailer
43 Closed to pedestrians
44 No left (or right) turns

45 46 47 48

49 50 51 52

53 54 55 56

57 58

45 No U turns
46 No passing
47 No passing by trucks
48 Passing permitted

49 Speed limit
50 Speed limits for light and heavy motor vehicles
51 End of speed limit
52 End of speed limit

53 Use of horn prohibited
54 Priority (right of way) to be given to vehicles coming in the opposite direction
55 Stop: Customs
56 No parking – on left on uneven dates; on right on even dates

57 No parking
58 Stopping prohibited

MANDATORY SIGNS

59

60

61

62

63

59 Direction to be followed
60 Rotary
61 Compulsory cycle track
62 Compulsory minimum speed
63 Compulsory way for pedestrians

INFORMATIVE   SIGNS

64 Priority (right of way) over traffic coming in the opposite direction

65 End of two-way traffic

66 Parking

67 Hospital

68 First-aid station

69 Mechanical help

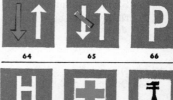
64   65   66

67   68   69

70 Telephone
71 Filling Station
72 Camping site

73 Trailer Court
74 Youth hostel
75 No through road

76 Superhighway
77 End of superhigh-way
78 Road reserved for motor traffic
79 Danger from cross winds

80 One-way traffic
81 Priority road
82 End of priority road

RULE OF THE ROAD

The rule of the road in Europe is to keep to the right except in Great Britain, Northern Ireland and the Republic of Ireland where traffic moves on the left-hand side of the road.

Road signs which conform to the international system are in use in the following countries:

Austria	Haiti	Rumania
Belgium	Hungary	Rwanda
Bulgaria	Iceland	San Marino
Cambodia	Israel	Senegal
Cuba	Italy	Spain
Czechoslovakia	Lebanon	Sweden
Denmark	Luxembourg	Switzerland
Dominican Republic	Monaco	Thailand
Ecuador	Morocco	Tunisia
Egypt	Netherlands	Uganda
Finland	Niger	United Kingdom
France	Norway	U.S.S.R.
Germany	Poland	Vatican City
Greece	Portugal	Yugoslavia

LIGHT SIGNALS

Red light	**Stop**
Amber light	**Stop**, the **Red** will follow
Flashing Amber	**Caution**, proceed with care
Green light	**Go**
Flashing Green	indicates green time is coming to an end; **Stop** if you can
Green Arrow	you may proceed in the direction indicated
Red Arrow	it is **Prohibited** to proceed in the direction Indicated

SIGNS AND NOTICES

SPANISH	ENGLISH
ABIERTO	ON; OPEN
ADELANTE	GO
ALTO	STOP
AVISO	ATTENTION
BADEN	DIP
BAJADA	STEEP GRADE
CABALLEROS	MEN (MEN'S ROOM)
CABLES A ALTA TENSIÓN	HIGH TENSION LINES
CAMINO ESTRECHO	NARROW ROAD
CAMINO SINUOSO	WINDING ROAD
CERRADO	CLOSED; OFF
CONSERVE SU DERECHA	KEEP TO YOUR RIGHT
CONSERVE SU IZQUIERDA	KEEP TO YOUR LEFT
CRUCE	CROSSROADS
CUIDESE DEL PERRO	BEWARE OF DOG
CURVA	CURVE
CURVA PELIGROSA	DANGEROUS CURVE
DAMAS	WOMEN (LADIES' ROOM)
DE CERCANÍAS	LOCAL
DEPRESIÓN	DIP
DESPACIO	SLOW
DESVÍO	DETOUR
EMPUJE	PUSH
ENCRUCIJADA	CROSSROADS

SPANISH	ENGLISH
ENTRADA	ENTRANCE
ESCUELA	SCHOOL
ESTACIONAMIENTO	PARKING
EXPRESOS	EXPRESS
FERROCARRIL	RAILROAD (CROSSING)
HALE	PULL
HOMBRES	MEN (MEN'S ROOM)
——— KILÓMETROS POR HORA	——— KILOMETERS PER HOUR
LAVABOS	LAVATORY
LAVATORIA	LAVATORY
MANEJE CON CUIDADO	DRIVE CAREFULLY
MUJERES	WOMEN (LADIES' ROOM)
NO FUNCIONA	OUT OF ORDER
NO HAY PASO	NO THOROUGHFARE
NO HAY SALIDA	DEAD END
OBRAS	ROAD REPAIRS
OBREROS	MEN WORKING
PARE	STOP
PASAJEROS	PASSENGERS
PASO A NIVEL	GRADE CROSSING
PELIGRO	DANGER
PRECAUCIÓN	CAUTION
PRIVADO	PRIVATE

SPANISH	ENGLISH
PROHIBIDO ANDAR SOBRE EL CESPED	KEEP OFF THE GRASS
PROHIBIDO DOBLAR	NO TURN
PROHIBIDO DOBLAR EN U	NO U-TURN
PROHIBIDO FUMAR	NO SMOKING
PROHIBIDO EL PASO	KEEP OUT
PROHIBIDO ENTRAR	KEEP OUT
PROHIBIDO ESCUPIR	NO SPITTING
PROHIBIDO ESTACIONAR	NO PARKING
PROHIBIDO PASAR	NO PASSING
PROHIBIDO VIRAR	NO TURN
PROHIBIDO VIRAR A LA DERECHA	NO RIGHT TURN
PROHIBIDO VIRAR A LA IZQUIERDA	NO LEFT TURN
SALIDA	EXIT
SECCIÓN DE OBJETOS PERDIDOS	LOST AND FOUND
SEÑORAS	LADIES (LADIES' ROOM)
SEÑORES	MEN (MEN'S ROOM)
SENTIDO UNICO	ONE WAY
TIRE	PULL
TOCAR BOCINA	SOUND YOUR HORN
VELOCIDAD MÁXIMA _____ KILÓMETROS POR HORA	SPEED LIMIT _____ KILOMETERS PER HOUR
VIRAJE	DOUBLE CURVE
VIRAJE RAPIDO	SHARP TURN

ENGLISH	SPANISH	PRONUNCIATION
a (an)	un, una	*oon,* OO-*nah*
able (capable)	capaz	*kah-*PAHSS
aboard	a bordo	*ah* BOHR-*thoh*
about (concerning)	sobre	SOH-*breh*
abroad (in foreign land)	en el extranjero	*ehn ehl ehss-trahn-*HEH-*roh*
absence	ausencia, f.	*ow-*SEHN-*syah*
absent	ausente	*ow-*SEHN-*teh*
accent (speech)	acento, m.	*ah-*SEHN-*toh*
accept, to	aceptar	*ah-sehp-*TAHR
accident (mishap)	accidente, m.	*ahk-see-*THEHN-*teh*
accommodate (have room for), to	hospedar	*ohss-peh-*THAHR
accompany (go along with), to	acompañar	*ah-kohm-pah-*NYAHR
accord (agreement)	acuerdo, m.	*ah-*KWEHR-*thoh*
according to (in accordance with)	según	*seh-*GOON
account (bank account)	cuenta, f.	KWEHN-*tah*
accountant	contador, m.	*kohn-tah-*THOHR
accurate	exacto	*ehk-*SAHK-*toh*
accuse, to	acusar	*ah-koo-*SAHR
accustom oneself, to	acostumbrarse	*ah-kohss-toom-*BRAHR-*seh*
ache	dolor, m.	*doh-*LOHR
ache, to	doler	*doh-*LEHR
acknowledge (note receipt of), to	acusar recibo	*ah-koo-*SAHR *rreh-*SEE-*boh*
acquaintance (knowledge)	conocimiento, m.	*koh-noh-see-*MYEHN-*toh*
acquaintance (person known)	conocido, m.	*koh-noh-*SEE-*thoh*

ENGLISH	SPANISH	PRONUNCIATION
across (beyond)	al otro lado de	*ahl* OH-*troh* LAH-*thoh deh*
across (to the other side)	a través de	*ah trah-*BEHSS *deh*
act (deed)	acto, m.	AHK-*toh*
act (dramatic unit)	acto, m.	AHK-*toh*
act (behave), to	portarse	*pohr-*TAHR-*seh*
act (do), to	obrar	*oh-*BRAHR
action (deed)	acción, f.	*ahk-*SYOHN
actor (player)	actor, m.	*ahk-*TOHR
actress	actriz, f.	*ahk-*TREESS
add (include), to	añadir	*ah-nyah-*THEER
address (postal directions)	dirección, f.	*dee-rehk-*SYOHN
address (speech)	discurso, m.	*deess-*KOOR-*soh*
addressee	destinatario, m.	*dehss-tee-nah-*TAH-*ryoh*
adjust (regulate), to	ajustar	*ah-hooss-*TAHR
admire, to	admirar	*ahd-mee-*RAHR
admission (right to enter)	entrada, f.	*ehn-*TRAH-*thah*
admit (permit to enter), to	dar entrada	*dahr ehn-*TRAH-*thah*
advance (go forward), to	avanzar	*ah-bahn-*SAHR
adventure	aventura, f.	*ah-behn-*TOO-*rah*
advertise (give notice of), to	anunciar	*ah-noon-*SYAHR
advertisement	anuncio, m.	*ah-*NOON-*syoh*
advice	consejo, m.	*kohn-*SEH-*hoh*
aerial (antenna)	antena, f.	*ahn-*TEH-*nah*
affect (influence), to	influir en	*een-floo-*EER *ehn*
afford (have the means), to	permitirse	*pehr-mee-*TEER-*seh*
afraid	temeroso	*teh-meh-*ROH-*soh*
after (conj.)	después (de) que	*dehss-*PWEHSS *(deh) keh*

ENGLISH	SPANISH	PRONUNCIATION
after (prep.)	después de	*dehss*-PWEHSS *deh*
afternoon	tarde, f.	TAHR-*theh*
afterward (later)	después	*dehss*-PWEHSS
again	otra vez	OH-*trah* BEHSS
against	contra	KOHN-*trah*
age (accumulated years)	edad, f.	*eh*-THAHTH
agent (representative)	agente, m.	*ah*-HEHN-*teh*
agree (assent), to	asentir	*ah*-sehn-TEER
agreeable (pleasing)	agradable	*ah*-grah-THAH-*bleh*
agreement (mutual understanding)	acuerdo, m.	*ah*-KWEHR-*thoh*
agree with, to	estar de acuerdo con	*ehss*-TAHR *deh* *ah*-KWEHR-*thoh*
ahead (forward)	adelante	*ah*-theh-LAHN-*teh*
ahead (in front)	delante	*deh*-LAHN-*teh*
aim (purpose)	propósito, m.	*proh*-POH-*see-toh*
air (atmosphere)	aire, m.	AH-*ee-reh*
air conditioning	acondiciona-miento del aire, m.	*ah*-kohn-dee-syoh-nah-MYEHN-*toh* *dehl* AH-*ee-reh*
air mail	correo aéreo, m.	*koh*-RREH-*oh* *ah*-EH-*reh-oh*
airplane	aeroplano, m.	*ah-eh-roh*-PLAH-*noh*
airport	aeropuerto, m.	*ah-eh-roh*-PWEHR-*toh*
aisle (passageway)	pasillo, m.	*pah*-SEE-*yoh*
alcohol	alcohol, m.	*ahl-koh*-OHL
alive	vivo	BEE-*boh*
all (entirely, adv.)	enteramente	*ehn-teh-rah*-MEHN-*teh*
all (every, adj.)	todo	TOH-*thoh*
all (everything, n.)	todo, m.	TOH-*thoh*
all (whole of, adj.)	todo	TOH-*thoh*

ENGLISH	SPANISH	PRONUNCIATION
allergy	alergia, f.	*ah-lehr-*HEE-*ah*
allow (permit), to	permitir	*pehr-mee-*TEER
almost	casi	KAH-*see*
alone	solo	SOH-*loh*
aloud	en voz alta	*ehn* BOHSS AHL-*tah*
already	ya	YAH
also	también	*tahm-*BYEHN
although	aunque	OWN-*keh*
altogether (entirely)	enteramente	*ehn-teh-rah-*MEHN-*teh*
always	siempre	SYEHM-*preh*
ambassador	embajador, m.	*ehm-bah-hah-*THOHR
ambulance	ambulancia, f.	*ahm-boo-*LAHN-*syah*
America	América	*ah-*MEH-*ree-kah*
American (adj.)	norteamericano	*nohr-teh-ah-meh-ree-*KAH-*noh*
amid	en medio de	*ehn* MEH-*thyoh deh*
among	entre	EHN-*treh*
amount	cantidad, f.	*kahn-tee-*THAHTH
amount to, to	montar a	*mohn-*TAHR *ah*
amuse, to	divertir	*dee-behr-*TEER
amusement	diversión, f.	*dee-behr-*SYOHN
ancestor	ascendiente, m.	*ahss-sehn-*DYEHN-*teh*
anchor	ancla, f.	AHN-*klah*
ancient	antiguo	*ahn-*TEE-*gwoh*
and	y, e	*ee, eh*
angry	enojado	*ehn-oh-*HAH-*thoh*
animal	animal, m.	*ah-nee-*MAHL
ankle	tobillo, m.	*toh-*BEE-*yoh*
anniversary	aniversario, m.	*ah-nee-behr-*SAH-*ryoh*
announce, to	anunciar	*ah-noon-*SYAHR
announcement	anuncio, m.	*ah-*NOON-*syoh*

ENGLISH	SPANISH	PRONUNCIATION
annoy (irk), to	fastidiar	*fahss-tee-*THYAHR
annual	anual	*ah-*NWAHL
another (different one, pron.)	otro	OH-*troh*
another (one more, adj.)	otro	OH-*troh*
answer	respuesta, f.	*rrehss-*PWEHSS-*tah*
answer (address reply to), to	responder a	*rrehss-pohn-*DEHR *ah*
anticipate (expect), to	anticipar (se)	*ahn-tee-see-*PAHR *(-seh)*
antiquity (ancientness)	antigüedad, f.	*ahn-tee-gweh-*THAHTH
anxious (uneasy)	inquieto	*een-*KYEH-*toh*
any (any at all, adj.)	cual(es) quier(a)	*kwahl(-ehss)-*KYEHR*(-ah)*
any (any one, adj.)	cualquier(a)	*kwahl-*KYEHR *(-ah)*
anybody (anybody whosoever)	cualquier persona	*kwahl-*KYEHR *pehr-*SOH-*nah*
anybody (not . . . anybody)	nadie	NAH-*thyeh*
anyhow (in any case)	de todos modos	*deh* TOH-*thohss* MOH-*thohss*
anything (anything whatever)	cualquier cosa	*kwahl-*KYEHR KOH-*sah*
apartment	departamento, m.	*deh-pahr-tah-*MEHN-*toh*
apologize, to	disculparse	*deess-kool-*PAHR-*seh*
apparent (obvious)	aparente	*ah-pah-*REHN-*teh*
appeal to (entreat), to	suplicar	*soo-plee-*KAHR
appear (seem), to	parecer	*pah-reh-*SEHR
appearance (aspect)	apariencia, f.	*ah-pah-*RYEHN-*syah*

ENGLISH	SPANISH	PRONUNCIATION
appendicitis	apendicitis, f.	*ah-pehn-dee-*SEE-*teess*
appetite	apetito, m.	*ah-peh-*TEE-*toh*
apple	manzana, f.	*mahn-*SAH-*nah*
application (request)	solicitud, f.	*soh-lee-see-*TOOTH
appointment (meeting)	cita, f.	SEE-*tah*
appraisal	valoración, f.	*bah-loh-rah-*SYOHN
appreciate (be grateful for) to	agradecer	*ah-grah-deh-*SEHR
approach (come near to), to	acercarse (a)	*ah-sehr-*KAHR-*seh ah*
apricot	albaricoque, m.	*ahl-bah-ree-*KOH-*keh*
arch (curved structure)	arco, m.	AHR-*koh*
area (extent)	área, f.	AH-*reh-ah*
area (region)	región, f.	*rreh-*HYOHN
argue (maintain), to	sostener	*sohss-teh-*NEHR
argument (dispute)	disputa, f.	*deess-*POO-*tah*
arm	brazo, m.	BRAH-*soh*
arrange (plan), to	hacer arreglos (para)	*ah-*SEHR *ah-*RREH-*glohss (pah-rah)*
arrangement (order)	colocación, f.	*koh-loh-kah-*SYOHN
arrest (take into custody), to	arrestar	*ah-rrehss-*TAHR
arrival	llegada, f.	*yeh-*GAH-*thah*
arrive, to	llegar	*yeh-*GAHR
art	arte, m., f.	AHR-*teh*
arthritis	artritis, f.	*ahr-*TREE-*teess*
article (literary composition)	artículo, m.	*ahr-*TEE-*koo-loh*
article (thing)	cosa, f.	KOH-*sah*
artificial	artificial	*ahr-tee-fee-*SYAHL

ENGLISH	SPANISH	PRONUNCIATION
artist	artista, m., f.	*ahr*-TEESS-*tah*
as (in the same way, conj.)	como	KOH-*moh*
ascend (go upward along), to	ascender	*ahss-sehn*-DEHR
ashamed (mortified)	avergonzado	*ah-behr-gohn*-SAH-*thoh*
ash tray	cenicero, m.	*seh-nee*-SEH-*roh*
ask (put question to), to	preguntar	*preh-goon*-TAHR
ask (request), to	pedir	*peh*-THEER
ask about, to	preguntar por	*preh-goon*-TAHR *pohr*
asleep (sleeping)	dormido	*dohr*-MEE-*thoh*
asparagus	esparrago, m.	*ehss*-PAH-*rrah-goh*
aspect (phase)	aspecto, m.	*ahss*-PEHK-*toh*
aspirin	aspirina, f.	*ahss-pee*-REE-*nah*
assent, to	asentir	*ah-sehn*-TEER
assist, to	ayudar	*ah-yoo*-THAHR
assistance	ayuda, f.	*ah*-YOO-*thah*
assistant	ayudante, m.	*ah-yoo*-THAHN-*teh*
association (body of persons)	asociación, f.	*ah-soh-syah*-SYOHN
assume (take for granted), to	dar por sentado	*dahr pahr sehn*-TAH-*thoh*
astonish, to	asombrar	*ah-sohm*-BRAHR
at (in)	en	*ehn*
at (near)	a	*ah*
at (on)	en	*ehn*
at (to, toward)	a	*ah*
athlete	atleta, m.	*aht*-LEH-*tah*
atmosphere (air)	atmósfera, f.	*aht*-MOHSS-*feh-rah*
attach (join), to	acompañar	*ah-kohm-pah*-NYAHR
attack (assault physically), to	agredir	*ah-greh*-THEER

ENGLISH	SPANISH	PRONUNCIATION
attempt, to	procurar	*proh-koo-*RAHR
attend (be present at), to	asistir	*ah-seess-*TEER
attendance (presence)	asistencia, f.	*ah-seess-*TEHN-*syah*
attention (heed)	atención, f.	*ah-tehn-*SYOHN
attorney	abogado, m.	*ah-boh-*GAH-*thoh*
attractive (pleasing)	atractivo	*ah-trahk-*TEE-*boh*
auction (sale)	subasta, f.	*soo-*BAHSS-*tah*
audience	auditorio, m.	*ow-thee-*TOH-*ryoh*
auditorium	salón de actos, m.	*sah-*LOHN *deh* AHK-*tohss*
aunt	tía, f.	TEE-*ah*
Austria	Austria	OWSS-*tryah*
Austrian (adj.)	austríaco	*owss-*TRYAH-*koh*
author	autor, m.	*ow-*TOHR
authority (power)	autoridad, f.	*ow-toh-ree-*THAHTH
authorization	autorización, f.	*ow-toh-ree-sah-*SYOHN
automobile	automóvil, m.	*ow-toh-*MOH-*beel*
autumn	otoño, m.	*oh-*TOH-*nyoh*
available	disponible	*deess-poh-*NEE-*bleh*
avenue (street)	avenida, f.	*ah-beh-*NEE-*thah*
average (ordinary, adj.)	mediano	*meh-*THYAH-*noh*
avert (prevent), to	impedir	*eem-peh-*THEER
aviator	aviador, m.	*ah-byah-*THOHR
avoid, to	evitar	*eh-bee-*TAHR
await, to	esperar	*ehss-peh-*RAHR
awful	terrible	*teh-*RREE-*bleh*
awkward	torpe	TOHR-*peh*
baby	criatura, f.	*kree-ah-*TOO-*rah*
back (rearward, adv.)	atrás	*ah-*TRAHSS
back (reverse side)	dorso, m.	DOHR-*soh*

ENGLISH	SPANISH	PRONUNCIATION
bacon	tocino, m.	*toh*-SEE-*noh*
bad, worse, worst	malo, peor, (el) peor	MAH-*toh, peh*-OHR, *(ehl) peh*-OHR
bag (purse)	bolsa, f.	BOHL-*sah*
bag (sack)	saco, m.	SAH-*koh*
baggage (luggage)	equipaje, m.	*eh-kee*-PAH-*heh*
bake (be cooking), to	cocer en horno	*koh*-SEHR *ehn* OHR-*noh*
baker	panadero, m.	*pah-nah*-THEH-*roh*
bald (hairless)	calvo	KAHL-*boh*
ball-point pen	bolígrafo	*boh*-LEE-*grah-foh*
banana	plátano, m.	PLAH-*toh-noh*
band (ribbon)	cinta, f.	SEEN-*tah*
bandage	venda, f.	BEHN-*dah*
bank (shore)	ribera, f.	*rree*-BEH-*rah*
bank (treasury)	banco, m.	BAHN-*koh*
banker	banquero, m.	*bahn*-KEH-*roh*
bankruptcy	quiebra, f.	KYEH-*brah*
banner	pendón, m.	*pehn*-THOHN
banquet	banquete, m.	*bahn*-KEH-*teh*
bar (barroom)	bar; cantina, f.	BAHR; *kahn*-TEE-*nah*
barber	barbero, m.	*bahr*-BEH-*roh*
bare (nude)	desnudo	*dehss*-NOO-*thoh*
bargain (advantageous purchase)	ganga, f.	GAHN-*gah*
bargain (agreement)	trato, m.	TRAH-*toh*
bargain (negotiate), to	negociar	*neh-goh*-SYAHR
barrier	barrera, f.	*bah*-RREH-*rah*
baseball	béisbol, m.	BEYSS-*bohl*
basement	sótano, m.	SOH-*tah-noh*
bashful	vergonzoso	*behr-gohn*-SOH-*soh*
basket	cesta,f.	SEHSS-*tah*
bathe (take a bath), to	bañarse	*bah*-NYAHR-*seh*

ENGLISH	SPANISH	PRONUNCIATION
bathing suit	traje de baño, m.	TRAH-*heh deh* BAH-*nyoh*
bathroom	(cuarto de) baño, m.	(KWAHR-*toh deh*) BAH-*nyoh*
bathtub	bañera, f.	bah-NYEH-*rah*
battery (primary cell)	pila seca, f.	PEE-*lah* SEH-*kah*
battle	batalla, f.	bah-TAH-*yah*
Bavaria	Baviera	bah-BYEH-*rah*
bay (inlet)	bahía, f.	bah-EE-*ah*
be, to	ser; estar	SEHR; ehss-TAHR
beach (strand)	playa, f.	PLAH-*yah*
bead (jewelry)	cuenta, f.	KWEHN-*tah*
beam (ray)	rayo, m.	RAH-*yoh*
bean (string bean)	haba, f.	AH-*bah*
bear (carry), to	llevar	yeh-BAHR
beard	barba, f.	BAHR-*bah*
beautiful	bello	BEH-*yoh*
beauty	belleza, f.	beh-YEH-*sah*
because (conj.)	porque	POHR-*keh*
because of (adv.)	a causa de	ah KOW-*sah deh*
become, to	hacerse	ah-SEHR-*seh*
bed	cama, f.	KAH-*mah*
bedroom	alcoba, f.	ahl-KOH-*bah*
bee	abeja, f.	ah-BEH-*hah*
beef	carne de vaca, f.	KAHR-*neh deh* BAH-*kah*
beer	cerveza, f.	sehr-BEH-*sah*
before (ahead, adv.)	adelante	ah-theh-LAHN-*teh*
before (earlier, adv.)	antes	AHN-*tehss*
beg (solicit alms), to	mendigar	mehn-dee-GAHR
begger	mendigo, m.	mehn-DEE-*goh*
begin (start to do), to	comenzar	koh-mehn-SAHR
beginning	principio, m.	preen-SEE-*pyoh*
behave (conduct oneself), to	conducirse	kohn-doo-SEER-*seh*

ENGLISH	SPANISH	PRONUNCIATION
behavior	conducta, f.	*kohn-*DOOK-*tah*
behind (in the rear, adv.)	detrás	*deh-*TRAHSS
behind (prep.)	detrás de	*deh-*TRAHSS *deh*
Belgium	Bélgica	BEHL-*hee-kah*
believe (accept), to	creer	*kreh-*EHR
belly (abdomen)	vientre, m.	BYEHN-*treh*
belong to (be the property of), to	pertenecer	*pehr-teh-neh-*SEHR
belt (article of clothing)	cinto, m.	SEEN-*toh*
beneath (below, adv.)	abajo	*ah-*BAH-*hoh*
benefit (advantage)	ventaja, f.	*behn-*TAH-*hah*
berry (fruit)	baya, f.	BAH-*yah*
berth (train bunk)	litera, f.	*lee-*TEH-*rah*
besides (other than, prep.)	además de	*ah-theh-*MAHSS *deh*
bet, to	apostar	*ah-pohss-*TAHR
better (adj.)	mejor	*meh-*HOHR
between (prep.)	entre	EHN-*treh*
beware of, to	guardarse de	*gwahr-*THAHR-*seh deh*
beyond (farther on than, prep.)	más allá de	*mahss ah-*YAH *deh*
Bible	Biblia, f.	BEE-*blyah*
bicycle	bicicleta, f.	*bee-see-*KLEH-*tah*
bid (amount offered)	postura, f.	*poh-*STOO-*rah*
big	grande	GRAHN-*deh*
bill (currency)	billete, m.	*bee-*YEH-*teh*
bill (invoice)	factura, f.	*fahk-*TOO-*rah*
bill of sale	carta de venta, f.	KAHR-*tah deh* BEHN-*tah*
billiards	billar, m.	*bee-*YAHR
bird	ave, f.	AH-*beh*
birthday	cumpleaños, m.	*koom-pleh-*AH-*nyohss*

ENGLISH	SPANISH	PRONUNCIATION
bit (small part)	poquito, m.	*poh*-KEE-*toh*
bite, to	morder	*mohr*-THEHR
bitter	amargo	*ah*-MAHR-*goh*
black	negro	NEH-*groh*
blackberry	mora, f.	MOH-*rah*
blackboard	pizarra, f.	*pee*-SAH-*rrah*
bladder	vejiga, f.	*beh*-HEE-*gah*
blame, to	culpar	*kool*-PAHR
blanket	manta, f.	MAHN-*tah*
bleach (make white), to	blanquear	*blahn-keh*-AHR
bleed (lose blood), to	sangrar	*sahn*-GRAHR
blind (lacking sight)	ciego	SYEH-*goh*
blister	ampolla, f.	*ahm*-POH-*yah*
blond	rubio	ROO-*byoh*
blood	sangre, f.	SAHN-*greh*
bloom, to	florecer	*floh-reh*-SEHR
blouse (shirtwaist)	blusa, f.	BLOO-*sah*
blow (breathe out), to	soplar	*soh*-PLAHR
blue	azul	*ah*-SOOL
blush, to	ruborizarse	*rroo-boh-ree-*SAHR-*seh*
boarding house	pensión, f.	*pehn*-SYOHN
boat	barco, m.	BAHR-*koh*
body	cuerpo, m.	KWEHR-*poh*
boil (bubble up), to	hervir	*ehr*-BEER
bolt (lock)	cerrojo, m.	*seh*-RROH-*hoh*
bone	hueso, m.	WEH-*soh*
book	libro, m.	LEE-*broh*
book (engage space), to	reservar	*rreh-sehr*-BAHR
boot (footgear)	bota, f.	BOH-*tah*

ENGLISH	SPANISH	PRONUNCIATION
boredom	aburrimiento, m.	*ah-boo-rree-*MYEHN-*toh*
borrow, to	tomar (pedir) prestado	*toh*-MAHR *(peh-*THEER*) prehss-*TAH-*thoh*
bosom	seno, m.	SEH-*noh*
boss (master)	patrón, m.	*pah*-TROHN
both (adj.)	los dos	*lohss* DOHSS
both (pron.)	los dos	*lohss* DOHSS
bother (annoy), to	molestar	*moh-lehss-*TAHR
bottle	botella, f.	*boh*-TEH-*yah*
bottom	fondo, m.	FOHN-*doh*
boundary (limit line)	límite, m.	LEE-*mee-teh*
bow (nod)	inclinación, f.	*een-klee-nah-*SYOHN
bowels	intestinos, m. pl.	*een-tehss-*TEE-*nohss*
bowl (dish)	cuenco, m.	KWEHN-*koh*
box (container)	caja, f.	KAH-*hah*
boy (lad)	muchacho, m.	*moo-*CHAH-*choh*
bracelet	pulsera, f.	*pool-*SEH-*rah*
brain	cerebro, m.	*seh-*REH-*broh*
brake	freno, m.	FREH-*noh*
brand (trade mark)	marca (de fá-brica), f.	MAHR-*kah (deh* FAH-*bree-kah)*
brandy	aguardiente, m.	*ah-gwahr-*THYEHN-*teh*
brass	latón, m.	*lah-*TOHN
brassiere	sostén, m.	*sohss-*TEHN
bread	pan, m.	PAHN
breadth (width)	anchura, f.	*ahn-*CHOO-*rah*
break (come apart), to	romperse	*rrohm-*PEHR-*seh*
break (cause to break), to	romper	*rrohm-*PEHR

ENGLISH	SPANISH	PRONUNCIATION
breakfast	desayuno, m.	deh-sah-YOO-noh
breast	pecho, m.	PEH-choh
breath	aliento, m.	ah-LYEHN-toh
breathe (draw breath), to	respirar	rrehss-pee-RAHR
breeze	brisa, f.	BREE-sah
bribe, to	sobornar	soh-bohr-NAHR
bridge (span)	puente, m.	PWEHN-teh
briefcase	cartera, f.	kahr-TEH-rah
bright (shining)	brillante	bree-YAHN-teh
bring, to	traer	trah-EHR
British (adj.)	británico	bree-TAH-nee-koh
broad (wide)	ancho	AHN-choh
broadcasting	radiodifusión, f.	rrah-thyoh-dee-foo-SYOHN
bronchitis	bronquitis, f.	brohn-KEE-teess
bronze (n.)	bronce, m.	BROHN-seh
brooch	broche, m.	BROH-cheh
broom	escoba, f.	ehss-KOH-bah
brother	hermano, m.	ehr-MAH-noh
brother-in-law	cuñado, m.	koo-NYAH-thoh
brown	pardo (castaño)	PAHR-thoh (kahss-TAH-nyoh)
bruise	cardenal, m.	kahr-theh-NAHL
budget (n.)	presupuesto, m.	preh-soo-PWEHSS-toh
bug (insect)	insecto, m.	een-SEHK-toh
building	edificio, m.	eh-thee-FEE-syoh
bulb (light bulb)	bombilla, f.	bohm-BEE-yah
bundle (parcel)	paquete, m.	pah-KEH-teh
bureau (chest)	cómoda, f.	KOH-moh-thah
bureau (office)	oficina, f.	oh-fee-SEE-nah
burglar	ladrón, m.	lah-THROHN
burial	entierro, m.	ehn-TYEH-rroh
burn (be on fire), to	arder	ahr-THEHR
bury (entomb), to	enterrar	ehn-teh-RRAHR

ENGLISH	SPANISH	PRONUNCIATION
bus	ómnibus, m.	OHM-*nee-booss*
bush (plant)	arbusto, m.	*ahr*-BOOSS-*toh*
business (commerce)	negocio, m.	*neh*-GOH-*syoh*
businessman	hombre de negocios, m.	OHM-*breh deh neh*-GOH-*syohss*
busy (occupied)	ocupado	*oh-koo*-PAH-*thoh*
but (yet, conj.)	pero	PEH-*roh*
butcher	carnicero, m.	*kahr-nee*-SEH-*roh*
butter	mantequilla	*mahn-teh*-KEE-*yah*
button	botón, m.	*boh*-TOHN
buy, to	comprar	*kohm*-PRAHR
by (near, prep.)	junto a	HOON-*toh ah*
by (prior to, prep.)	antes de	AHN-*tehss deh*
cab (taxi)	taxi, m.	TAHK-*see*
cabbage	col, f.	KOHL
cabin (of ship)	camarote, m.	*kah-mah*-ROH-*teh*
cablegram	cablegrama, m.	*kah-bleh*-GRAH-*mah*
cake (dessert)	torta, f.	TOHR-*tah*
calendar	calendario, m.	*kah-lehn*-DAH-*ryoh*
call (shout), to	gritar	*gree*-TAHR
call (summon), to	llamar	*yah*-MAHR
camera	cámara, f.	KAH-*mah-rah*
can (tin)	lata, f.	LAH-*tah*
canal	canal, m.	*kah*-NAHL
cancel (revoke), to	cancelar	*kahn-seh*-LAHR
cancer	cáncer, m.	KAHN-*sehr*
candle	vela, f.	BEH-*lah*
candy	dulce, m.	DOOL-*seh*
cane (walking stick)	bastón, m.	*bahss*-TOHN
cap (hat)	gorra, f.	GOH-*rrah*
capital (city)	capital, f.	*kah-pee*-TAHL
captain (officer)	capitán, m.	*kah-pee*-TAHN
car (auto)	coche, m.	KOH-*cheh*

ENGLISH	SPANISH	PRONUNCIATION
car, railroad	vagón, m.	*bah*-GOHN
carbon copy	copia (en papel carbón), f.	KOH-*pyah (ehn pah*-PEHL *kahr*-BOHN)
card, calling	tarjeta de visita, f.	*tahr*-HEH-*tah deh bee*-SEE-*tah*
card, playing	naipe, m.	NAH-*ee-peh*
card, postal	tarjeta, f.	*tahr*-HEH-*tah*
cardboard	cartón, m.	*kahr*-TOHN
care (custody)	custodia, f.	*kooss*-TOH-*thyah*
care (be concerned), to	interesarse en	*een-teh-reh*-SAHR-*seh ehn*
careful (cautious)	cuidadoso	*kwee-thah*-THOH-*soh*
cargo	cargamento, m.	*kahr-gah*-MEHN-*toh*
carpet	alfombra, f.	*ahl*-FOHM-*brah*
carriage (horse-drawn vehicle)	coche, m.	KOH-*cheh*
carrot	zanahoria, f.	*sah-nah*-OH-*ree-ah*
carry (bear), to	llevar	*yeh*-BAHR
cart	carro, m.	KAH-*rroh*
case (instance)	caso, m.	KAH-*soh*
cash (money)	efectivo, m.	*eh-fehk*-TEE-*boh*
cash (receive cash for), to	hacer efectivo	*ah*-SEHR *eh-fehk*-TEE-*boh*
cashier	cajero, m.	*kah*-HEH-*roh*
castle	castillo, m.	*kahss*-TEE-*yoh*
cat	gato, m.	GAH-*toh*
cathedral	catedral, f.	*kah-teh*-DRAHL
Catholic (adj.)	católico	*kah*-TOH-*lee-koh*
cattle	ganado vacuno, m.	*gah*-NAH-*thoh bah*-KOO-*noh*
cauliflower	coliflor, f.	*koh-lee*-FLOHR
cause	causa, f.	KAH-*oo-sah*
caution (warn), to	advertir	*ahd-behr*-TEER
ceiling (of room)	techo, m.	TEH-*choh*

ENGLISH	SPANISH	PRONUNCIATION
celery	apio, m.	AH-*pyoh*
cellar	bodega, f.;	boh-THEH-*gah;*
	sótano, m.	SOH-*tah-noh*
cemetery	cementerio, m.	seh-mehn-TEH-*ryoh*
center	centro, m.	SEHN-*troh*
century	siglo, m.	SEE-*gloh*
cereal (grain)	cereal, m.	seh-reh-AHL
ceremony	ceremonia, f.	seh-reh-MOH-*nyah*
certain (sure)	cierto	SYEHR-*toh*
certainly (of course!, interj.)	por cierto	pohr SYEHR-*toh*
certify, to	certificar	sehr-tee-fee-KAHR
chair	silla, f.	SEE-*yah*
chance (opportunity)	ocasión, f.	oh-kah-SYOHN
chance (possibility)	posibilidad, f.	poh-see-bee-lee-THAHTH
change (become different), to	alterarse	ahl-teh-RAHR-*seh*
channel (strait)	canal, m.	kah-NAHL
chapel	capilla, f.	kah-PEE-*yah*
character (person portrayed)	personaje, m.	pehr-soh-NAH-*heh*
charge (price)	precio, m.	PREH-*syoh*
charge account	cuenta cor-riente, f.	KWEHN-*tah koh-*RRYEHN-*teh*
charming	encantador	ehn-kahn-tah-THOHR
chat, to	charlar	chahr-LAHR
cheap (inexpensive)	barato	bah-RAH-*toh*
cheat (defraud), to	engañar	ehn-gah-NYAHR
check (bank check)	cheque, m.	CHEH-*keh*
cheek	mejilla, f.	meh-HEE-*yah*
cheer (applaud), to	aplaudir	ah-plah-oo-THEER
cheerful (joyful)	jovial	hoh-BYAHL
cheese	queso, m.	KEH-*soh*
cherry (fruit)	cereza, f.	seh-REH-*sah*

ENGLISH	SPANISH	PRONUNCIATION
chess	ajedrez, m.	*ah-heh-*DREHSS
chest	pecho, m.	PEH-*choh*
chew, to	mascar	*mahss-*KAHR
chicken	pollo, m.	POH-*yoh*
chicken pox	varicela, f.	*bah-ree-*SEH-*lah*
chief (leading)	principal	*preen-see-*PAHL
child	niño, m.	NEE-*nyoh*
chimney	chimenea, f.	*chee-meh-*NEH-*ah*
chocolate	chocolate, m.	*choh-koh-*LAH-*teh*
choke, to	ahogar	*ah-oh-*GAHR
cholera	cólera (asiático), m.	KOH-*leh-rah (ah-*SYAH-*tee-koh)*
choose (select), to	escoger	*ehss-koh-*HEHR
Christmas	Navidad, f.	*nah-bee-*THAHTH
church	iglesia, f.	*ee-*GLEH-*syah*
cigar	cigarro, m.	*see-*GAH-*rroh*
cigarette	cigarrillo, m.	*see-gah-*REE-*yoh*
citizen	ciudadano, m.	*syoo-thah-*THAH-*noh*
city	ciudad, f.	*syoo-*THAHTH
claim, to	reclamar	*rreh-klah-*MAHR
clap (applaud), to	aplaudir	*ah-plah-oo-*THEER
class (kind)	clase, f.	KLAH-*seh*
classroom	aula, f.; clase, f.	AH-*oo-lah;* KLAH-*seh*
clean	limpio	LEEM-*pyoh*
clear	claro	KLAH-*roh*
clearance (customs clearance)	despacho de aduana, m.	*dehss-*PAH-*choh deh ah-*THWAH-*nah*
clerk (salesperson)	dependiente, m.	*deh-pehn-*DYEHN-*teh*
clever	hábil	AH-*beel*
climate (weather)	clima, m.	KLEE-*mah*
climb (scale), to	escalar	*ehss-kah-*LAHR
cloak (apparel)	capa, f.	KAH-*pah*
clock	reloj, m.	*rreh-*LOH

ENGLISH	SPANISH	PRONUNCIATION
close (shut), to	cerrar	*seh*-RRAHR
cloth	tela, f.	TEH-*lah*
clothing	ropa, f.	RROH-*pah*
cloud	nube, f.	NOO-*beh*
cloudy (overcast)	nublado	*noo*-BLAH-*thoh*
coach, railroad	vagón, m.	*bah*-GOHN
coal	carbón, m.	*kahr*-BOHN
coarse	tosco	TOHSS-*koh*
coast (seaboard)	costa, f.	KOHSS-*tah*
coat (man's overcoat)	gabán, m. abrigo, m.	*gah*-BAHN; *ah*-BREE-*goh*
coat (woman's overcoat)	abrigo de mujer m.	*ah*-BREE-*goh deh moo*-HEHR
cocktail	coctel, m.	*kohk*-TEHL
cocoa	cacao, m.	*kah*-KAH-*oh*
coffee	café, m.	*kah*-FEH
coffin	ataúd, m.	*ah-tah*-OOTH
coin	moneda, f.	*moh*-NEH-*thah*
cold (adj.)	frío	FREE-*oh*
cold (disease)	resfriado, m.	*rrehss-free*-AH-*thoh*
collar	cuello, m.	KWEH-*yoh*
color	color, m.	*koh*-LOHR
column (pillar)	columna, f.	*koh*-LOOM-*nah*
comb (for hair)	peine, m.	PEH-*ee-neh*
combine (make join), to	combinar	*kohm-bee*-NAHR
come, to	venir	*beh*-NEER
comedy (comic play)	comedia, f.	*koh*-MEH-*thyah*
comfort (ease)	comodidad, f.	*koh-moh-thee*-THAHTH
comfort (console), to	consolar	*kohn-soh*-LAHR
comfortable	cómodo	KOH-*moh-thoh*
command (order), to	mandar	*mahn*-DAHR
comment, to	comentar	*koh-mehn*-TAHR
commercial	comercial	*koh-mehr*-SYAHL
common (usual)	ordinario	*ohr-thee*-NAH-*ryoh*

ENGLISH	SPANISH	PRONUNCIATION
communism	comunismo, m.	*koh-moo-*NEEZ-*moh*
community (neighborhood)	barrio	BAH-*rryoh*
companion	compañero, m.	*kohm-pah-*NYEH-*roh*
company (bus.)	compañía, f.	*kohm-pah-*NYEE-*ah*
compare (consider relatively), to	comparar	*kohm-*PRAHR
comparison	comparación, f.	*kohm-pah-rah-*SYOHN
compartment (of train)	compartimiento, m.	*kohm-pahr-tee-*MYEHN-*toh*
complain, to	quejarse	*keh-*HAHR-*seh*
complaint	queja, f.	KEH-*hah*
complete (entire)	completo	*kohm-*PLEH-*toh*
compliment	cumplimiento, m.	*koom-plee-*MYEHN-*toh*
comrade	camarada, m., f.	*kah-mah-*RAH-*thah*
conceal, to	ocultar	*oh-kool-*TAHR
concern (business firm)	casa, f.	KAH-*sah*
concern (affect), to	concernir	*kohn-sehr-*NEER
concerning (regarding)	respecto a	*rrehss-*PEHK-*toh ah*
concert (musical performance)	concierto, m.	*kohn-*SYEHR-*toh*
condition (state)	condición, f.	*kohn-dee-*SYOHN
conductor (mus.)	director, m.	*dee-rehk-*TOHR
conductor (ticket collector)	revisor, m.	*rreh-bee-*SOHR
confident (self-assured)	confiado en sí mismo	*kohn-fee-*AH-*thoh ehn see* MEEZ-*moh*
confidential (private)	confidencial	*kohn-fee-thehn-*SYAHL

ENGLISH	SPANISH	PRONUNCIATION
confirm (corroborate), to	confirmar	*kohn-feer-*MAHR
confirmation (corroboration)	confirmación, f.	*kohn-feer-mah-*SYOHN
confusion (disorder)	confusión, f.	*kohn-foo-*SYOHN
congregation (religious community)	feligreses, m. pl.	*feh-lee-*GREH-*sehss*
connection (relationship)	relación, f.	*rreh-lah-*SYOHN
conquer, to	conquistar	*kohn-keess-*TAHR
conscious (aware)	consciente	*kohn-*SYEHN-*teh*
consequently	por consiguiente	*pohr kohn-see-*GHYEHN-*teh*
consider (reflect on), to	considerar	*kohn-see-theh-*RAHR
consideration (regard)	consideración, f.	*kohn-see-theh-rah-*SYOHN
consist of (comprise), to	consistir en	*kohn-seess-*TEER *ehn*
constitute, to	constituir	*kohn-stee-too-*EER
construct, to	construir	*kohn-stroo-*EER
consul	cónsul, m.	KOHN-*sool*
consult (seek professional advice of), to	consultar	*kohn-sool-*TAHR
contain, to	contener	*kohn-teh-*NEHR
contemporary (modern)	contemporáneo	*kohn-tehm-poh-*RAH-*neh-oh*
contempt (scorn)	desprecio, m.	*dehss-*PREH-*syoh*
content (satisfied)	contento	*kohn-*TEHN-*toh*
contents	contenido, m.	*kohn-teh-*NEE-*thoh*
continent	continente, m.	*kohn-tee-*NEHN-*teh*
continual	continuo	*kohn-*TEE-*noo-oh*
continuation	continuación, f.	*kohn-tee-noo-ah-*SYOHN
contraband	contrabando, m.	*kohn-trah-*BAHN-*doh*

ENGLISH	SPANISH	PRONUNCIATION
contradict (deny), to	contradecir	*kohn-trah-deh-*SEER
contrary (opposite)	contrario	*kohn-*TRAH-*ryoh*
contribute, to	contribuir	*kohn-tree-boo-*EER
contribution	contribución, f.	*kohn-tree-boo-*SYOHN
convenience	comodidad, f.	*koh-moh-thee-*THAHTH
convenient	cómodo	KOH-*moh-thoh*
conversation	conversación, f.	*kohn-behr-sah-*SYOHN
convince, to	convencer	*kohn-behn-*SEHR
cook	cocinero, m.	*koh-see-*NEH-*roh*
cook (heat food), to	cocer	*koh-*SEHR
cook (prepare meals), to	cocinar	*koh-see-*NAHR
cool (having low temperature)	fresco	FREHSS-*koh*
cool (make less hot), to	enfriar	*ehn-free-*AHR
cooperation	cooperación, f.	*koh-oh-peh-rah-*SYOHN
copper	cobre, m.	KOH-*breh*
copy (duplicate)	copia, f.	KOH-*pyah*
copy (of a publication)	ejemplar, m.	*eh-hehm-*PLAHR
copy (imitate), to	copiar	*koh-*PYAHR
cord (rope)	cuerda, f.	KWEHR-*thah*
cork (stopper)	corcho, m.	KOHR-*choh*
corn (maize)	maíz, m.	*mah-*EESS
corpse	cadáver, m.	*kah-*THAH-*behr*
correspondence (letters)	correspondencia, f.	*kah-rrehss-pohn-*DEHN-*syah*
correspond with (write to), to	corresponderse con	*koh-rrehss-pohn-*DEHR-*seh kohn*
cosmetic (n.)	cosmético, m.	*kohss-*MEH-*tee-koh*

ENGLISH	SPANISH	PRONUNCIATION
cost (price)	costa, f.	KOHSS-*tah*
cost, to	costar	*kohss*-TAHR
cotton (boll)	algodón, m.	*ahl-goh*-THOHN
cotton (fabric)	(tela de) algodón, (f.) m.	(TEH-*lah deh*) *ahl-goh*-THOHN
cough	tos, f	TOHSS
council	consejo, m.	*kohn*-SEH-*hoh*
counsel (advice)	consejo, m.	*kohn*-SEH-*hoh*
counsel (lawyer)	abogado, m.	*ah-boh*-GAH-*thoh*
count (enumerate), to	contar	*kohn*-TAHR
counterfeit (adj.)	falso	FAHL-*soh*
country (countryside)	campo, m.	KAHM-*poh*
country (nation)	país, m.	*pah*-EES
couple (pair, n.)	pareja, f.	*pah*-REH-*hah*
court (of law)	tribunal, m.	*tree-boo*-NAHL
courteous (polite)	cortés	*kohr*-TEHSS
cousin	primo, m.	PREE-*moh*
cover (lid)	tapa, f.	TAH-*pah*
cover, to	tapar	*tah*-PAHR
cow	vaca, f.	BAH-*kah*
crab (shellfish)	cangrejo, m.	*kahn*-GREH-*hoh*
cradle	cuna, f.	KOO-*nah*
cramp (med.)	calambre, m.	*kah*-LAHM-*breh*
crazy	loco	LOH-*koh*
cream	nata, f.	NAH-*tah*
create, to	crear	*kreh*-AHR
credit	crédito, m.	KREH-*thee-toh*
crew	tripulación, f.	*tree-poo-lah*-SYOHN
crime	crimen, m.	KREE-*mehn*
criminal (n.)	criminal, m.	*kree-mee*-NAHL
crisp (brittle)	crujiente	*kroo*-HYEHN-*teh*
criticism (judgment)	crítica, f.	KREE-*tee-kah*
cross (crucifix)	cruz, f.	KROOSS

ENGLISH	SPANISH	PRONUNCIATION
cross (traverse), to	atravesar	*ah-trah-beh-*SAHR
crossing (ocean voyage)	travesía, f.	*trah-beh-*SEE-*ah*
crossroads	encrucijada, f.	*ehn-kroo-see-*HAH-*thah*
crowd	muchedumbre, f.	*moo-cheh-*THOOM-*breh*
cruel	cruel	*kroo-*EHL
cruise (voyage)	viaje por mar, m.	BYAH-*heh pohr* MAHR
crumb	migaja, f.	*mee-*GAH-*hah*
crutch	muleta, f.	*moo-*LEH-*tah*
cry (weep), to	llorar	*yoh-*RAHR
cucumber	pepino, m.	*peh-*PEE-*noh*
cuff (of sleeve)	puño, m.	POO-*nyoh*
cuff (of trouser)	vuelta, f.	BWEHL-*tah*
cup	taza, f.	TAH-*sah*
cupboard	armario, m.	*ahr-*MAH-*ryoh*
curb (edge of street)	bordillo, m.	*bohr-*THEE-*yoh*
cure (healing)	curación, f.	*koo-rah-*SYOHN
cure (heal), to	curar	*koo-*RAHR
curious	curioso	*koo-*RYOH-*soh*
currency (money)	moneda corriente, f.	*moh-*NEH-*thah koh-*RRYEHN-*teh*
current (contemporary, adj.)	corriente	*koh-*RRYEHN-*teh*
curse	maldición, f.	*mahl-dee-*SYOHN
curse (swear), to	blasfemar	*blahss-feh-*MAHR
curtain (drape)	cortina, f.	*kohr-*TEE-*nah*
custom (habit)	costumbre, f.	*kohss-*TOOM-*breh*
customer (buyer)	cliente, m., f.	*klee-*EHN-*teh*
customhouse	aduana, f.	*ah-*THWAH-*nah*
customs (tax)	derechos de aduana, m. pl.	*deh-*REH-*chohss deh ah-*THWAH-*nah*
cut (divide into parts), to	cortar	*kohr-*TAHR

ENGLISH	SPANISH	PRONUNCIATION
daily (adj.)	diario	DYAH-*ryoh*
dairy	lechería, f.	*leh-cheh*-REE-*ah*
damage (injury)	daño, m.	DAH-*nyoh*
damage (injure), to	dañar	*dah*-NYAHR
damp (moist)	húmedo	HOO-*meh-thoh*
danger	peligro, m.	*peh*-LEE-*groh*
dangerous	peligroso	*peh-lee*-GROH-*soh*
dark (in color, adj.)	o(b)scuro	*ohss*-KOO-*roh*
dark (without light, adj.)	o(b)scuro	*ohss*-KOO-*roh*
darkness	o(b)scuridad, f.	*ohss-koo-ree*-THAHTH
darn (mend), to	zurcir	*soor*-SEER
date (appointment)	cita, f.	SEE-*tah*
date (fruit)	dátil, m.	DAH-*teel*
daughter	hija, f.	EE-*hah*
daughter-in-law	nuera, f.	NWEH-*rah*
dawn (daybreak)	alba, f.	AHL-*bah*
day (daytime)	día, m.	DEE-*ah*
day (24-hour period)	día, m.	DEE-*ah*
dead	muerto	MWEHR-*toh*
deaf	sordo	SOHR-*thoh*
dealer (trader)	negociante, m.	*neh-goh*-SYAHN-*teh*
dear (beloved, adj.)	querido	*keh*-REE-*thoh*
death	muerte, f.	MWEHR-*teh*
debt	deuda, f.	DEH-*oo-thah*
debtor	deudor, m.	*deh-oo*-THOHR
deceive (delude), to	engañar	*ehn-gah*-NYAHR
decent (respectable)	decente	*deh*-SEHN-*teh*
decide (make up one's mind), to	decidir	*deh-see*-DEER
decision (judgment)	decisión, f.	*deh-see*-SYOHN
deck (of cards)	baraja, f.	*bah*-RAH-*hah*
deck (of ship)	cubierta, f.	*koo*-BYEHR-*tah*

ENGLISH	SPANISH	PRONUNCIATION
declare (state), to	declarar	*deh-klah-*RAHR
decorate (adorn), to	decorar	*deh-koh-*RAHR
decoration (decor)	decoración, f.	*deh-koh-rah-*SYOHN
deed (act)	hecho, m.	EH-*choh*
deep (in extent)	hondo	OHN-*doh*
defect (flaw)	defecto, m.	*deh-*FEHK-*toh*
defend (protect), to	defender	*deh-fehn-*DEHR
definite	definido	*deh-fee-*NEE-*thoh*
degree (unit of measurement)	grado, m.	GRAH-*thoh*
delay	retraso, m.	*rreh-*TRAH-*soh*
delay (postpone), to	diferir	*dee-feh-*REER
deliberate (intentional)	deliberado	*deh-lee-beh-*RAH-*thoh*
delicious	delicioso	*deh-lee-*SYOH-*soh*
delightful	deleitoso	*deh-leh-ee-*TOH-*soh*
demand (ask for), to	exigir	*ehk-see-*HEER
demonstrate (show), to	demostrar	*deh-mohss-*TRAHR
demonstration (proof)	demostración, f.	*deh-mohss-trah-*SYOHN
dentist	dentista, m.	*dehn-*TEESS-*tah*
department store	almacén, m.	*ahl-mah-*SEHN
departure (setting out)	partida, f.	*pahr-*TEE-*thah*
depend (rely) on, to	contar con	*kohn-*TAHR *kohn*
deposit, to (fin.)	depositar	*deh-poh-see-*TAHR
depot (station)	estación, f.	*ehss-tah-*SYOHN
depth (deepness)	profundidad, f.	*proh-foon-dee-*THAHTH
descend (move downward), to	descender	*dehss-sehn-*DEHR
descendant (offspring)	descendiente, m., f.	*dehss-sehn-*DYEHN-*teh*

ENGLISH	SPANISH	PRONUNCIATION
describe (portray), to	describir	*dehss-kree-*BEER
description (account)	descripción, f.	*dehss-kreep-*SYOHN
desert	desierto, m.	*deh-*SYEHR*-toh*
deserve, to	merecer	*meh-reh-*SEHR
design (intention)	propósito, m.	*proh-*POH*-see-toh*
design (pattern)	diseño, m.	*dee-*SEH*-nyoh*
desire (long for), to	desear	*deh-seh-*AHR
desk	escritorio, m.	*ehss-kree-*TOH*-ryoh*
despite (prep.)	a despecho de	*ah dehss-*PEH*-choh deh*
dessert	postre, m.	POHSS*-treh*
destination	destino, m.	*dehss-*TEE*-noh*
destiny	destino, m.	*dehss-*TEE*-noh*
detail (minor item)	detalle, m.	*deh-*TAH*-yeh*
determine (make up one's mind), to	decidir	*deh-see-*THEER
detour	desviación, f.	*dehss-byah-*SYOHN
devotion (loyal attachment)	devoción, f.	*deh-boh-*SYOHN
dew	rocío, m.	*rroh-*SEE*-oh*
diabetes	diabetes, f.	*dee-ah-*BEH*-tehss*
dice (marked cubes)	dados, m. pl.	DAH*-thohss*
dictate (for transcription), to	dictar	*deek-*TAHR
dictionary	diccionario, m.	*deek-syoh--*NAH*-ryoh*
die, to	morir (se)	*moh-*REER*(-seh)*
diet (restricted food allowance)	dieta, f.	*dee-*EH*-tah*
difference (dissimilarity)	diferencia, f.	*dee-feh-*REHN*-syah*
different (unlike)	diferente	*dee-feh-*REHN*-teh*

ENGLISH	SPANISH	PRONUNCIATION
difficult	difícil	*dee-*FEE-*seel*
difficulty (hardness)	dificultad, f.	*dee-fee-kool-*TAHTH
dig (excavate), to	cavar	*kah-*BAHR
digest, to	digerir	*dee-heh-*REER
dim	semio(b)scuro	*seh-mee-ohss-*KOO-*roh*
dine, to	comer	*koh-*MEHR
dining room	comedor, m.	*koh-meh-*THOHR
dinner	comida, f.	*koh-*MEE-*thah*
direct (immediate)	directo	*dee-*REHK-*toh*
direction (course)	dirección, f.	*dee-rehk-*SYOHN
director	director, m.	*dee-rehk-*TOHR
dirt (unclean matter)	suciedad, f.	*soo-syeh-*THAHTH
dirty (soiled)	sucio	soo-*syoh*
disagree (differ), to	disentir	*dee-sehn-*TEER
disagreeable	desagradable	*deh-sah-grah-*THAH-*bleh*
disappear, to	desaparecer	*deh-sah-pah-reh-*SEHR
disappoint, to	decepcionar	*deh-sehp-syoh-*NAHR
dissappointment	decepción, f.	*deh-sehp-*SYOHN
discover, to	descubrir	*dehss-koo-*BREER
discuss, to	discutir	*deess-koo-*TEER
discussion	discusión, f.	*deess-koo-*SYOHN
disease	enfermedad, f.	*ehn-fehr-meh-*THAHTH
dish (food)	plato, m.	PLAH-*toh*
dishes (tableware)	vajilla, f.	*bah-*HEE-*yah*
dislike, to	tener aversión a	*teh-*NEHR *ah-behr-*SYOHN *ah*
dispatch (communication)	parte, m.	PAHR-*teh*
display (exhibit), to	exhibir	*ehk-see-*BEER
dispute	disputa, f.	*dees-*POO-*tah*

ENGLISH	SPANISH	PRONUNCIATION
distance	distancia, f.	*deess*-TAHN-*syah*
distant (far off)	lejano	*leh*-HAN-*noh*
distinct (different)	distinto	*deess*-TEEN-*toh*
distinction (difference)	distinción, f.	*deess-teen*-SYOHN
distinguish (differentiate), to	distinguir	*deess-teen*-GHEER
distinguished (notable)	distinguido	*deess-teen*-GHEE-*thoh*
distress	apuro, m.	*ah*-POO-*roh*
distribute (allot), to	repartir	*rreh-pahr*-TEER
distinct (locality)	comarca, f.	*koh*-MAHR-*kah*
disturb, to	perturbar	*pehr-toor*-BAHR
dive, to	zambullirse	*sahm-boo*-YEER-*seh*
divine (adj.)	divino	*dee*-BEE-*noh*
division (portion)	división, f.	*dee-bee*-SYOHN
divorce (law)	divorcio, m.	*dee*-BOHR-*syoh*
dizzy (unsteady)	aturdido	*ah-toor*-THEE-*thoh*
do, to	hacer	*ah*-SEHR
dock	muelle, m.	MWEH-*yeh*
doctor	médico, m.	MEH-*thee-koh*
dog	perro, m.	PEH-*rroh*
domestic (not foreign)	nacional	*nah-syoh*-NAHL
donkey	asno, m.	AHSS-*noh*
door	puerta, f.	PWEHR-*tah*
doubt	duda, f.	DOO-*thah*
doubt (be uncertain about), to	dudar	*doo*-THAHR
doubtful	dudoso	*doo*-THOH-*soh*
doubtless	sin duda	*seen* DOO-*thah*
down (downward, adv.)	abajo	*ah*-BAH-*hoh*
down payment	primer pago, m.	*pree*-MEHR PAH-*goh*

ENGLISH	SPANISH	PRONUNCIATION
downstairs (on a lower floor)	abajo	*ah*-BAH-*hoh*
dozen	docena, f.	*doh*-SEH-*nah*
draft (air current)	corriente de aire, f.	*koh*-RRYEHN-*teh deh* AH-*ee-reh*
draft (check)	giro, m.	HEE-*roh*
draw (pull along), to	tirar	*tee*-RAHR
draw (sketch), to	dibujar	*dee-boo*-HAHR
drawing (sketch)	dibujo, m.	*dee*-BOO-*hoh*
dreadful	horrendo	*oh*-RREHN-*doh*
dream	sueño, m.	SWEH-*nyoh*
dream, to	soñar	*soh*-NYAHR
dress (frock)	vestido, m.	*behss*-TEE-*thoh*
dress (clothe), to	vestir	*behss*-TEER
dress (get dressed), to	vestirse	*behss*-TEER-*seh*
dresser (bureau)	tocador, m.	*toh-kah*-THOHR
dressing (sauce)	salsa, f.	SAHL-*sah*
drink (beverage)	bebida, f.	*beh*-BEE-*thah*
drink, to	beber	*beh*-BEHR
drive (a vehicle), to	guiar	*ghee*-AHR
driver (of automobile)	chófer, m.	CHOH-*fehr*
drop (droplet)	gota, f.	GOH-*tah*
drown (die by drowning), to	ahogarse	*ah-oh*-GAHR-*seh*
drug (medicine)	droga, f.	DROH-*gah*
drunk (intoxicated)	borracho	*boh*-RRAH-*choh*
dry	seco	SEH-*koh*
dry (make dry), to	secar	*seh*-KAHR
duck	pato, m.	PAH-*toh*
duplicate (copy, n.)	duplicado, m.	*doo-plee*-KAH-*thoh*
during	durante	*doo*-RAHN-*teh*
dust	polvo, m.	POHL-*boh*

ENGLISH	SPANISH	PRONUNCIATION
dusty	polvoriento	*pohl-boh-*RYEHN-*toh*
duty (obligation)	deber, m.	*deh-*BEHR
duty (tax)	derechos de aduana, m. pl.	*deh-*REH-*chohss deh ah-*THWAH-*nah*
duty-free	libre de derechos	LEE-*breh deh deh-*REH-*chohss*
dwell (reside), to	residir	*rreh-see-*THEER
dwelling	habitación, f.	*ah-bee-tah-*SYOHN
dye, to	teñir	*teh-*NYEER
dysentery	disentería, f.	*dee-sehn-teh-*REE-*ah*
each (every, adj.)	cada	KAH-*thah*
each one (pron.)	cada uno	KAH-*thah* OO-*noh*
ear (external ear)	oreja, f.	*oh-*REH-*hah*
earache	dolor de oído, m.	*doh-*LOHR *deh oh-*EE-*thoh*
earn (be paid), to	ganar	*gah-*NAHR
earnest	serio	SEH-*ryoh*
earring	arete, m.	*ah-*REH-*teh*
earth (land)	tierra, f.	TYEH-*rrah*
earthquake	terremoto, m.	*teh-rreh-*MOH-*toh*
east	este, m.	EHSS-*teh*
Easter	Pascuas	PAHSS-*kwahss*
easy (not difficult)	fácil	FAH-*seel*
eat, to	comer	*koh-*MEHR
economical (thrifty)	económico	*eh-koh-*NOH-*mee-koh*
economy (thrift)	economía, f.	*eh-koh-noh-*MEE-*ah*
edge (border)	borde, m.	BOHR-*theh*
edge (sharp side)	filo, m.	FEE-*loh*
edition	edición, f.	*eh-thee-*SYOHN
educate, to	educar	*eh-thoo-*KAHR
education (schooling process)	educación, f.	*eh-thoo-kah-*SYOHN

ENGLISH	SPANISH	PRONUNCIATION
effort	esfuerzo, m.	ehss-FWEHR-soh
egg	huevo, m.	WEH-boh
either (one or the other, adj.)	uno u otro	OO-noh oo OH-troh
either . . . or (conj.)	o . . . o	oh . . . oh
elbow	codo, m.	KOH-thoh
elect, to	elegir	eh-leh-HEER
electric	eléctrico	eh-LEHK-tree-koh
electricty	electricidad, f.	eh-lehk-tree-see-THAHTH
element	elemento, m.	eh-leh-MEHN-toh
elevator (passenger lift)	ascensor, m.	ahss-sehn-SOHR
else (different, adj.)	otro	OH-troh
else (instead, adv.)	de otro modo	deh OH-troh MOH-thoh
elsewhere	en otra parte	ehn OH-trah PAHR-teh
embarrassment	desconcierto, m.	dehss-kohn-SYEHR-toh
emergency (n.)	emergencia, f.	eh-mehr-HEHN-syah
emotion	emoción, f.	eh-moh-SYOHN
employ (hire), to	emplear	ehm-pleh-AHR
employ (use), to	emplear	ehm-pleh-AHR
employee	empleado, m.	ehm-pleh-AH-thoñ
employer (boss)	patrón, m.	pah-TROHN
employment (work)	empleo, m.	ehm-PLEH-oh
empty	vacío	bah-SEE-oh
empty (remove contents of), to	vaciar	bah-SYAHR
enclose (include in envelope), to	incluir	een-kloo-EER
encourage, to	animar	ah-nee-MAHR
end (conclusion)	fin, m.	FEEN
end (bring to an end), to	terminar	tehr-mee-NAHR

ENGLISH	SPANISH	PRONUNCIATION
end (come to an end), to	terminarse	*tehr-mee-*NAHR-*seh*
endeavor, to	empeñarse	*ehm-peh-*NYAHR-*seh*
endorsement (signature)	endoso, m.	*ehn-*DOH-*soh*
endure (bear), to	soportar	*soh-pohr-*TAHR
enema	enema, f.	*eh-*NEH-*mah*
energy	energía, f.	*eh-nehr-*HEE-*ah*
engagement (appointment)	cita, f.	SEE-*tah*
engagement (betrothal)	noviazgo	*noh-*BYAHSS-*goh*
engine (locomotive)	locomotora, f.	*loh-koh-moh-*TOH-*rah*
engine (motor)	motor, m.	*moh-*TOHR
English (adj.)	inglés	*een-*GLEHSS
enjoy (derive joy from), to	gozar de	*goh-*SAHR *deh*
enter (come or go into), to	entrar	*ehn-*TRAHR
enterprise (undertaking)	empresa, f.	*ehm-*PREH-*sah*
entertain (amuse), to	divertir	*dee-behr-*TEER
entertain (be host to), to	agasajar	*ah-gah-sah-*HAHR
entertainment	entretenimiento, m.	*ehn-treh-teh-nee-*MYEHN-*toh*
entrance	entrada, f.	*ehn-*TRAH-*thah*
epidemic	epidemia, f.	*eh-pee-*THEH-*myah*
equal (adj.)	igual	*ee-*GWAHL
errand	mandado, m.	*mahn-*DAH-*thoh*
escape, to	escapar(se)	*ehss-kah-*PAHR (-*seh*)
escort (social companion)	acompañante, m.	*ah-kohm-pah-*NYAHN-*teh*

ENGLISH	SPANISH	PRONUNCIATION
especially	especialmente	*ehss-peh-syahl-*MEHN-*teh*
establishment (firm)	establecimiento, m.	*ehss-tah-bleh-see-*MYEHN-*toh*
evening	anochecer, m.	*ah-noh-cheh-*SEHR
ever (at all times)	siempre	SYEHM-*preh*
ever (at any time)	alguna vez	*ahl-*GOO-*nah* BEHSS
every	cada	KAH-*thah*
everybody	todo el mundo	TOH-*thoh ehl* MOON-*doh*
everyone	cada uno	KAH-*thah* OO-*noh*
everything (pron.)	todo	TOH-*thoh*
everywhere	en todas partes	*ehn* TOH-*thahss* PAHR-*tehss*
evident	evidente	*eh-bee-*THEHN-*teh*
exact (precise)	exacto	*ehk-*SAHK-*toh*
examination (test)	examen, m.	*ehg-*SAH-*mehn*
example	ejemplo, m.	*eh-*HEHM-*plah*
excellent	excelente	*ehss-seh-*LEHN-*teh*
except (prep.)	excepto	*ehss-*SEHP-*toh*
exception (unusual case)	excepción, f.	*ehss-sehp-*SYOHN
exchange (barter)	trueque, m.	TRWEH-*keh*
exclude, to	excluir	*ehss-kloo-*EER
exclusive (not including)	exclusivo	*ehss-kloo-*SEE-*boh*
excuse (pardon), to	excusar	*ehss-koo-*SAHR
exempt (adj.)	exento	*ehg-*SEHN-*toh*
exercise (physical exertion)	ejercicio, m.	*eh-hehr-*SEE-*syoh*
exist, to	existir	*ehg-seess-*TEER
exit	salida, f.	*sah-*LEE-*thah*
expedition (journey)	expedición, f.	*ehss-peh-thee-*SYOHN
expense (cost)	costo, m.	KOHSS-*toh*
expensive	costoso	*kohss-*TOH-*soh*

ENGLISH	SPANISH	PRONUNCIATION
experience (conscious event)	experiencia, f.	*ehss-peh-*RYEHN-*syah*
expire to	expirar	*ehss-pee-*RAHR
explain (account for), to	explicar	*ehss-plee-*KAHR
explanation	explicación, f.	*ehss-plee-kah-*SYOHN
export, to	exportar	*ehss-pohr-*TAHR
express (state), to	expresar	*ehss-preh-*SAHR
expression (sign of feeling; word or phrase)	expresión, f.	*ehss-preh-*SYOHN
extend (stretch out), to	extender	*ehss-tehn-*DEHR
extensive	extenso	*ehss-*TEHN-*soh*
extent (magnitude)	grado, m.	GRAH-*thoh*
exterior (adj.)	exterior	*ehss-teh-*RYOHR
extra (additional)	de sobra	*deh* SOH-*brah*
extraordinary	extraordinario	*ehss-trah-ohr-thee-*NAH-*ryoh*
eye	ojo, m.	OH-*hoh*
eyebrow	ceja, f.	SEH-*hah*
eyelash	pestaña, f.	*pehss-*TAH-*nyah*
eyelid	párpado, m.	PAHR-*pah-thoh*
fabric (cloth)	tela, f.	TEH-*lah*
face	cara, f.	KAH-*rah*
fact	hecho, m.	EH-*choh*
factor (element)	factor, m.	*fahk-*TOHR
factory	fábrica, f.	FAH-*bree-kah*
fade (lose color), to	descolorar	*dehss-koh-loh-*RAHR
fail (be unsuccessful), to	fracasar	*frah-kah-*SAHR
fail (neglect) to, to	dejar de	*deh-*HAHR *deh*
failure (lack of success)	fracaso, m.	*frah-*KAH-*soh*

ENGLISH	SPANISH	PRONUNCIATION
faint, to	desmayarse	*dehss-mah-*YAHR-*seh*
fair (impartial)	justo	HOOSS-*toh*
fair (not cloudy)	despejado	*dehss-peh-*HAH-*thoh*
faith (creed)	credo, m.	KREH-*thoh*
faith (trust)	fe, f.	FEH
fall (autumn, n.)	otoño, m.	*oh-*TOH-*nyoh*
fall, to	caer	*kah-*EHR
false (erroneous)	erróneo	*eh-*RROH-*neh-oh*
falsehood (lie)	falsedad, f.	*fahl-seh-*THAHTH
familiar (well-known)	familiar	*fah-mee-*LYAHR
family	familia, f.	*fah-*MEE-*lyah*
famous	famoso	*fah-*MOH-*soh*
fan, electric	abanico eléctrico m.	*ah-bah-*NEE-*koh eh-*LEHK-*tree-koh*
fancy (imagine), to	figurarse	*fee-goo-*RAHR-*seh*
fancy (ornamental, adj.)	de ornato	*deh ohr-*NAH-*toh*
far (afar, adv.)	lejos	LEH-*hohss*
far (distant, adj.)	lejano	*leh-*HAH-*noh*
fare (transp.)	pasaje, m.	*pah-*SAH-*heh*
farewell (leave-taking)	adiós, m.	*ah-*THYOHSS
farm	granja, f.	GRAHN-*hah*
farmer	agricultor, m.	*ah-gree-kool-*TOHR
fashion (current style)	moda, f.	MOH-*thah*
fast (quick, adj.)	rápido	RRAH-*pee-thoh*
fast (quickly, adv.)	de prisa	*deh* PREE-*sah*
fat (obese, adj.)	gordo	GOHR-*thoh*
fate	destino, m.	*dehss-*TEE-*noh*
father	padre, m.	PAH-*threh*
father-in-law	suegro, m.	SWEH-*groh*
faucet	llave, f.	YAH-*beh*

ENGLISH	SPANISH	PRONUNCIATION
favorite (adj.)	favorito	*fah-boh-*REE*-toh*
fear	temor, m.	*teh-*MOHR
fear (be afraid of), to	temer	*teh-*MEHR
feather	pluma, f.	PLOO-*mah*
feature (part of face)	facciones, f. pl.	*fahk-*SYOH*-nehss*
fee	honorario, m.	*oh-noh-*RAH*-ryoh*
feed (give food to), to	dar de comer	DAHR *deh koh-*MEHR
feel (experience), to	sentir	*sehn-*TEER
feel (touch), to	tocar	*toh-*KAHR
feeling (emotion)	sentimiento, m.	*sehn-tee-*MYEHN*-toh*
feeling (sensation	sensación, f.	*sehn-sah-*SYOHN
female (adj.)	hembra	EHM-*brah*
feminine	feminino	*feh-mee-*NEE*-noh*
fence (barrier)	cerca, f.	SEHR-*kah*
ferry (boat)	barco de tras-bordo, m.	BAHR-*koh deh trahss-*BOHR*-thoh*
festival	festival, m.	*fehss-tee-*BAHL
fever	fiebre, f.	FYEH-*breh*
few (not many, adj.)	pocos	POH-*kohss*
few, a	algunos	*ahl-*GOO*-nohss*
fig	higo, m.	EE-*goh*
fight	pelea, f.	*peh-*LEH*-ah*
figure (human form)	figura, f.	*fee-*GOO*-rah*
figure (numeral)	cifra, f.	SEE-*frah*
fill (make full), to	llenar	*yeh-*NAHR
film (photog.)	película, f.	*peh-*LEE*-koo-lah*
fine (good)	bueno	BWEH-*noh*
fine (penalty, n.)	multa, f.	MOOL-*tah*
finger	dedo, m.	DEH-*thoh*
finish (complete), to	terminar	*tehr-mee-*NAHR
fire	fuego, m.	FWEH-*goh*

ENGLISH	SPANISH	PRONUNCIATION
fireplace	chimenea, f.	*chee-meh-*NEH-*ah*
firm (business company)	casa, f.	KAH-*sah*
first (adj.)	primer(o)	*pree-*MEHR*(-oh)*
fish (food)	pescado, m.	*pehss-*KAH-*thoh*
fish, to	pescar	*pehss-*KAHR
fix (repair), to	reparar	*rreh-pah-*RAHR
flag	bandera, f.	*bahn-*DEH-*rah*
flashlight	linterna eléc- trica, f.	*leen-*TEHR-*nah eh-*LEHK-*tree- kah*
flat (level, adj.)	plano	PLAH-*noh*
flavor (savor)	sabor, m.	*sah-*BOHR
flesh	carne, f.	KAHR-*neh*
flight (journey by air)	vuelo, m.	BWEH-*loh*
flood	inundación, f.	*ee-noon-dah-* SYOHN
floor (bottom surface)	piso, m.	PEE-*soh*
floor (story)	piso, m.	PEE-*soh*
flour	harina, f.	*ah-*REE-*nah*
flow (circulate), to	fluir	*floo-*EER
flower (blossom)	flor, f.	FLOHR
fly (housefly)	mosca, f.	MOHSS-*kah*
fly, to	volar	*boh-*LAHR
fog (mist)	niebla, f.	NYEH-*blah*
food	alimento, m.	*ah-lee-*MYEHN-*toh*
foolish	bobo	BOH-*boh*
foot	pie, m.	PYEH
forbidden	prohibido	*proh-ee-*BEE-*thoh*
force (coercion)	fuerza, f.	FWEHR-*sah*
force, to	forzar	*fohr-*SAHR
forehead	frente, f.	FREHN-*teh*
foreign	extranjero	*ehss-trahn-*HEH- *roh*

ENGLISH	SPANISH	PRONUNCIATION
foreigner	extranjero, m.	*ehss-trahn-*HEH-*roh*
forest	bosque, m.	BOHSS-*keh*
forever	para siempre	*pah-rah* SYEHM-*preh*
forget, to	olvidar	*ohl-bee-*THAHR
forgive, to	perdonar	*pehr-thoh-*NAHR
forgotten	olvidado	*ohl-bee-*THAH-*thoh*
fork (eating utensil)	tenedor, m.	*teh-neh-*THOHR
form (shape)	forma, f.	FOHR-*mah*
form (shape), to	formar	*fohr-*MAHR
former (first of two, adj.)	primer(o)	*pree-*MEHR*(-oh)*
former (preceding, adj.)	anterior	*ahn-teh-*RYOHR
fort	fuerte, m.	FWEHR-*teh*
fortunate	afortunado	*ah-fohr-too-*NAH-*thoh*
foul (filthy)	inmundo	*een-*MOON-*doh*
fountain	fuente, f.	FWEHN-*teh*
fowl (poultry)	pollo, m.	POH-*yoh*
fracture (med.)	fractura, f.	*frahk-*TOO-*rah*
free (gratuitous)	gratuito	*grah-*TWEE-*toh*
free (independent)	libre	LEE-*breh*
freeze (turn to ice), to	congelar	*kohn-heh-*LAHR
freight	flete, m.	FLEH-*teh*
French (adj.)	francés	*frahn-*SEHSS
fresh (not stale)	fresco	FREHSS-*koh*
friend	amigo, m.	*ah-*MEE-*goh*
friendly	amistoso	*ah-meess-*TOH-*soh*
friendship	amistad, f.	*ah-meess-*TAHTH
frighten (make afraid), to	espantar	*ehss-pahn-*TAHR
from	de	*deh*

ENGLISH	SPANISH	PRONUNCIATION
front (forward part)	frente, f.	FREHN-*teh*
frontier	frontera, f.	*frohn*-TEH-*rah*
frost	escarcha, f.	*ehss*-KAHR-*chah*
frown, to	fruncir el ceño	*froon*-SEER *ehl* SEH-*nyoh*
frozen	congelado	*kohn-heh*-LAH-*thoh*
fruit	fruta, f.	FROO-*tah*
fry (be cooked in fat), to	freír	*freh*-EER
fuel	combustible, m.	*kohm-booss*-TEE-*bleh*
full (complete)	completo	*kohm*-PLEH-*toh*
full (filled)	lleno	YEH-*noh*
fun	diversión, f.	*dee-behr*-SYOHN
fund	fondo, m.	FOHN-*doh*
funds	fondos, m. pl.	FOHN-*dohss*
funeral	funerales, m. pl.	*foo-neh*-RAH-*lehss*
funny (comical)	cómico	KOH-*mee-koh*
furious	furioso	*foo*-RYOH-*soh*
furnace (home heater)	horno, m.	OHR-*noh*
furniture	muebles, m. pl.	MWEH-*blehss*
fuse (elec.)	fusible, m.	*foo*-SEE-*bleh*
fuss (ado)	melindres, m. pl.	*meh*-LEEN-*drehss*
future (adj.)	futuro	*foo*-TOO-*roh*
future (n.)	porvenir, m.	*pohr-beh*-NEER
gain (increase)	aumento, m.	*ow*-MEHN-*toh*
gain (get), to	ganar	*gah*-NAHR
galoshes	chanclos, m. pl.	CHAHN-*klohss*
game (contest)	juego, m.	HWEH-*goh*
garage	garaje, m.	*gah*-RAH-*heh*
garbage	desperdicios, m. pl.	*dehss-pehr*-THEE-*syohss*
garden	jardín, m.	*hahr*-THEEN

ENGLISH	SPANISH	PRONUNCIATION
garlic	ajo, m.	AH-*hoh*
garment	prenda de vestir, f.	PREHN-*dah deh behss*-TEER
garter	liga, f.	LEE-*gah*
gas	gas, m.	GAHSS
gasoline	gasolina, f.	*gah-soh*-LEE-*nah*
gate	portón, m.	*pohr*-TOHN
gather (bring together), to	recoger	*rreh-koh*-HEHR
gather (congregate), to	reunir	*rreh-oo*-NEER
gear (mech.)	engranaje, m.	*ehn-grah*-NAH-*heh*
general (adj.)	general	*heh-neh*-RAHL
generous	generoso	*heh-neh*-ROH-*soh*
gentle (soothing)	suave	SWAH-*beh*
gentleman	caballero, m.	*kah-bah*-YEH-*roh*
genuine	genuino	*heh*-NWEE-*noh*
German (adj.)	alemán	*ah-leh*-MAHN
get (obtain), to	obtener	*ohb-teh*-NEHR
gift (present)	regalo, m.	*rreh*-GAH-*loh*
girl	muchacha, f.	*moo*-CHAH-*chah*
give (bestow), to	dar	DAHR
glad	contento	*kohn*-TEHN-*toh*
glass (material)	vidrio, m.	BEE-*thryoh*
glass (vessel)	vaso, m.	BAH-*soh*
glasses (spectacles)	anteojos, m. pl.	*ahn-teh*-OH-*hohss*
glide, to	deslizarse	*dehss-lee*-SAHR-*seh*
gloomy (melancholy)	melancólico	*meh-lahn*-KOH-*lee-koh*
glorious (resplendent)	glorioso	*gloh*-RYOH-*soh*
glove	guante, m.	GWAHN-*teh*
go (ride), to	ir	EER
go (walk), to	ir	EER
God	Dios, m.	DYOHSS

ENGLISH	SPANISH	PRONUNCIATION
gold	oro, m.	OH-*roh*
good, better, best	bueno, mejor, (lo) mejor	BWEH-*noh,* meh-HOHR, *(loh)* meh-HOHR
good-by	adiós	*ah*-THYOHSS
goods	mercancías, f. pl.	*mehr-kahn*-SEE-*ahss*
government	gobierno, m.	*goh*-BYEHR-*noh*
governor	gobernador, m.	*goh-behr-nah*-THOHR
grade (school division)	año, m.	AH-*nyoh*
grain (cereal)	grano, m.	GRAH-*noh*
grammar	gramática, f.	*grah*-MAH-*tee-kah*
grand (imposing)	grandioso	*grahn*-DYOH-*soh*
granddaughter	nieta, f.	NYEH-*tah*
grandfather	abuelo, m.	*ah*-BWEH-*loh*
grandmother	abuela, f.	*ah*-BWEH-*lah*
grandson	nieto, m.	NYEH-*toh*
grape	uva, f.	OO-*bah*
grass	hierba, f.	YEHR-*bah*
grateful	agradecido	*ah-grah-theh*-SEE-*thoh*
gratitude	gratitud, f.	*grah-tee*-TOOTH
grave (serious)	grave	GRAH-*beh*
gray	gris	GREESS
grease (cooking fat)	grasa, f.	GRAH-*sah*
great	grande	GRAHN-*deh*
greatness (eminence)	grandeza, f.	*grahn*-DEH-*sah*
greedy	ávido	AH-*bee-thoh*
Greek (adj.)	griego	GRYEH-*goh*
green (color)	verde	BEHR-*theh*
greet (salute), to	saludar	*sah-loo*-THAHR
greeting	saludo, m.	*sah-*LOO-*thoh*
grief	aflicción, f.	*ah-fleek*-SYOHN

ENGLISH	SPANISH	PRONUNCIATION
grocery	tienda de comestibles, f.	TYEHN-*dah deh koh-mehss-*TEE-*blehss*
ground	tierra, f.	TYEH-*rrah*
group	grupo, m.	GROO-*poh*
grow (expand), to	crecer	*kreh-*SEHR
growth (development)	desarrollo, m.	*deh-sah-*RROH-*yoh*
guard (watcher)	guarda, m.	GWAHR-*thah*
guardian	tutor, m.	*too-*TOHR
guess (suppose), to	suponer	*soo-poh-*NEHR
guest (visitor)	huésped, m.	WEHSS-*pehth*
guide (one who guides)	guía, m.	GHEE-*ah*
gulf (large bay)	golfo, m.	GOHL-*foh*
gum	encía, f.	*ehn-*SEE-*ah*
gum (chewing gum)	chicle, m.	CHEE-*kleh*
gun	arma de fuego, f.	AHR-*mah deh* FWEH-*goh*
gutter (of street)	arroyo, m.	*ah-*RROH-*yoh*
gymnasium (athletic arena)	gimnasio, m.	*heem-*NAH-*syoh*
habit (custom)	hábito, m.	AH-*bee-toh*
hail (ice)	granizo, m.	*grah-*NEE-*soh*
hail (precipitate hail), to	granizar	*grah-nee-*SAHR
hair	pelo, m.	PEH-*loh*
half (adj.)	medio	MEH-*thyoh*
half (n.)	mitad, f.	*mee-*TAHTH
hall (corridor)	pasillo, m.	*pah-*SEE-*yoh*
hall (meeting room)	salón, m.	*sah-*LOHN
halt (come to a stop), to	pararse	*pah-*RAHR-*seh*
handkerchief	pañuelo, m.	*pah-*NYWEH-*loh*
handle	mango, m.	MAHN-*goh*
happen (occur), to	acontecer	*ah-kohn-teh-*SEHR

ENGLISH	SPANISH	PRONUNCIATION
happiness	felicidad, f.	*fel-lee-see-*THAHTH
happy (glad)	feliz	*feh-*LEESS
harbor	puerto, m.	PWEHR-*toh*
hard (difficult)	difícil	*dee-*FEE-*seel*
hard (not soft)	duro	DOO-*roh*
hardly (barely)	apenas	*ah-*PEH-*nahss*
hardship (privation)	privación, f.	*pree-bah-*SYOHN
hardware	quincalla, f.	*keen-*KAH-*yah*
harm (damage), to	dañar	*dah-*NYAHR
haste	prisa, f.	PREE-*sah*
hat	sombrero, m.	*sohm-*BREH-*roh*
hate (hatred)	odio, m.	*oh-*THYOH
hate, to	odiar	*oh-*THYAHR
have, to	tener	*teh-*NEHR
he	él	EHL
head	cabeza, f.	*kah-*BEH-*sah*
head (leader)	jefe, m.	HEH-*feh*
headache	dolor de cabeza, m.	*doh-*LOHR *deh kah-*BEH-*sah*
headquarters	cuartel general, m.	*kwahr-*TEHL *heh-neh-*RAHL
heal (cure), to	curar	*koo-*RAHR
health	salud, f.	*sah-*LOOTH
healthy	sano	SAH-*noh*
hear, to	oír	*oh-*EER
heart	corazón, m.	*koh-rah-*SOHN
hearty (cordial)	cordial	*kohr-*THYAHL
heat	calor, m.	*kah-*LOHR
heat, to	calentar	*kah-lehn-*TAHR
heaven	cielo, m.	SYEH-*loh*
heavy	pesado	*peh-*SAH-*thoh*
heel	talón, m.	*tah-*LOHN
height (highness)	altura, f.	*ahl-*TOO-*rah*
helicopter	helicóptero, m.	*eh-lee-*KOHP-*teh-roh*

ENGLISH	SPANISH	PRONUNCIATION
help (assistance)	ayuda, f.	*ah*-YOO-*thah*
help, to	ayudar	*ah*-yoo-THAHR
helper	ayudante, m.	*ah*-yoo-THAHN-*teh*
helpful (useful)	útil	OO-*teel*
helpless	desvalido	*dehss*-BAH-*lee thoh*
hem	bastilla, f.	*bahss*-TEE-*yah*
hemisphere	hemisferio, m.	*eh-meess*-FEH-*ryoh*
herb	hierba, f.	YEHR-*bah*
herring	arenque, m.	*ah*-REHN-*keh*
hide (conceal), to	esconder	*ehss-kohn*-DEHR
high	alto	AHL-*toh*
highway	carretera, f.	*kah-rreh*-TEH-*rah*
hill	colina, f.	*koh*-LEE-*nah*
hinder, to	estorbar	*ehss-tohr*-BAHR
hip	cadera, f.	*kah*-THEH-*rah*
hire (employ), to	emplear	*ehm-pleh*-AHR
history	historia, f.	*eess*-TOH-*ryah*
hit (strike), to	golpear	*gohl-peh*-AHR
hog (animal)	puerco, m.	PWEHR-*koh*
hold, to	tener	*teh*-NEHR
holiday	día festivo, m.	DEE-*ah fehss*-TEE-*boh*
hollow (adj.)	hueco	WEH-*koh*
holy	sagrado	*sah*-GRAH-*thoh*
home	hogar, m.	*oh*-GAHR
homesick	nostálgico	*nohss*-TAHL-*hee-koh*
honest	honrado	*ohn*-RAH-*thoh*
honesty	honradez, f.	*ohn-rah*-THEHSS
honey	miel, f.	MYEHL
honor	honor, m.	*oh*-NOHR
honor (respect), to	honrar	*ohn*-RAHR
hood (auto.)	cubierta, f.	*koo*-BYEHR-*tah*

ENGLISH	SPANISH	PRONUNCIATION
hook	gancho, m.	GAHN-*choh*
hope	esperanza, f.	*ehss-peh-*RAHN-*sah*
hope, to	esperar	*ehss-peh-*RAHR
horn (auto.)	bocina, f.	*boh-*SEE-*nah*
horn (mus.)	corneta, f.	*kohr-*NEH-*tah*
horse	caballo, m.	*kah-*BAH-*yoh*
hospital	hospital, m.	*ohss-pee-*TAHL
hot	caliente	*kah-*YEHN-*teh*
hotel	hotel, m.	*oh-*TEHL
hour	hora, f.	OH-*rah*
house	casa, f.	KAH-*sah*
how (interrog. adv.)	cómo	KOH-*moh*
however (nevertheless)	sin embargo	*seen ehm-*BAHR-*goh*
human (adj.)	humano	*oo-*MAH-*noh*
hunger	hambre, f.	AHM-*breh*
hungry	hambriento	*ahm-*BRYEHN-*toh*
hungry, to be	tener hambre	*teh-*NEHR AHM-*breh*
hunting (sport)	caza, f.	KAH-*sah*
hurry (haste)	prisa, f.	PREE-*sah*
hurry (hasten), to	apresurarse	*ah-preh-soo-*RAHR-*seh*
hurt (be painful), to	dolerle (a uno)	*doh-*LEHR-*leh (ah oo-noh)*
husband	marido, m.	*mah-*REE-*thoh*
I	yo	YOH
ice (frozen water)	hielo, m.	YEH-*loh*
icebox	nevera, f.	*neh-*BEH-*rah*
ice-cream	helado, m.	*eh-*LAH-*thoh*
idea	idea, f.	*ee-*THEH-*ah*
idle (not busy)	desocupado	*deh-soh-koo-*PAH-*thoh*
if (supposing that)	si	*see*
if (whether)	si	*see*
ignorant	ignorante	*eeg-noh-*RAHN-*teh*

ENGLISH	SPANISH	PRONUNCIATION
ill (sick)	enfermo	*ehn*-FEHR-*moh*
illegal	ilegal	*ee-leh*-GAHL
illness	enfermedad, f.	*ehn-fehr-meh-*THAHTH
illuminate (light up), to	iluminar	*ee-loo-mee-*NAHR
imagination	imaginación, f.	*ee-mah-hee-nah-*SYOHN
imagine (picture mentally) to	imaginar	*ee-mah-hee-*NAHR
immediately (instantly)	inmediatemente	*een-meh-thyah-tah-*MEHN-*teh*
impatient	impaciente	*eem-pah-*SYEHN-*teh*
importance	importancia, f.	*eem-pohr-*TAHN-*syah*
important	importante	*eem-pohr-*TAHN-*teh*
impossibility	imposibilidad, f.	*eem-poh-see-bee-lee-*THAHTH
impossible	imposible	*eem-poh-*SEE-*bleh*
impress (affect deeply), to	impresionar	*eem-preh-syoh-*NAHR
improve (make better), to	mejorar	*meh-hoh-*RAHR
improvement (betterment)	mejoramiento, m.	*meh-hoh-rah-*MYEHN-*toh*
in (during, prep.)	en	*ehn*
in (inside, prep.)	en	*ehn*
in (into, prep.)	en	*ehn*
include (contain), to	incluir	*een-kloo-*EER
income	ingresso, m.	*een-*GREH-*soh*
income tax	impuesto sobre rentas, m.	*eem-*PWEHSS-*toh soh-breh* RREHN-*tahss*
inconvenience	inconveniencia, f.	*een-kohm-beh-*NYEHN-*syah*

ENGLISH	SPANISH	PRONUNCIATION
indeed (adv.)	de veras	*deh* BEH-*rahss*
independence	independencia, f.	*een-deh-pehn-*DEHN-*syah*
independent	independiente	*een-deh-pehn-*DYEHN-*teh*
indicate (point out), to	indicar	*een-dee-*KAHR
indifferent (unconcerned)	indiferente	*een-dee-feh-*REHN-*teh*
indigestion	indigestión, f.	*een-dee-hehss-*TYOHN
individual (person, n.)	individuo, m.	*een-dee-*BEE-*thwoh*
indoors (adv.)	dentro	DEHN-*troh*
infant (n.)	infante, m.	*een-*FAHN-*teh*
infection	infección, f.	*een-fehk-*SYOHN
inferior (mediocre)	inferior	*een-feh-*RYOHR
inflammation	inflamación, f.	*een-flah-mah-*SYOHN
inform (appraise), to	informar	*een-fohr-*MAHR
information (knowledge)	información, f.	*een-fohr-mah-*SYOHN
inhabit, to	habitar	*ah-bee-*TAHR
inhabitant	habitante, m.	*ah-bee-*TAHN-*teh*
initial (letter)	letra inicial, f.	LEH-*trah ee-nee-*SYAHL
injection (med.)	inyección, f.	*een-yehk-*SYOHN
injury	lesión, f.	*leh-*SYOHN
ink	tinta, f.	TEEN-*tah*
inn	posada, f.	*poh-*SAH-*thah*
innocent (guiltless)	inocente	*ee-noh-*SEHN-*teh*
inquire (ask), to	preguntar	*preh-goon-*TAHR
inquiry (question)	pregunta, f.	*preh-*GOON-*tah*
insect	insecto, m.	*een-*SEHK-*toh*
inspection (scrutiny)	inspección, f.	*een-spehk-*SYOHN

ENGLISH	SPANISH	PRONUNCIATION
install (set up for use), to	instalar	*een-stah-*LAHR
installment	plazo, m.	PLAH-*soh*
instance (example)	ejemplo, m.	*eh-*HEHM-*ploh*
instead of	en lugar de	*ehn loo-*GAHR *deh*
instruct (teach), to	instruir	*een-stroo-*EER
instruction (teaching)	instrucción, f.	*een-strook-*SYOHN
instrument (implement)	instrumento, m.	*een-stroo-*MEHN-*toh*
insurance	seguro, m.	*seh-*GOO-*roh*
intelligence (understanding)	inteligencia, f.	*een-teh-lee-*HEHN-*syah*
intelligent	inteligente	*een-teh-lee-*HEHN-*teh*
intend (propose), to	intentar	*een-tehn-*TAHR
intention	intención, f.	*een-tehn-*SYOHN
interest (attention)	atención, f.	*ah-tehn-*SYOHN
interest (money rate)	interés, m.	*een-teh-*REHSS
interest, to	interesar	*een-teh-reh-*SAHR
interesting	interesante	*een-teh-reh-*SAHN-*teh*
interfere (meddle), to	intervenir	*een-tehr-beh-*NEER
interior (inside, n.)	interior, m.	*een-teh-*RYOHR
interpret (explain), to	interpretar	*een-tehr-preh-*TAHR
interrupt, to	interrumpir	*een-teh-rroom-*PEER
interval (period of time)	intervalo, m.	*een-tehr-*BAH-*loh*
intimate (personal)	íntimo	EEN-*tee-moh*
into (to the inside)	adentro	*ah-*THEHN-*troh*
introduce (make acquainted), to	presentar	*preh-sehn-*TAHR

ENGLISH	SPANISH	PRONUNCIATION
invest, to	invertir	*een-behr-*TEER
invitation	invitación, f.	*een-bee-tah-*SYOHN
invite, to	invitar	*een-bee-*TAHR
involve (entail), to	envolver	*ehn-bohl-*BEHR
iodine (antiseptic)	yodo, m.	YOH-*thoh*
Irish (adj.)	irlandés	*eer-lahn-*DEHSS
iron (metal)	hierro, m.	YEH-*rroh*
iron, electric	planca eléctrica, f.	PLAHN-*chah eh-*LEHK-*tree-kah*
island (geog.)	isla, f.	EESS-*lah*
isthmus	istmo, m.	EEST-*moh*
Italian (adj.)	italiano	*ee-tah-*LYAH-*noh*
jacket (shortcoat)	chaqueta, f.	*chah-*KEH-*tah*
jail	cárcel, f.	KAHR-*sehl*
Japanese (adj.)	japonés	*hah-pah-*NEHSS
jar (vessel)	jarra, f.	HAH-*rrah*
jaw	quijada, f.	*kee-*HAH-*thah*
jelly	jalea, f.	*hah-*LEH-*ah*
Jew (n.)	judío, m.	*hoo-*THEE-*ah*
jewel	joya, f.	HOH-*yah*
jewelry	joyas, f. pl.	HOH-*yahss*
Jewish (adj.)	judío	*hoo-*THEE-*oh*
job (employment)	empleo, m.	*ehm-*PLEH-*oh*
job (task)	tarea, f.	*tah-*REH-*ah*
joke (jest)	chiste, m.	CHEESS-*teh*
joke (jest), to	chancearse	*chahn-seh-*AHR-*seh*
journey	viaje, m.	BYAH-*heh*
joy	júbilo, m.	HOO-*bee-loh*
judge	juez, m.	HWEHSS
judge, to	juzgar	*hooss-*GAHR
juice	jugo, m.	HOO-*goh*
jump (bound), to	saltar	*sahl-*TAHR
jury	jurado, m.	*hoo-*RAH-*thoh*
just (merely)	solamente	*soh-lah-*MEHN-*teh*
keep (retain), to	guardar	*gwahr-*THAHR

ENGLISH	SPANISH	PRONUNCIATION
kettle	caldera, f.	*kahl*-DEH-*rah*
key	llave, f.	YAH-*beh*
kidney	riñon, m.	*ree*-NYOHN
kill, to	matar	*mah*-TAHR
kind (adj.)	bondadoso	*bohn-dah*-THOH-*soh*
kind (n.)	especie, f.	*ehss*-PEH-*syeh*
kindness (goodness)	bondad, f.	*bohn*-DAHTH
king	rey, m.	RREY
kiss	beso, m.	BEH-*soh*
kiss, to	besar	*beh*-SAHR
kitchen	cocina, f.	*koh*-SEE-*nah*
knee	rodilla, f.	*rroh*-THEE-*yah*
knife	cuchillo, m.	*koo*-CHEE-*yoh*
knock, to	tocar	*toh*-KAHR
knot	nudo, m.	NOO-*thoh*
know (be acquainted with), to	conocer	*koh-noh*-SEHR
knowledge (information)	conocimiento, m.	*koh-noh-see-*MYEHN-*toh*
known (familiar)	conocido	*koh-noh-*SEE-*thoh*
label	rótulo, m.	RROH-*too-loh*
lace (fabric)	encaje, m.	*ehn*-KAH-*heh*
lace (shoelace)	cordón, m.	*kohr*-THOHN
lack (be without), to	faltar	*fahl*-TAHR
lady	dama, f.	DAH-*mah*
lake	lago, m.	LAH-*goh*
lamb	cordero, m.	*kohr*-THEH-*roh*
lamb chop	chuleta de carnero, f.	*choo*-LEH-*tah deh kahr*-NEH-*roh*
lamp	lámpara, f.	LAHM-*pah-rah*
land (ground)	tierra, f.	TYEH-*rrah*
land (property)	bienes raíces, m. pl.	BYEH-*nehss rrah*-EE-*sehss*
land (region)	territorio, m.	*teh-rree*-TOH-*ryoh*

ENGLISH	SPANISH	PRONUNCIATION
land (from a ship), to	desembarcar	*deh-sehm-bahr-*KAHR
landscape (scenery)	paisaje, m.	*pah-ee-*SAH-*heh*
language	lengua, f.	LEHN-*gwah*
large	grande	GRAHN-*deh*
last (final, adj.)	último	*ool-tee-moh*
last (most recent, adj.)	último	*ool-tee-moh*
late (at relative time, adv.)	tarde	TAHR-*theh*
late (tardily, adv.)	tardíamente	*tahr-*THEE-*ah-mehn-teh*
latter (second of two, adj.)	último	OOL-*tee-moh*
laugh, to	reír	*rreh-*EER
laughter	risa, f.	RREE-*sah*
laundry (articles laundered)	ropa lavada, f.	RROH-*pah lah-*BAH-*thah*
lawful	legal	*leh-*GAHL
lawyer	abogado, m.	*ah-boh-*GAH-*thoh*
lay (put down), to	colocar	*koh-loh-*KAHR
lead (guide), to	guiar	*ghee-*AHR
learn (acquire knowledge), to	aprender	*ah-prehn-*DEHR
least (adv.)	menos	MEH-*nohss*
leather (n.)	cuero, m.	KWEH-*roh*
leave (depart), to	partir	*pahr-*TEER
leave (let remain), to	dejar	*deh-*HAHR
left (adj.)	izquierdo	*eess-*KYEHR-*thoh*
left (adv.)	a la izquierda	*ah lah eess-*KYEHR-*thah*
leg	pierna, f.	PYEHR-*nah*
legal	legal	*leh-*GAHL
leisure	ocio, m.	OH-*syoh*

ENGLISH	SPANISH	PRONUNCIATION
lemon	limón, m.	*lee*-MOHN
lend, to	prestar	*prehss*-TAHR
length	largo, m.	LAHR-*goh*
less (adv.)	menos	MEH-*nohss*
less (minus, prep.)	menos	MEH-*nohss*
lesson (assignment)	lección, f.	*lehk*-SYOHN
let (permit), to	dejar	*deh*-HAHR
letter (character)	letra, f.	LEH-*trah*
letter (epistle)	carta, f.	KAHR-*tah*
level (flat)	plano	PLAH-*noh*
liability (responsibility)	responsabilidad, f.	*rrehss-pohn-sah-bee-lee*-THAHTH
liable (responsible)	responsable	*rrehss-pohn*-SAH-*bleh*
liberty (freedom)	libertad, f.	*lee-behr*-TAHTH
library	biblioteca, f.	*bee-blyoh*-TEH-*kah*
license (permit)	licencia, f.	*lee*-SEHN-*syah*
lid (cover)	tapa, f.	TAH-*pah*
lie (be located), to	estar	*ehss*-TAHR
lie (be prone), to	tenderse	*tehn*-DEHR-*seh*
lie (prevaricate), to	mentir	*mehn*-TEER
lie down, to	acostarse	*ah-kohss*-TAHR-*seh*
life	vida, f.	BEE-*thah*
lift (raise), to	levantar	*leh-bahn*-TAHR
light (illumination)	luz, f.	LOOSS
light (of little weight)	ligero	*lee*-HEH-*roh*
light (set fire to), to	encender	*ehn-sehn*-DEHR
lightning	relámpago, m.	*rreh*-LAHM-*pah-goh*
like (adj.)	semejante	*seh-meh*-HAHN-*teh*
like (adv.)	como	KOH-*moh*
like (be fond of), to	gustarle (a uno)	*gooss*-TAHR-*leh (ah* OO-*noh)*
likely (probable, adj.)	probable	*pro*-BAH-*bleh*
limb	miembro, m.	MYEHM-*broh*

ENGLISH	SPANISH	PRONUNCIATION
limit	límite, m.	LEE-*mee-teh*
limit, to	limitar	*lee-mee*-TAHR
line (row)	fila, f.	FEE-*lah*
linen (fabric)	lino, m.	LEE-*noh*
liner, ocean	vapor de travesía, m.	*bah*-POHR *deh trah-beh-*SEE-*ah*
lip	labio, m.	LAH-*byoh*
lipstick	lápiz para los labios, m.	LAH-*peess pah-rah lohss* LAH-*byohss*
listen (hearken), to	escuchar	*ehss-koo-*CHAHR
litter (stretcher)	camilla, f.	*kah-*MEE-*yah*
little (not much, adj.)	poco	POH-*koh*
little (small, adj.)	pequeño	*peh-*KEH-*nyoh*
little (small amount, n.)	poco, m.	POH-*koh*
live (adj.)	vivo	BEE-*boh*
live (be alive), to	vivir	*bee-*BEER
liver	hígado, m.	EE-*gah-thoh*
living (livelihood)	subsistencia, f.	*soob-seess-*TEHN-*syah*
load (burden)	carga, f.	KAHR-*gah*
loaf	hogaza, f.	*oh-*GAH-*sah*
lobster	langosta, f.	*lahn-*GOHSS-*tah*
local (regional)	local	*loh-*KAHL
locality (place)	localidad, f.	*loh-kah-lee-*THAHTH
locate (find), to	encontrar	*ehn-kohn-*TRAHR
lock (fastening)	cerradura, f.	*seh-rrah-*THOO-*rah*
lock (fasten with key), to	cerrar con llave	*seh-*RRAHR *kohn* YAH-*beh*
lodging (temporary quarters)	hospedaje, m.	*ohss-peh-*THAH-*heh*
lone (solitary)	solitario	*soh-lee-*TAH-*ryoh*
lonely (unfrequented)	solitario	*soh-lee-*TAH-*ryoh*
lonesome	solo	SOH-*loh*

ENGLISH	SPANISH	PRONUNCIATION
long (not short)	largo	LAHR-*goh*
long for, to	anhelar	*ah-neh*-LAHR
look (gaze), to	mirar	*mee*-RAHR
look (seem), to	parecer	*pah-reh*-SEHR
look for, to	buscar	*booss*-KAHR
lose, to	perder	*pehr*-THEHR
loss	pérdida, f.	PEHR-*thee-thah*
loud (resounding)	fuerte	FWEHR-*teh*
love	amor, m.	*ah*-MOHR
love, to	amar	*ah*-MAHR
low	bajo	BAH-*hoh*
luck	suerte, f.	SWEHR-*teh*
lucky (fortunate)	afortunado	*ah-fohr-too*-NAH-*thoh*
luggage	equipaje, m.	*eh-kee*-PAH-*heh*
lunch (midday meal)	almuerzo, m.	*ahl*-MWEHR-*soh*
lung	pulmón, m.	*pool*-MOHN
machine	máquina, f.	MAH-*kee-nah*
mad (insane)	loco	LOH-*koh*
magazine (periodical)	revista, f.	*rreh*-BEESS-*tah*
maid (servant)	sirvienta, f.	*seer*-BYEHN-*tah*
maiden name	apellido de sol-tera, m.	*ah-peh*-YEE-*thoh deh sohl*-TEH-*rah*
mail (letters exchanged)	correspondencia, f.	*koh-rrehss-pohn*-DEHN-*syah*
mail (postal system)	correo, m.	*koh*-RREH-*oh*
mail (post), to	echar al correo	*eh*-CHAHR *ahl koh*-RREH-*oh*
main (principal)	principal	*preen-see*-PAHL
make, to	hacer	*ah*-SEHR
malaria	malaria, f.	*mah*-LAH-*ryah*
male (adj.)	macho	MAH-*choh*
man	hombre, m.	OHM-*breh*

ENGLISH	SPANISH	PRONUNCIATION
manage (administer), to	dirigir	*dee-ree-*HEER
management (administration)	dirección, f.	*dee-rehk-*SYOHN
manager (administrator)	administrador, m.	*ahd-mee-neess-trah-*THORH
manual (small book)	manual, m.	*mah-*NWAHL
many, more, most	muchos, más, (el) más	MOO-*chohss,* MAHSS, *(ehl)* MAHSS
map	mapa, m.	MAH-*pah*
mark (designate), to	señalar	*seh-nyah-*LAHR
market (trading center)	mercado, m.	*mehr-*KAH-*thoh*
marriage	matrimonio, m.	*mah-tree-*MOH-*nyoh*
married	casado	*kah-*SAH-*thoh*
marry, to	casarse (con)	*kah-*SAHR-*seh (kohn)*
marvelous	maravilloso	*mah-rah-bee-*YOH-*soh*
master (great artist)	maestro, m.	*mah-*EHSS-*troh*
match (lucifer)	fósforo, m.	FOHSS-*foh-roh*
material (substance)	material, m.	*mah-teh-*RYAHL
matinee (theater performance)	matinée, m.	*mah-tee-*NEH
matter (affair)	asunto, m.	*ah-*SOON-*toh*
mattress	colchón, m.	*kohl-*CHOHN
maybe	quizás	*kee-*SAHSS
mayor	alcalde, m.	*ahl-*KAHL-*deh*
meal (repast)	comida, f.	*koh-*MEE-*thah*
mean (have in mind), to	querer decir	*keh-*REHR *deh-*SEER
mean (intend), to	tener intención	*teh-*NEHR *een-tehn-*SYOHN
meaning (sense)	sentido, m.	*sehn-*TEE-*thoh*
meantime (n.)	ínterin, m.	EEN-*teh-reen*

ENGLISH	SPANISH	PRONUNCIATION
meanwhile (adv.)	mientras tanto	MYEHN-*trahss* TAHN-*toh*
measles	sarampión, m.	*sah-rahm*-PYOHN
meat	carne, f.	KAHR-*neh*
mechanic	mecánico, m.	*meh*-KAH-*nee-koh*
medical	médico	MEH-*thee-koh*
medicine (medicament)	medicina, f.	*meh-thee*-SEE-*nah*
meet (be introduced to), to	ser presentado a	*sehr preh-sehn*-TAH-*thoh ah*
meet (come together), to	reunirse	*rreh-oo*-NEER-*seh*
meet (encounter), to	encontrar	*ehn-kohn*-TRAHR
memory (recollection)	memoria, f.	*meh*-MOH-*ryah*
mend (repair), to	reparar	*rreh-pah*-RAHR
mention, to	mencionar	*mehn-syoh*-NAHR
menu	menú, m.	*meh*-NOO
merchant	comerciante, m.	*koh-mehr*-SYAHN-*teh*
merciful	misericordioso	*mee-seh-ree-kohr*-THYOH-*soh*
mercy	misericordia, f.	*mee-seh-ree*-KOHR-*thyah*
merely	meramente	*meh-rah*-MEHN-*teh*
merit, to	merecer	*meh-reh*-SEHR
messenger (courier)	mensajero, m.	*mehn-sah*-HEH-*roh*
metal (n.)	metal, m.	*meh*-TAHL
middle (center)	medio, m.	MEH-*thyoh*
midnight	medianoche, f.	*meh-thyah*-NOH-*cheh*
milk	leche, f.	LEH-*cheh*
mind (opinion)	parecer, m.	*pah-reh*-SEHR
mineral	mineral, m.	*mee-neh*-RAHL
minister (clergyman)	pastor, m.	*pahss*--TOHR
minute (unit of time)	minuto, m.	*mee*-NOO-*toh*

ENGLISH	SPANISH	PRONUNCIATION
mirror	espejo, m.	ehss-PEH-hoh
miscellaneous	misceláneo	meess-seh-LAH-neh-oh
mischief (harm)	daño, m.	DAH-nyoh
miserable (unhappy)	miserable	mee-seh-RAH-bleh
misfortune	desgracia, f.	dehss-GRAH-syah
mislay, to	extraviar	ehss-trah-BYAHR
Miss	(la) señorita, f.	(lah) seh-nyoh-REE-tah
miss (fail to do), to	dejar de	deh-HAHR deh
miss (feel the loss of), to	echar de menos	eh-CHAHR deh MEM-nohss
mist	neblina, f.	neh-BLEE-nah
mistake	error, m.	eh-RROHR
mitten	mitón, m.	mee-TOHN
mix (make blend), to	mezclar	mehss-KLAHR
mixture	mezcla, f.	MEHSS-klah
mob (disorderly crowd)	populacho, m.	poh-poo-LAH-choh
model (exemplar)	modelo, m.	moh-THEH-loh
model (small copy)	modelo, m.	moh-THEH-loh
modest	modesto	moh-THEHSS-toh
moist	húmedo	OO-meh-thoh
moldy	mohoso	moh-OH-soh
moment (instant)	momento, m.	moh-MEHN-toh
monastery	monasterio, m.	moh-nahss-TEH-ryoh
money	dinero, m.	dee-NEH-roh
money order	giro postal, m.	HEE-roh pohss-TAHL
monk	monje, m.	MOHN-heh
monkey	mono, m.	MOHN-noh
month	mes, m.	MEHSS

ENGLISH	SPANISH	PRONUNCIATION
monthly (every month, adj.)	mensual	*mehn*-SWAHL
monument	monumento, m.	*moh-noo*-MEHN-*toh*
mood (humor)	humor, m.	OO-MOHR
moon	luna, f.	LOO-*nah*
more (adj.)	más	MAHSS
moreover	además	*ah-theh*-MAHSS
morning	mañana, f.	*mah*-NYAH-*nah*
morrow	mañana, f.	*mah*-NYAH-*nah*
mosquito	mosquito, m.	*mohss*-KEE-*toh*
most (adv.)	más	MAHSS
most (n.)	(el) más, m.	*(ehl)* MAHSS
mostly	principalmente	*preen-see-pahl*-MEHN-*teh*
moth	polilla, f.	*poh*-LEE-*yah*
mother	madre, f.	MAH-*threh*
mother-in-law	suegra, f.	SWEH-*grah*
motor (engine)	motor, m.	*moh*-TOHR
mountain	montaña, f.	*mohn*-TAH-*nyah*
mountainous	montañoso	*mohn-tah*-NYOH-*soh*
mouse	ratón, m.	*rrah*-TOHN
mouth	boca, f.	BOH-*kah*
move (change residence), to	mudarse	*moo*-THAHR-*seh*
move (shift the position of), to	mover	*moh*-BEHR
movement (motion)	movimiento, m.	*moh-bee*-MYEHN-*toh*
movies	cine, m.	SEE-*neh*
Mr.	(el) señor, m.	*(ehl) seh*-NYOHR
Mrs.	(la) señora, f.	*(lah) seh*-NYOH-*rah*
much, more, most	mucho, más, (el) más	MOO-*choh*, MAHSS, *(ehl)* MAHSS
mud	lodo, m.	LOH-*thoh*

ENGLISH	SPANISH	PRONUNCIATION
muscle	músculo, m.	MOOSS-*koo-loh*
museum	museo, m.	*moo-*SEH*-oh*
mushroom (n.)	seta, f.	SEH-*tah*
music	música, f.	MOO-*see-kah*
musician	músico, m.	MOO-*see-koh*
mustache	bigote, m.	*bee-*GOH*-teh*
mustard	mostaza, f.	*mohss-*TAH*-sah*
mutton	carne de carnero, f.	KAHR-*neh deh kahr-*NEH*-roh*
mutual	mutuo	MOO-*too-oh*
nail	uña, f.	OO-*nyah*
nail (hardware)	clavo, m.	KLAH-*boh*
name	nombre, m.	NOHM-*breh*
namely	a saber	*ah sah-*BEHR
nap	siesta, f.	SYEHSS-*tah*
napkin	servilleta, f.	*sehr-bee-*YEH*-tah*
narrow	estrecho	*ehss-*TREH*-choh*
national (adj.)	nacional	*nah-syoh-*NAHL
natural	natural	*nah-too-*RAHL
near (not far, adv.)	cerca	SEHR-*kah*
near (prep.)	cerca de	SEHR-*kah deh*
nearly (almost)	casi	KAH-*see*
necessary	necesario	*neh-seh-*SAH*-ryoh*
necessity	necesidad, f.	*neh-seh-see-*THAHTH
neck	cuello, m.	KWEH-*yoh*
necklace	collar, m.	*koh-*YAHR
need	necesidad, f.	*neh-seh-see-*THAHTH
need (require), to	necesitar	*neh-seh-see-*TAHR
needle	aguja, f.	*ah-*GOO*-hah*
neglect (slight), to	despreciar	*dehss-preh-*SYAHR
Negro	negro, m.	NEH-*groh*
neighbor	vecino, m.	*beh-*SEE*-noh*
neighborhood	vecindad, f.	*beh-seen-*THAHTF
neither (adj.)	ni el uno . . .	*nee ehl* OO-*noh* . . .

ENGLISH	SPANISH	PRONUNCIATION
neither (pron.)	ninguno	*neen-*GOO*-noh*
neither . . . nor (conj.)	ni . . . ni	*nee . . . nee*
nephew	sobrino, m.	*soh-*BREE*-noh*
nervous (high-strung)	nervioso	*nehr-*BYOH*-soh*
never	nunca	NOON*-kah*
new	nuevo	NWEH*-boh*
newspaper	periódico, m.	*peh-*RYOH*-thee-koh*
newstand	puesto de perió-dicos, m.	PWEHSS*-toh deh peh-*RYOH*-thee-kohss*
New Year's Day	día de año nuevo m.	DEE*-ah deh* AH*-nyoh* NWEH*-boh*
next (adv.)	luego	LWEH*-goh*
next (following, adj.)	siguiente	*see-*GHYEHN*-teh*
next to (alongside of, prep.)	junto a	HOON*-toh ah*
nice (agreeable)	agradable	*ah-grah-*THAH*-bleh*
nickname	mote, m.	MOH*-teh*
niece	sobrina, f.	*soh-*BREE*-nah*
night	noche, f.	NOH*-cheh*
nightgown	camisa de dormir, f.	*kah-*MEE*-sah deh dohr-*MEER
no (nay)	no	*noh*
no (not any, adj.)	ninguno	*neen-*GOO*-noh*
nobody (pron.)	nadie	NAH*-thyeh*
noise (din)	ruido, m.	RWEE*-thoh*
noisy	ruidoso	*rwee-*THOH*-soh*
none (pron.)	ninguno	*neen-*GOO*-noh*
nonsense (absurdity)	disparate, m.	*deess-pah-*RAH*-teh*
nonsense (stupidity)	tontería	*tohn-teh-*REE*-ah*
noon	mediodía, m.	*meh-thyoh-*THEE*-ah*
nor	ni	*nee*
normal (adj.)	normal	*nohr-*MAHL

ENGLISH	SPANISH	PRONUNCIATION
north (adv.)	al norte	*ahl* NOHR-*teh*
north (n.)	norte, m.	NOHR-*teh*
North America	Norte América	NOHR-*teh ah-*MEH-*ree-kah*
nose	nariz, f.	*nah-*REESS
nostril	ventana de la nariz, f.	*behn-*TAH-*nah deh lah nah-*REESS
not	no	*noh*
notary	notario, m.	*noh-*TAH-*ryoh*
nothing (n.)	nada	NAH-*thah*
notice (notification)	notificación, f.	*noh-tee-fee-kah-*SYOHN
notice (see), to	observar	*ohb-sehr-*BAHR
notify, to	notificar	*noh-tee-fee-*KAHR
nourish, to	nutrir	*noo-*TREER
nourishment	nutrimento, m.	*noo-tree-*MEHN-*toh*
novel (book)	novela, f.	*noh-*BEH-*lah*
now (adv.)	ahora	*ah-*OH-*rah*
nowhere	en ninguna parte	*ehn neen-*GOO-*nah* PAHR-*teh*
number (numeral)	número, m.	NOO-*meh-roh*
number (quantity)	número, m.	NOO-*meh-roh*
nurse	enfermera, f.	*ehn-fehr-*MEH-*rah*
nut (food)	nuez, f.	NWEHSS
oath (vow)	juramento, m.	*hoo-rah-*MEHN-*toh*
obedience (compliance)	obediencia, f.	*oh-beh-*THYEHN-*syah*
obedient	obediente	*oh-beh-*THYEHN-*teh*
obey, to	obedecer	*oh-beh-theh-*SEHR
object (aim)	propósito, m.	*proh-*POH-*see-toh*
object (thing)	objeto, m.	*ohb-*HEH-*toh*
obligation (duty)	obligación, f.	*oh-blee-gah-*SYOHN
oblige (compel), to	obligar	*oh-blee-*GAHR
observe (remark), to	observar	*ohb-sehr-*BAHR
observe (watch), to	observar	*ohb-sehr-*BEHR

ENGLISH	SPANISH	PRONUNCIATION
obstacle	obstáculo, m.	*ohb*-STAH-*koo-loh*
obtain (get), to	obtener	*ohb-teh*-NEHR
obvious	obvio	OHB-*vyoh*
occasion	ocasión, f.	*oh-kah*-SYOHN
occupation (calling)	ocupación, f.	*oh-koo-pah*-SYOHN
occupy (make busy), to	ocupar	*oh-koo*-PAHR
occur (happen), to	ocurrir	*oh-koo*-REER
ocean	océano, m.	*oh*-SEH-*ah-noh*
odor (scent)	olor, m.	*oh*-LOHR
of	de	*deh*
office (place of business)	oficina, f.	*oh-fee*-SEE-*nah*
often	a menudo	*ah meh*-NOO-*thoh*
oil	aceite, m.	*ah*-SEH-*ee-teh*
old (elderly)	viejo	BYEH-*hoh*
omit (leave out), to	omitir	*oh-mee*-TEER
on (prep.)	en	*ehn*
once (one time, adv.)	una vez	OO-*nah* BEHSS
once (formerly, adv.)	en otro tiempo	*ehn*-OH-*troh* TYEHM-*poh*
onion	cebolla, f.	*seh*-BOH-*yah*
only (merely)	solamente	*soh-lah*-MEHN-*teh*
only (sole)	único	OO-*nee-koh*
open (adj.)	abierto	*ah*-BYEHR-*toh*
open (make open), to	abrir	*ah*-BREER
operation (med.)	operación, f.	*oh-peh-rah*-SYOHN
opinion	opinión, f.	*oh-pee*-NYOHN
opportunity	oportunidad, f.	*oh-pohr-too-nee*-THAHTH
opposite (n.)	contrario, m.	*kohn*-TRAH-*ryoh*
opposite (prep.)	frente a	FREHN-*teh ah*
or	o, u	*oh, oo*
orange (fruit)	naranja, f.	*nah*-RAHN-*hah*
order (command)	orden, f.	OHR-*thehn*

ENGLISH	SPANISH	PRONUNCIATION
order (purchase)	pedido, m.	*peh*-THEE-*thoh*
order (sequence)	orden, m.	OHR-*thehn*
order (command), to	ordenar	*ohr-theh*-NAHR
order (purchase), to	pedir	*peh*-THEER
ordinary (usual)	ordinario	*ohr-thee*-NAH-*ryoh*
original (first)	original	*oh-ree-hee*-NAHL
ornament	ornamento, m.	*ohr-nah*-MEHN-*toh*
orphan (n.)	huérfano, m.	WEHR-*fah-noh*
other (adj.)	otro	OH-*troh*
other (pron.)	otro	OH-*troh*
otherwise (under other conditions)	de otro modo	*deh* OH-*troh* MOH-*thoh*
out (forth, adv.)	fuera	FWEH-*rah*
out (not in, adv.)	afuera	*ah*-FWEH-*rah*
outdoors (adv.)	al aire libre	*ahl* AH-*ee-reh* LEE-*breh*
outfit (equipment)	equipo, m.	*eh*-KEE-*poh*
outside (adj.)	exterior	*ehss-teh*-RYOHR
outside (adv.)	afuera	*ah*-FWEH-*rah*
outside (n.)	exterior, m.	*ehss-teh*-RYOHR
oven	horno, m.	OHR-*noh*
over (above, prep.)	sobre	SOH-*breh*
overcoat	sobretodo, m.	*soh-breh*-TOH-*thoh*
overlook (disregard), to	pasar por alto	*pah*-SAHR *pohr* AHL-*toh*
oversea(s) (adj.)	ultramar	*ool-trah*-MAHR
owe, to	deber	*deh*-BEHR
own (adj.)	propio	PROH-*pyoh*
own (possess), to	poseer	*poh-seh*-EHR
owner	propietario, m.	*proh-pyeh*-TAH-*ryoh*
oyster	ostra, f.	OHSS-*trah*
pack (wrap), to	empacar	*ehm-pah*-KAHR
package	paquete, m.	*pah*-KEH-*teh*
page (leaf)	página, f.	PAH-*hee-nah*

ENGLISH	SPANISH	PRONUNCIATION
pail	balde, m.	BAHL-*deh*
pain (ache)	dolor, m.	*doh*-LOHR
painful	doloroso	*doh-loh*-ROH-*soh*
painter (artist)	pintor, m.	*peen*-TOHR
painting (picture)	pintura, f.	*peen*-TOO-*rah*
pair	par, m.	PAHR
pajamas	pijamas, m. pl.	*pee*-HAH-*mahss*
pal	compañero, m.	*kohm-pah*-NYEH-*roh*
palace	palacio, m.	*pah*-LAH-*syoh*
pale (wan)	pálido	PAH-*lee-thoh*
pane, window	cuadro de vidrio, m.	KWAH-*throh deh* BEE-*thryoh*
paper	papel, m.	*pah*-PEHL
parade (procession)	desfile, m.	*dehss*-FEE-*leh*
paragraph	párrafo, m.	PAH-*rrah-foh*
parcel (package)	paquete, m.	*pah*-KEH-*teh*
parcel post	paquete postal, m	*pah*-KEH-*teh pohss*-TAHL
parents	padres, m. pl.	PAH-*threhss*
park	parque, m.	PAHR-*keh*
park (put in place), to	estacionar	*ehss-tah-syoh*-NAHR
parlor (living room)	sala, f.	SAH-*lah*
part (portion)	parte, f.	PAHR-*teh*
part (leave each other)	separarse	*seh-pah*-RAHR-*seh*
participate, to	participar	*pahr-tee-see*-PAHR
particular (detail, n.)	detalle, m.	*deh*-TAH-*yeh*
particular (specific, adj.)	particular	*pahr-tee-koo*-LAHR
partly	en parte	*ehn* PAHR-*teh*
partner (bus.)	socio, m.	SOH-*syoh*
party	partido, f.	*pahr*-TEE-*thoh*
party (social gathering)	tertulia, f.	*tehr*-TOO-*lyah*

ENGLISH	SPANISH	PRONUNCIATION
pass (go by), to	pasar	*pah*-SAHR
passage (passageway)	pasaje, m.	*pah*-SAH-*heh*
passenger	pasajero, m.	*pah-sah*-HEH-*roh*
passport	pasaporte, m.	*pah-sah*-POHR-*teh*
past (beyond, prep.)	más allá de	*mahss ah*-YAH-*deh*
past (bygone, adj.)	pasado	*pah*-SAH-*thoh*
past (n.)	pasado, m.	*pah*-SAH-*thoh*
pastor	pastor, m.	*pahss*-TOHR
patch (repair)	parche, m.	PAHR-*cheh*
patience	paciencia, f.	*pah*-SYEHN-*syah*
patient (forbearing)	paciente	*pah*-SYEHN-*teh*
patient (invalid)	paciente, m., f.	*pah*-SYEHN-*teh*
patron (customer)	cliente, m., f.	KLYEHN-*teh*
pattern (design)	diseño, m.	*dee*-SEH-*nyoh*
pavement	pavimento, m.	*pah-bee*-MEHN-*toh*
pawn, to	empeñar	*ehm-peh*-NYAHR
pawnshop	casa de empeño, f.	KAH-*sah deh ehm*-PEH-*nyoh*
pay, to	pagar	*pah*-GAHR
payable (due)	pagadero	*pah-gah*-THEH-*roh*
payment	pago, m.	PAH-*goh*
peace	paz, f.	PAHSS
peach	melocotón, m.	*meh-loh-koh*-TOHN
pear	pera, f.	PEH-*rah*
pearl (gem)	perla, f.	PEHR-*lah*
peculiar (odd)	singular	*seen-goo*-LAHR
peel (take skin from), to	descortezar	*dehss-kohr-teh*-SAHR
pen, fountain	pluma fuente, f.	PLOO-*mah* FWEHN-*teh*
pencil	lápiz, m.	LAH-*peess*
peninsula	península, f.	*peh*-NEEN-*soo-lah*
people (persons)	gente, f.	HEHN-*teh*
pepper (seasoning)	pimienta, f.	*pee*-MYEHN-*tah*
perfect (flawless)	perfecto	*pehr*-FEHK-*toh*

ENGLISH	SPANISH	PRONUNCIATION
perform (do), to	ejecutar	*eh-heh-koo-*TAHR
performance (stage presentation)	representación, f.	*rreh-preh-sehn-tah-*SYOHN
perfume	perfume, m.	*pehr-*FOO*-meh*
perhaps	tal vez	*tahl* BEHSS
period (of time)	período, m.	*peh-*REE*-oh-thoh*
permanent (adj.)	permanente	*pehr-mah-*NEHN*-teh*
permission	permiso, m.	*pehr-*MEE*-soh*
permit (allow), to	permitir	*pehr-mee-*TEER
person	persona, f.	*pehr-*SOH*-nah*
personal	personal	*pehr-soh-*NAHL
persuade, to	persuadir	*pehr-swah-*THEER
pet (animal)	animal mimado, m.	*ah-nee-*MAHL *mee-*MAH*-thoh*
petticoat	enaguas, f. pl.	*eh-*NAH*-gwahss*
pharmacist	farmacéutico, m.	*fahr-mah-*SEH*-oo-tee-koh*
pharmacy (drug store)	farmacia, f.	*fahr-*MAH*-syah*
phone, to	telefonear	*teh-leh-foh-neh-*AHR
phonograph	fonógrafo, m.	*foh-*NOH*-grah-foh*
photograph	fotografía, f.	*foh-toh-grah-*FEE*-ah*
physician	médico, m.	MEH*-thee-koh*
piano (n.)	piano, m.	PYAH*-noh*
pick (choose), to	escoger	*ehss-koh-*HEHR
picture (depiction)	cuadro, m.	KWAH*-throh*
pie	pastel, m.	*pahss-*TEHL
piece (bit)	pedazo, m.	*peh-*THAH*-soh*
pig (animal)	cerdo, m.	SEHR*-thoh*
pigeon	paloma, f.	*pah-*LOH*-mah*
pill	píldora, f.	PEEL*-doh-rah*
pillow	almohada, f.	*ahl-moh-*AH*-thah*
pin (sewing accessory)	alfiler, m.	*ahl-fee-*LEHR

ENGLISH	SPANISH	PRONUNCIATION
pipe (tobacco pipe)	pipa, f.	PEE-*pah*
pitcher (container)	jarro, m.	HAH-*rroh*
pity (compassion)	compasión, f.	*kohm-pah-*SYOHN
pity, to	compadecer	*kohm-pah-theh-*SEHR
place (locality)	lugar, m.	*loo-*GAHR
place (lay), to	colocar	*koh-loh-*KAHR
plain (clear)	claro	KLAH-*roh*
plane (airplane)	aeroplano, m.	*ah-eh-roh-*PLAH-*noh*
plant (flora)	planta, f.	PLAHN-*tah*
plate (shallow dish)	plato, m.	PLAH-*toh*
platform, railroad	andén, m.	*ahn-*THEHN
play (stage presentation)	representación, f.	*rreh-preh-sehn-tah-*SYOHN
play (engage in recreation), to	jugar	*hoo-*GAHR
play (perform music upon), to	tocar	*toh-*KAHR
playmate	compañero de juego, m.	*kohm-pah-*NYEH-*roh deh* HWEH-*goh*
pleasant	agradable	*ah-grah-*THAH-*bleh*
please (satisfy), to	complacer	*kohm-plah-*SEHR
pleasure	placer, m.	*plah-*SEHR
plenty (n.)	abundancia, f.	*ah-boon-*DAHN-*syah*
plug (elec.)	enchufe, m.	*ehn-*CHOO-*feh*
plum (fruit)	ciruela, f.	*see-*RWEH-*lah*
pneumonia	pulmonía, f.	*pool-moh-*NEE-*ah*
pocket	bolsillo, m.	*bohl-*SEE-*yoh*
poem	poema, m.	*poh-*EH-*mah*
poet	poeta, m.	*poh-*EH-*tah*
poetry	poesía, f.	*poheh-*SEE-*ah*
point (indicate), to	indicar	*een-dee-*KAHR

ENGLISH	SPANISH	PRONUNCIATION
poison	veneno, m.	*beh*-NEH-*noh*
poison, to	envenenar	*ehn-beh-neh-*NAHR
police	policía, f.	*poh-lee-*SEE-*ah*
policeman	policía, m.	*poh-lee-*SEE-*ah*
polish, to	pulir	*poo-*LEER
polite	cortés	*kohr-*TEHSS
political	político	*poh-*LEE-*tee-koh*
politician	político, m.	*poh-*LEE-*tee-koh*
politics	política, f.	*poh-*LEE-*tee-kah*
pool (standing water)	charco, m.	CHAHR-*koh*
poor (needy)	pobre	POH-*breh*
poor (unfortunate)	pobre	POH-*breh*
pope	papa, m.	PAH-*pah*
popular (prevalent)	popular	*poh-poo-*LAHR
population (number of people)	población, f.	*pohb-lah-*SYOHN
porcelain (n.)	porcelana f.	*pohr-seh-*LAH-*nah*
pork	carne de cerdo, f.	KAHR-*neh deh* SEHR-*thoh*
pork chop	chuleta de cerdo, f.	*choo-*LEH-*tah deh* SEHR-*thoh*
port (harbor)	puerto, m.	PWEHR-*toh*
porter (baggage carrier)	mozo, m.	MOH-*soh*
possess, to	poseer	*poh-seh-*EHR
possession (ownership)	posesión, f.	*poh-seh-*SYOHN
possibility	posibilidad, f.	*poh-see-bee-lee-*THAHTH
possible	posible	*poh-*SEE-*bleh*
postage (postal charge)	franqueo, m.	*frahn-*KEH-*oh*
post office	correo, m.	*koh-*RREH-*oh*
postpone, to	posponer	*pohss-poh-*NEHR
potato (white)	papa, f.	PAH-*pah*

ENGLISH	SPANISH	PRONUNCIATION
poverty	pobreza, f.	poh-BREH-sah
powder (cosmetic)	polvos, m. pl.	POHL-bohss
power (authority)	poder, m.	poh-THEHR
powerful	poderoso	poh-theh-ROH-soh
practice (custom)	práctica, f.	PRAHK-tee-kah
praise, to	elogiar	eh-loh-HYAHR
pray, to	rezar	rreh-SAHR
prayer (petition)	oración, f.	oh-rah-SYOHN
prefer (like better), to	preferir	preh-feh-REER
prejudice	prejuicio, m.	preh-HWEE-syoh
prescription (med.)	receta, f.	rreh-SEH-tah
present (give), to	regalar	rreh-gah-LAHR
present (introduce), to	presentar	preh-sehn-TAHR
press (newspapers and periodicals)	prensa, f.	PREHN-sah
press (iron), to	planchar	plahn-CHAHR
pretend (feign), to	fingir	feen-HEER
pretty	bonito	boh-NEE-toh
prevent (stop), to	prevenir	preh-beh-NEER
previous	previo	PREH-byoh
price	precio, m.	PREH-syoh
priest	sacerdote, m.	sah-sehr-DOH-teh
principal (main)	principal	preen-see-PAHL
principle (basic truth)	principio, m.	preen-SEE-pyoh
print (printed reproduction)	impresión, f.	eem-preh-SYOHN
print, to	imprimir	eem-pree-MEER
prison	prisión, f.	pree-SYOHN
prisoner	prisionero, m.	pree-syoh-NEH-roh
private (personal)	privado	pree-BAH-thoh
privilege	privilegio, m.	pree-bee-LEH-hyoh
prize (trophy)	premio, m.	PREH-myoh
probable (likely)	probable	proh-BAH-bleh
product	producto, m.	proh-DOOK-toh

ENGLISH	SPANISH	PRONUNCIATION
production (manufacture)	producción, f.	*proh-dook-*SYOHN
profession (occupation)	profesión, f.	*proh-feh-*SYOHN
professor (teacher)	profesor, m.	*proh-feh-*SOHR
profit	ganancia, f.	*gah-*NAHN-*syah*
prohibition	prohibición, f.	*proh-ee-bee-*SYOHN
prominent (eminent)	sobresaliente	*soh-breh-sah-*LYEHN-*teh*
promise (pledge)	promesa, f.	*proh-*MEH-*sah*
promise (pledge), to	prometer	*proh-meh-*TEHR
prompt (quick)	pronto	PROHN-*toh*
pronounce (enunciate), to	pronunciar	*proh-noon-*SYAHR
proper (acceptable)	correcto	*koh-*RREHK-*toh*
property (possession)	propiedad, f.	*proh-pyeh-*THAHTH
propose (suggest), to	proponer	*proh-poh-*NEHR
prosperity	prosperidad, f.	*prohss-peh-ree-*THAHTH
prosperous	próspero	PROHSS-*peh-roh*
protect, to	proteger	*proh-teh-*HEHR
proud (taking pride in)	orgulloso	*ohr-goo-*YOH-*soh*
prove (verify), to	probar	*proh-*BAHR
prune	ciruela pasa, f.	*see-*RWEH-*lah* PAH-*sah*
public (common, adj.)	público	POO-*blee-koh*
publication (published work)	publicación, f.	*poo-blee-kah-*SYOHN
publish, to	publicar	*poo-blee-*KAHR
publisher	editor, m.	*eh-thee-*TOHR
pudding	budín, m.	*boo-*THEEN
pull (draw), to	tirar de	*tee-*RAHR *deh*
punctual	puntual	*poon-*TWAHL

ENGLISH	SPANISH	PRONUNCIATION
punish, to	castigar	*kahss-tee-*GAHR
punishment	castigo, m.	*kahss-*TEE*-goh*
pupil	discípulo, m.	*deess-*SEE*-poo-loh*
purchase (act of buying)	compra, f.	KOHM*-prah*
pure (unadulterated)	puro	POO*-roh*
purpose (aim)	propósito, m.	*proh-*POH*-see-toh*
purse (coin pouch)	portamonedas, m.	*pohr-tah-moh-*NEH*-thahss*
pursue (chase), to	perseguir	*pehr-seh-*GHEER
push (above), to	empujar	*ehm-poo-*HAHR
put (place), to	colocar	*koh-loh-*KAHR
quaint (unusual)	raro	RRAH*-roh*
quantity (amount)	cantidad, f.	*kahn-tee-*THAHTH
quarrel (dispute)	riña, f.	RREE*-nyah*
quarrel (dispute), to	reñirse	*rreh-*NYEER*-seh*
quarter (one-fourth)	cuarto	KWAHR*-toh*
queen	reina, f.	RREH*-ee-nah*
queer	extraño	*ehss-*TRAH*-nyoh*
question (query)	pregunta, f.	*preh-*GOON*-tah*
question (doubt), to	dudar	*doo-*THAHR
question (query), to	interrogar	*een-teh-rroh-*GAHR
quick (rapid)	rápido	RRAH*-pee-thoh*
quiet (silent, adj.)	silencioso	*see-lehn-*SYOH*-soh*
quiet (stillness)	quietud, f.	*kyeh-*TOOTH
quite (considerably)	bastante	*bahss-*TAHN*-teh*
rabbi	rabino, m.	*rrah-*BEE*-noh*
rabbit	conejo, m.	*koh-*NEH*-hoh*
race	carrera, f.	*kah-*RREH*-rah*
radiator (heater)	radiador, m.	*rrah-thyah-*THOHR
radio (receiving set)	radio, m.	RRAH*-thyoh*
rag	trapo, m.	TRAH*-poh*
rail (bar on track)	riel, m.	RRYEHL
railroad	ferrocarril, m.	*feh-rroh-kah-*RREEL

ENGLISH	SPANISH	PRONUNCIATION
rain	lluvia, f.	YOO-*byah*
rain, to	llover	*yoh*-BEHR
rainbow	arco iris, m.	AHR-*koh* EE-*reess*
raincoat	impermeable, m.	*eem-pehr-meh*-AH-*bleh*
rainy	lluvioso	*yoo*-BYOH-*soh*
raisin	pasa, f.	PAH-*sah*
range (of mountains)	cordillera, f.	*kohr-thee*-YEH-*rah*
rapid (adj.)	rápido	RRAH-*pee-thoh*
rare (uncommon)	raro	RRAH-*roh*
raspberry	frambuesa, f.	*frahm*-BWEH-*sah*
rat	rata, f.	RRAH-*tah*
rate (degree of speed)	velocidad, f.	*beh-loh-see*-THAHTH
rate (exchange)	tipo de cambio, m.	TEE-*poh deh* KAHM-*byoh*
rather (somewhat)	algo	AHL-*goh*
raw (in natural state)	crudo	KROO-*thoh*
ray (beam)	rayo, m.	RRAH-*yoh*
rayon	rayón, m.	*rrah*-YOHN
razor	navaja de afeitar f.	*nah*-BAH-*hah deh ah-fey*-TAHR
razor blade	hoja de afeitar, f.	OH-*hah deh ah-fey*-TAHR
reach (arrive at), to	llegar a	*yeh*-GAHR *ah*
read, to	leer	*leh*-EHR
ready (prepared)	listo	LEESS-*toh*
real (actual)	real	*rreh*-AHL
really (actually)	realmente	*rreh-ahl*-MEHN-*teh*
reason (ground)	razón, f.	*rrah*-SOHN
reason (intellect)	razón, f.	*rrah*-SOHN
reasonable (rational)	razonable	*rrah-soh*-NAH-*bleh*
recall (remember), to	recordar	*rreh-kohr*-THAHR

ENGLISH	SPANISH	PRONUNCIATION
receipt (voucher)	recibo, m.	*rreh-*SEE-*boh*
recent	reciente	*rreh-*SYEHN-*teh*
recently	recientemente	*rreh-syehn-teh-*MEHN-*teh*
recipe	receta, f.	*rreh-*SEH-*tah*
reckon (compute), to	computar	*kohm-poo-*TAHR
recognition (acknowledgment)	reconocimiento, m.	*rreh-koh-noh-see-*MYEHN-*toh*
recognize (identify), to	reconocer	*rreh-koh-noh-*SEHR
recommend (advise), to	recomendar	*rreh-koh-mehn-*DAHR
recommendation	recomendación, f.	*rreh-koh-mehn-dah-*SYOHN
recover (get well), to	recuperar	*rreh-koo-peh-*RAHR
red	rojo	RROH-*hoh*
refer (allude), to	referirse	*rreh-feh-*REER-*seh*
reference (allusion)	referencia, f.	*rreh-feh-*REHN-*syah*
reflection (meditation)	reflexión, f.	*rreh-flehk-*SYOHN
refresh, to	refrescar	*rreh-frehss-*KAHR
refreshments	refrescos, m. pl.	*rreh-*FREHSS-*kohss*
refrigerator	nevera, f.	*neh-*BEH-*rah*
regard (consider), to	considerar	*kohn-see-theh-*RAHR
regarding (concerning)	tocante a	*toh-*KAHN-*teh ah*
region (area)	región, f.	*rreh-*HYOHN
register, to	registrar	*rreh-heess-*TRAHR
registered (postal designation)	certificado	*sehr-tee-fee-*KAH-*thoh*
regret, to	sentir	*sehn-*TEER
regular (normal)	regular	*rreh-goo-*LAHR

ENGLISH	SPANISH	PRONUNCIATION
reimburse, to	reintegrar	*rreh-een-teh-*GRAHR
related (connected)	relacionado	*rreh-lah-syoh-*NAH-*thoh*
relation (connection)	relación, f.	*rreh-lah-*SYOHN
relative (kinsman)	pariente, m., f.	*pah-*RYEHN-*teh*
reliable	digno de confianza	DEEG-*noh deh kohn-*FYAHN-*sah*
relieve (ease), to	aliviar	*ah-lee-*BYAHR
religion	religión, f.	*rreh-lee-*HYOHN
religious (adj.)	religioso	*rreh-lee-*HYOH-*soh*
remain (be left), to	quedar	*keh-*THAHR
remain (stay behind), to	quedarse	*keh-*THAHR-*seh*
remainder	resto, m.	RREHSS-*toh*
remark (comment)	advertencia, f.	*ahd-behr-*TEHN-*syah*
remark (say), to	comentar	*koh-mehn-*TAHR
remedy	remedio, m.	*rreh-*MEH-*thyoh*
remember (recollect), to	recordar	*rreh-kohr-*THAHR
remind, to	recordar	*rreh-kohr-*THAHR
remit (send payment), to	remesar	*rreh-meh-*SAHR
remittance	remesa, f.	*rreh-*MEH-*sah*
remote (far-off)	remoto	*rreh-*MOH-*toh*
remove (take away), to	quitar	*kee-*TAHR
renew, to	renovar	*rreh-noh-*BAHR
rent (payment)	alquiler, m.	*ahl-kee-*LEHR
rent (charge rent for), to	alquilar	*ahl-kee-*LAHR
rent (pay rent for), to	alquilar	*ahl-kee-*LAHR
repair (fix), to	reparar	*rreh-pah-*RAHR

ENGLISH	SPANISH	PRONUNCIATION
repay (reimburse), to	reembolsar	*rreh-ehm-bohl-*SAHR
repeat (reiterate), to	repetir	*rreh-peh-*TEER
repent, to	arrepentirse	*ah-rreh-pehn-*TEER-*seh*
reply	respuesta, f.	*rrehss-*PWEHSS-*tah*
reply, to	responder	*rrehss-pohn-*DEHR
represent (act for), to	representar	*rreh-preh-sehn-*TAHR
representation (pol.)	representación, f.	*rreh-preh-sehn-tah-*SYOHN
representative (deputy)	representante, m.	*rreh-preh-sehn-*TAHN-*teh*
reproach	reproche, m.	*rreh-*PROH-*cheh*
reproach, to	reprochar	*rreh-proh-*CHAHR
reputation	reputación, f.	*rreh-poo-tah-*SYOHN
request	solicitud, f.	*soh-lee-see-*TOOTH
request, to	solicitar	*soh-lee-see-*TAHR
resemble, to	asemejarse a	*ah-seh-meh-*HAHR-*seh ah*
reserve (order in advance), to	reservar	*rreh-sehr-*BAHR
residence (abode)	residencia, f.	*rreh-see-*THEHN-*syah*
resident (n.)	residente, m.	*rreh-see-*THEHN-*teh*
resist, to	resistir	*rreh-seess-*TEER
resistance	resistencia, f.	*rreh-seess--*TEHN-*syah*
resort (spa)	lugar de veraneo, m.	*loo-*GAHR *deh beh-rah-*NEH-*oh*
respect (esteem)	respeto, m.	*rrehss-*PEH-*toh*
respect (esteem), to	respetar	*rrehss-peh-*TAHR
respectable	respetable	*rrehss-peh-*TAH-*bleh*

ENGLISH	SPANISH	PRONUNCIATION
respective (adj.)	respectivo	*rrehss-pehk-*TEE-*boh*
respond (reply), to	responder	*rrehss-pohn-*DEHR
response (reply)	respuesta, f.	*rrehss-*PWEHSS-*tah*
responsibility (accountability)	responsabilidad, f.	*rrehss-pohn-sah-bee-lee-*THAHTH
responsible (answerable)	responsable	*rrehss-pohn-*SAH-*bleh*
rest (remainder)	resto, m.	RREHSS-*toh*
rest (repose)	descanso, m.	*dehss-*KAHN-*soh*
rest (repose), to	descansar	*dehss-kahn-*SAHR
restaurant	restaurante, m.	*rrehss-tah-oo-*RAHN-*teh*
result (consequence)	resultado, m.	*rreh-sool-*TAH-*thoh*
retire (stop working), to	retirarse	*rreh-tee-*RAHR-*seh*
return (coming or going back)	regreso, m.	*rreh-*GREH-*soh*
return (give back), to	devolver	*deh-bohl-*BEHR
return (go back), to	regresar	*rreh-greh-*SAHR
reverence (respect)	reverencia, f.	*rreh-beh-*REHN-*syah*
revolution (pol.)	revolución, f.	*rreh-boh-loo-*SYOHN
reward (recompense)	recompensa, f.	*rreh-kohm-*PEHN-*sah*
reward, to	recompensar	*rreh-kohm-pehn-*SAHR
rheumatism	reumatismo, m.	*rreh-oo-mah-*TEEZ-*moh*
rib	costilla, f.	*kohss-*TEE-*yah*
ribbon	listón, m.	*leess-*TOHN
rice	arroz, m.	*ah-*RROHSS
rich	rico	RREE-*koh*

ENGLISH	SPANISH	PRONUNCIATION
ride (in a car)	paseo en auto, m.	*pah-*SEH-*oh ehn* OW-*toh*
ride (in a car), to	pasear en auto	*pah-seh-*AHR *ehn* OW-*toh*
ridiculous	ridículo	*rree-*THEE-*koo-loh*
right (correct)	correcto	*koh-*RREHK-*toh*
right (on the right, adj.)	a la derecha	*ah lah deh-*REH-*chah*
right (right-hand side)	derecho, m.	*deh-*REH-*choh*
right (to the right, adv.)	a la derecha	*ah lah deh-*REH-*chah*
ring (jewelry)	anillo, m.	*ah-*NEE-*yoh*
ring (resound), to	resonar	*rreh-soh-*NAHR
ripe	maduro	*mah-*THOO-*roh*
rise (ascend), to	elevarse	*eh-leh-*BAHR-*seh*
rise (stand up), to	ponerse de pie	*poh-*NEHR-*seh dah* PYEH
risk (danger)	riesgo, m.	RRYEHZ-*goh*
river	río, m.	REE-*oh*
road	camino, m.	*kah-*MEE-*noh*
roast	asado, m.	*ah-*SAH-*thoh*
roast (be roasted), to	asarse	*ah-*SAHR-*seh*
rob (steal from), to	robar	*rroh-*BAHR
robber	ladrón, m.	*lah-*THROHN
robe (dressing gown)	bata, f.	BAH-*tah*
rock (large stone)	roca, f.	RROH-*kah*
rocky (rock-covered)	rocoso	*rroh-*KOH-*soh*
role	papel, m.	*pah-*PEHL
roll (bread)	panecillo, m.	*pah-neh-*SEE-*yoh*
romantic	romántico	*rroh-*MAHN-*tee-koh*
roof	techo, m.	TEH-*choh*
room (of house)	cuarto, m.	KWAHR-*toh*
room (space)	espacio, m.	*ehss-*PAH-*syoh*
rope	soga, f.	SOH-*gah*

ENGLISH	SPANISH	PRONUNCIATION
rotten (decayed)	podrido	*poh*-THREE-*thoh*
rouge	colorete, m.	*koh-loh*-REH-*teh*
rough (harsh)	grosero	*groh*-SEH-*roh*
rough (uneven)	áspero	AHSS-*peh-roh*
round (adj.)	redondo	*rreh*-THOHN-*doh*
rouse (awaken), to	despertar	*dehss-pehr*-TAHR
royal	real	*rreh*-AHL
rubber	caucho, m.	KAH-*oo-choh*
rubbers (overshoes)	chanclos, m. pl.	CHAHN-*klohss*
rubbish (litter)	basura, f.	*bah*-SOO-*rah*
rude (impolite)	rudo	RROO-*thoh*
rug	alfombra, f.	*ahl*-FOHM-*brah*
ruins, (remains)	ruinas, f. pl.	RWEE-*nahss*
rule (regulation)	regla, f.	RREH-*glah*
rule (govern), to	gobernar	*goh-behr*-NAHR
ruler (measuring instrument)	regla, f.	RREH-*glah*
run (extend), to	extenderse	*ehss-tehn*-DEHR-*seh*
run (flow), to	correr	*koh*-RREHR
run (sprint), to	correr	*koh*-RREHR
rural	rural	*rroo*-RAHL
rush (dash), to	apresurarse	*ah-preh-soo*-RAHR-*seh*
Russian (adj.)	ruso	ROO-*soh*
rust	orín, m.	*oh*-REEN
rusty	oxidado	*ohk-see*-THAH-*thoh*
sack (bag)	saco, m.	SAH-*koh*
sacred	sagrado	*sah*-GRAH-*thoh*
sad (sorrowful)	triste	TREESS-*teh*
sadness	tristeza, f.	*treess*-TEH-*sah*
safe (unharmed)	seguro	*seh*-GOO-*roh*
safe (without risk)	seguro	*seh*-GOO-*roh*
safety (n.)	seguridad, f.	*seh-goo-ree*-THAHTH
safety pin	imperdible, m.	*eem-pehr*-THEE-*bleh*
saint	santo, m.	SAHN-*toh*

ENGLISH	SPANISH	PRONUNCIATION
salad	ensalada, f.	*ehn-sah-*LAH*-thah*
sale (exchange)	venta, f.	BEHN*-tah*
salesman	vendedor, m.	*behn-deh-*THOHR
salmon	salmón, m.	*sahl-*MOHN
salt	sal, f.	SAHL
same (adj.)	mismo	MEEZ*-moh*
sample	muestra, f.	MWEHSS*-trah*
sandwich	sandwich, m.	SAHN*-weech*
sane	sano de mente	SAH*-noh deh* MEHN*-teh*
satin	raso, m.	RRAH*-soh*
satisfactory	satisfactorio	*sah-teess-fahk-*TOH*-ryoh*
satisfied (contented)	satisfecho	*sah-teess-*FEH*-choh*
satisfy, to	satisfacer	*sah-teess-fah-*SEHR
saucer	platillo, m.	*plah-*TEE*-yoh*
sausage	salchicha, f.	*sahl-*CHEE*-chah*
save (rescue), to	salvar	*sahl-*BAHR
save (store up), to	ahorrar	*ah-oh-*RRAHR
savings (money)	ahorros, m. pl.	*ah-*OH*-rrohss*
saw (tool)	sierra, f.	SYEH*-rrah*
say, to	decir	*deh-*SEER
scarce	escaso	*ehss-*KAH*-soh*
scare (frighten), to	espantar	*ehss-pahn-*TAHR
scarf (neck cloth)	bufanda, f.	*boo-*FAHN*-dah*
scarlet (adj.)	escarlata	*ehss-kahr-*LAH*-tah*
scarlet fever	escarlata, f.	*ehss-kahr-*LAH*-tah*
scene (dramatic unit)	cuadro, m.	KWAH*-throh*
scent (odor)	olor, m.	*oh-*LOHR
schedule (time-table)	horario, m.	*oh-*RAH*-ryoh*
school	escuela, f.	*ehss-*KWEH*-lah*
schooling (instruction)	instrucción, f.	*een-strook-*SYOHN

ENGLISH	SPANISH	PRONUNCIATION
science	ciencia, f.	SYEHN-*syah*
scientific	científico	*syehn*-TEE-*fee-koh*
scissors	tijeras, f. pl.	*tee*-HEH-*rahss*
Scotch (adj.)	escocés	*ehss-koh*-SEHSS
scrambled eggs	huevos revueltos, m. pl.	WEH-*bohss* rreh-BWEHL-*tohss*
scrap (fragment)	pedacito, m.	*peh-thah*-SEE-*toh*
scratch, to	rascar	*rrahss*-KAHR
screen (partition)	mampara, f.	*mahm*-PAH-*rah*
screw (threaded nail)	tornillo, m.	*tohr*-NEE-*yoh*
screw driver	destornillador, m.	*dehss-tohr-nee-yah*-THOHR
scrub, to	fregar	*freh*-GAHR
sculptor	escultor, m.	*ehss-kool*-TOHR
sea	mar, m., f.	MAHR
search (hunt)	búsqueda, f.	BOOSS-*keh-thah*
season (of year)	estación, f.	*ehss-tah*-SYOHN
second (adj.)	segundo	*seh*-GOON-*doh*
second (time unit)	segundo, m.	*seh*-GOON-*doh*
secret (n.)	secreto, m.	*seh*-KREH-*toh*
secretary (stenographer)	secretaria, f.	*seh-kreh*-TAH-*ryah*
secure (safe)	seguro	*seh*-GOO-*roh*
security (safety)	seguridad, f.	*seh-goo-ree*-THAHTH
seldom	rara vez	RRAH-*rah* BEHSS
select, to	seleccionar	*seh-lehk-syoh*-NAHR
selection (things chosen)	selección, f.	*seh-lehk*-SYOHN
sell, to	vender	*behn*-DEHR
send, to	enviar	*ehn*-BYAHR
sense (intelligence)	entendimiento, m.	*ehn-tehn-dee*-MYEHN-*toh*
sense (signification)	significado, m.	*seeg-nee-fee*-KAH-*thoh*

ENGLISH	SPANISH	PRONUNCIATION
sensible (reasonable)	sensato	*sehn*-SAH-*toh*
sensitive (susceptible)	sensible	*sehn*-SEE-*bleh*
sentence	frase, f.	FRAH-*seh*
separate	separado	*seh-pah*-RAH-*thoh*
separate (disconnect), to	separar	*seh-pah*-RAHR
series	serie, f.	SEH-*ryeh*
serious	serio	SEH-*ryoh*
servant (in a household)	sirviente, m.	*seer*-BYEHN-*teh*
serve, to	servir	*sehr*-BEER
service	servicio, m.	*sehr*-BEE-*syoh*
set (put), to	poner	*poh*-NEHR
settle (agree on), to	convenir	*kohn-beh*-NEER
several (a few, adj.)	varios	BAH-*ryohss*
severe (strict)	severo	*seh*-VEH-*roh*
sew, to	coser	*koh*-SEHR
sewing machine	máquina de coser, f.	MAH-*kee-nah* deh *koh*-SEHR
sex	sexo, m.	SEHK-*soh*
shade (window blind)	cortina, f.	*kohr*-TEE-*nah*
shadow	sombra, f.	SOHM-*brah*
shake, to	sacudir	*sah-koo*-THEER
shallow	poco profundo	POH-*koh* proh-FOON-*doh*
shame	vergüenza, f.	*behr*-GWEHN-*sah*
shape (contour)	forma, f.	FOHR-*mah*
share (part)	porción, f.	*pohr*-SYOHN
share, to	compartir	*kohm-pahr*-TEER
sharp	afilado	*ah-fee*-LAH-*thoh*
shave (oneself), to	afeitarse	*ah-fey*-TAHR-*seh*
shaver, electric	afeitadora eléctrica, f.	*ah-fey-tah*-THOH-*rah-eh*-LEHK-*tree-kah*

ENGLISH	SPANISH	PRONUNCIATION
shaving cream	crema de afeitar, f.	KREH-*mah deh ah-fey*-TAHR
she	ella	EH-*yah*
sheet (bedding)	sábana, f.	SAH-*bah-nah*
sheet (of paper)	hoja, f.	OH-*hah*
shelf	anaquel, m.	ah-nah-KEHL
shell (covering)	cáscara, f.	KAHSS-*kah-rah*
shine (gleam), to	brillar	bree-YAHR
shine (polish), to	dar brillo	DAHR BREE-*yoh*
ship	barco, m.	BAHR-*koh*
ship (send goods), to	despachar	dehss-pah-CHAHR
shipping agent	expedidor, m.	ehss-peh-thee-THOHR
shirt	camisa, f.	kah-MEE-*sah*
shoe (footwear)	zapato, m.	sah-PAH-*toh*
shoemaker	zapatero, m.	sah-pah-TEH-*roh*
shop (store)	tienda, f.	TYEHN-*dah*
shop, to	ir de compras	EER *deh* KOHM-*prahss*
shore	ribera, f.	rree-BEH-*rah*
short (brief)	corto	KOHR-*toh*
shoulder	hombro, m.	OHM-*broh*
show (exhibit)	exhibición, f.	ehg-see-bee-SYOHN
show, to	mostrar	mohss-TRAHR
shower (bath)	ducha, f.	DOO-*chah*
shower (rainfall)	aguacero, m.	ah-gwah-SEH-*roh*
shrill	chillón	chee-YOHN
shrimp	camarón, m.	kah-mah-ROHN
shudder, to	estremecerse	ehss-treh-meh-SEPR-*seh*
shut (make close), to	cerrar	seh-RRAHR
shy (bashful)	tímido	TEE-*mee-thoh*
sick (ailing)	enfermo	ehn-FEHR-*moh*
sickness	enfermedad, f.	ehn-fehr-meh-THAHTH

ENGLISH	SPANISH	PRONUNCIATION
side	lado, m.	LAH-*thoh*
sidewalk	acera, f.	*ah*-SEH-*rah*
sigh, to	suspirar	*sooss-pee*-RAHR
sight (eyesight)	vista, f.	BEESS-*tah*
sight (spectacle)	espectáculo, m.	*ehss-pehk*-TAH-*koo-loh*
sign (indication)	signo, m.	SEEG-*noh*
sign (endorse), to	firmar	*feer*-MAHR
signature (name)	firma, f.	FEER-*mah*
silk (n.)	seda, f.	SEH-*thah*
silly	tonto	TOHN-*toh*
silver (metal, n.)	plata, f.	PLAH-*tah*
similar	similar	*see-mee*-LAHR
similarity	semejanza, f.	*seh-meh*-HAHN-*sah*
simple (uninvolved)	simple	SEEM-*pleh*
since (after, prep.)	desde	DEHZ-*deh*
since (because conj.)	puesto que	PWWHSS-*toh keh*
since (from then to now, adv.)	desde entonces	DEHZ-*deh ehn*-TOHN-*sehss*
sing, to	cantar	*kahn*-TAHR
single (unmarried)	soltero	*sohl*-TEH-*roh*
singular	singular	*seen-goo*-LAHR
sink	fregadero, m.	*freh-gah*-THEH-*roh*
sir	señor, m.	*seh*-NYOHR
sister (n.)	hermana, f.	*ehr*-MAH-*nah*
sister-in-law	cuñada, f.	*koo*-NYAH-*thah*
sit (be sitting), to	estar sentado	*ehss*-TAHR *sehn*-TAH-*thoh*
sit down, to	sentarse	*sehn*-TAHR-*seh*
size (of hats)	medida, f.	*meh*-THEE-*thah*
size (of shoes, gloves)	número, m.	NOO-*meh-roh*
size (of suits, dresses, coats)	talla, f.	TAH-*yah*
skate, ice	patín de hielo, m	*pah*-TEEN *deh* YEH-*loh*

ENGLISH	SPANISH	PRONUNCIATION
ski, to	esquiar	*ehss-kee-*AHR
skin (animal hide)	piel, f.	PYEHL
skin (human skin)	cutis, m.	KOO-*teess*
skirt (garment)	falda, f.	FAHL-*dah*
sky	cielo, m.	SYEH-*loh*
sled	trineo, m.	*tree-*NEH-*oh*
sleep	sueño, m.	SWEH-*nyoh*
sleep, to	dormir	*dohr-*MEER
sleeve	manga, f.	MAHN-*gah*
slide, to	deslizarse	*dehss-lee-*SAHR-*seh*
slipper	zapatilla, f.	*sah-pah-*TEE-*yah*
slippery	resbaloso	*rrehss-bah-*LOH-*soh*
slow (not fast)	lento	LEHN-*toh*
smallpox	viruela, f.	*bee-*RWEH-*lah*
smell (odor)	olor, m.	*oh-*LOHR
smell (perceive odor), to	oler	*oh-*LEHR
smile	sonrisa, f.	*sohn-*REE-*sah*
smile, to	sonreírse	*sohn-reh-*EER-*seh*
smoke	humo, m.	OO-*moh*
smoke, to	fumar	*foo-*MAHR
smooth	liso	LEE-*soh*
snail	caracol, m.	*kah-rah-*KOHL
sneeze, to	estornudar	*ehss-tohr-noo-*THAHR
snow	nieve, f.	NYEH-*beh*
so (in order that, conj.)	para que	*pah-rah keh*
so (therefore, adv.)	por lo tanto	*pohr loh* TAHN-*toh*
so (to such a degree, adv.)	tan	*tahn*
soap	jabón, m.	*hah-*BOHN
social (societal)	social	*soh-*SYAHL
society (association)	sociedad, f.	*soh-syeh-*THAHTH

ENGLISH	SPANISH	PRONUNCIATION
sock (garment)	calcentín, m.	*kahl-seh-*TEEN
soft	blando	BLAHN-*doh*
soil (make dirty), to	ensuciar	*ehn-soo-*SYAHR
sole (of shoe)	suela, f.	SWEH-*lah*
solemn (grave)	solemne	*soh-*LEHM-*neh*
solution (solving)	solución, f.	*soh-loo-*SYOHN
solve, to	resolver	*rreh-sohl-*BEHR
some (a few, adj.)	algunos	*ahl-*GOO-*nohss*
some (unspecified, adj.)	algún, alguna	*ahl-*GOON, *ahl-*GOO-*nah*
some (a quantity, pron.)	algunos	*ahl-*GOO-*nohss*
some (a quantity of, adj.)	algo de	AHL-*goh deh*
somebody	alguien	AHL-*ghyehn*
somehow	de algún modo	*deh ahl-*GOON MOH-*thoh*
someone	alguien	AHL-*ghyehn*
something	algo	AHL-*goh*
sometimes	algunas veces	*ahl-*GOO-*nahss* BEH-*sehss*
son	hijo, m.	EE-*hoh*
song	canción, f.	*kahn-*SYOHN
son-in-law	yerno, m.	YEHR-*noh*
soon (shortly)	pronto	PROHN-*toh*
sore throat	mal de garganta, m.	MAHL *deh gahr-*GAHN-*tah*
sorrow (sadness)	pesar, m.	*peh-*SAHR
sorry, to be	sentir	*sehn-*TEER
sort	clase, f.	KLAH-*seh*
sound (healthy)	sano	SAH-*noh*
sound (noise)	sonido, m.	*soh-*NEE-*thoh*
soup	sopa, f.	SOH-*pah*
sour (tart)	agrio	AH-*gryoh*
south (n.)	sur, m.	SOOR
southern	meridional	*meh-ree-thyoh-*NAHL

ENGLISH	SPANISH	PRONUNCIATION
space (area)	espacio, m.	*ehss*-PAH-*syoh*
Spanish (adj.)	español	*ehss-pah*-NYOHL
spark	chispa, f.	CHEES-*pah*
speak (talk), to	hablar	*ah*-BLAHR
special	especial	*ehss-peh*-SYAHL
spectacles (glasses)	anteojos, m. pl.	*ahn-teh*-OH-*hohss*
speed (rapidity)	velocidad, f.	*beh-loh-see-*THAHTH
spell, to	deletrear	*deh-leh-treh-*AHR
spirit	espíritu, m.	*ehss-*PEE-*ree-too*
spit, to	escupir	*ehss-koo-*PEER
spoon (tablespoon)	cuchara, f.	*koo-*CHAH-*rah*
spoon (teaspoon)	cucharita, f.	*koo-chah-*REE-*tah*
sport (game)	deporte, m.	*deh-*POHR-*teh*
spot (place)	sitio, m.	SEE-*tyoh*
spot (stain)	mancha, f.	MAHN-*chah*
sprain, to	torcer	*tohr-*SEHR
square (adj.)	cuadrado	*kwah-*THRAH-*thoh*
square (plaza)	plaza, f.	PLAH-*sah*
squirrel	ardilla, f.	*ahr-*THEE-*yah*
staff (personnel)	personal, m.	*pehr-soh-*NAHL
stage (dais)	tablado, m.	*tah-*BLAH-*thoh*
stain	mancha, f.	MAHN-*chah*
stairway	escalera, f.	*ehss-kah-leh-*LEH-*rah*
stale	añejo	*ah-*NYEH-*hoh*
stall (stop going), to	pararse	*pah-*RAHR-*seh*
stamp, postage	sello, m.	SEH-*yoh*
stand (bear), to	soportar	*soh-pohr-*TAHR
stand (be upright), to	estar de pie	*ehss-*TAHR *deh* PYEH
stand up, to	ponerse de pie	*poh-*NEHR-*seh deh* PYEH
star	estrella, f.	*ehss-*TREH-*yah*
start (beginning)	comienzo, m.	*koh-*MYEHN-*soh*
start (initiate), to	comenzar	*koh-mehn-*SAHR
starve (die of hunger), to	morirse de hambre	*moh-*REER-*seh deh* AHM-*breh*

ENGLISH	SPANISH	PRONUNCIATION
state (condition)	estado, m.	*ehss*-TAH-*thoh*
station, railroad	estación, f.	*ehss-tah-*SYOHN
stationery (writing paper)	papelería, f.	*pah-peh-leh-*REE-*ah*
statue	estatua, f.	*ehss*-TAH-*too-ah*
stay (sojourn)	estada, f.	*ehss*-TAH-*thah*
stay (remain), to	permanecer	*pehr-mah-neh-*SEHR
steal, to	robar	*rroh-*BAHR
steam	vapor, m.	*bah-*POHR
steep (adj.)	empinado	*ehm-pee-*NAH-*thoh*
step (stair)	escalón, m.	*ehss-kah-*LOHN
step (stride)	paso, m.	PAH-*soh*
steward (attendant on ship)	camarero, m.	*kah-mah-*REH-*roh*
stick (small branch)	palo, m.	PAH-*loh*
stick (adhere), to	pegarse	*peh-*GAHR-*seh*
still (adv.)	aún	*ah-*OON
still (motionless, adj.)	inmóvil	*een-*MOH-*beel*
still (nevertheless, conj.)	no obstante	*noh ohb-*STAHN-*teh*
stocking	media, f.	MEH-*thyah*
stomach	estómago, m.	*ehss-*TOH-*mah-goh*
stone (piece of rock)	piedra, f.	PYEH-*thrah*
stop (halt)	parada, f.	*pah-*RAH-*thah*
stop (cease), to	dejar de	*deh-*HAHR *deh*
stop (come to a standstill), to	pararse	*pah-*RAHR-*seh*
store (shop)	tienda, f.	TYEHN-*dah*
storm	tormenta, f.	*tohr-*MEHN-*tah*
story (account)	cuento, m.	KWEHN-*toh*
story (floor)	piso, m.	PEE-*soh*
stove (for cooking)	estufa, f.	*ehss-*TOO-*fah*
strange (peculiar)	extraño	*ehss-*TRAH-*nyoh*
stranger (unknown person)	desconocido, m.	*dehss-koh-noh-*SEE-*thoh*

ENGLISH	SPANISH	PRONUNCIATION
strawberry	fresa, f.	FREH-*sah*
stream (rivulet)	arroyo, m.	*ah*-RROH-*yoh*
street	calle, f.	KAH-*yeh*
strength	fuerza, f.	FWEHR-*sah*
stretch (draw out), to	estirar	*ehss-tee*-RAHR
string (cord)	cordel, m.	*kohr*-DEHL
strip (band)	tira, f.	TEE-*rah*
strip (denude), to	desnudar	*dehss-noo*-THAHR
stroll, to	pasearse	*pah-seh*-AHR-*seh*
strong	fuerte	FWEHR-*teh*
structure (thing built)	construcción, f.	*kohn-strook*-SYOHN
stubborn	terco	TEHR-*koh*
student	estudiante, m., f.	*ehss-too*-THYAHN-*teh*
study (active learning)	estudio, m.	*ehss*-TOO-*thyoh*
study, to	estudiar	*ehss-too*-THYAHR
stupid	estúpido	*ehss*-TOO-*pee-thoh*
style (manner)	estilo, m.	*ehss*-TEE-*loh*
subject (topic)	tema, m.	TEH-*mah*
subscription (for periodicals, etc.)	subscripción, f.	*soob-skreep*-SYOHN
subsequent	subsecuente	*soob-seh*-KWEHN-*teh*
substitute (thing replacing another)	substituto, m.	*soob-stee*-TOO-*toh*
substitute (put in place of), to	substituir	*soob-stee-too*-EER
subtract, to	restar	*rrehss*-TAHR
subway (underground railway)	subterráneo, m.	*soob-teh*-RRAH-*neh-oh*
succeed (attain goal), to	tener éxito	*teh*-NEHR EHK-*see-toh*
success (attainment)	éxito, m.	EHK-*see-toh*
successful	próspero	PROHSS-*peh-roh*

ENGLISH	SPANISH	PRONUNCIACION
such (of that kind, adj.)	tal	*tahl*
sudden (unexpected)	imprevisto	*eem-preh-*BEESS-*toh*
sue (bring action against), to	demandar	*deh-mahn-*DAHR
suede (n.)	gamuza, f.	*gah-*MOO-*sah*
suffer (undergo), to	sufrir	SOO-FREER
sugar	azúcar, m.	*ah-*SOO-*kahr*
suggestion (proposal)	sugestión, f.	*soo-hehss-*TYOHN
suit (lawsuit)	pleito, m.	PLEH-*ee-toh*
suit, man's	traje, m.	TRAH-*heh*
suit, woman's	traje, m.	TRAH-*heh*
summer (n.)	verano, m.	*beh-*RAH-*noh*
summit	cumbre, f.	KOOM-*breh*
sun	sol, m.	SOHL
sunburn	quemadura de sol, f.	*keh-mah-*THOO-*rah deh* SOHL
sunglasses	gafas contra el sol, f. pl.	GAH-*fahss* KOHN-*trah ehl* SOHL
sunlight	luz solar, f.	LOOSS *soh-*LAHR
sunny	asoleado	*ah-soh-leh-*AH-*thoh*
sunrise	salida del sol, f.	*sah-*LEE-*thah dehl* SOHL
sunset	puesta del sol, f.	PWEHSS-*tah dehl* SOHL
sunshine	luz del sol, f.	LOOSS *dehl* SOHL
superstition	superstición, f.	*soo-pehr-stee-*SYOHN
supply (provide), to	proveer	*proh-beh-*EHR
surgeon	cirujano, m.	*see-roo-*HAH-*noh*
surname	apellido, m.	*ah-peh-*YEE-*thoh*
surprise	sorpresa, f.	*sohr-*PREH-*sah*
surprise (astonish), to	sorprender	*sohr-prehn-*DEHR

ENGLISH	SPANISH	PRONUNCIATION
surroundings	alrededores, m. pl.	*ahl-reh-theh-*THOH-*rehss*
suspect (distrust), to	sospechar	*sohss-peh-*CHAHR
suspenders	tirantes, m. pl.	*tee-*RAHN-*tehss*
suspicion	sospecha, f.	*sohss-*PEH-*chah*
swallow, to	tragar	*trah-*GAHR
swear (curse), to	blasfemar	*blahss-feh-*MAHR
sweat	sudor, m.	*soo-*THOHR
sweater	suéter, m.	SWEH-*tehr*
Swedish (adj.)	sueco	SWEH-*koh*
sweep (clean), to	barrer	*bah-*RREHR
sweet (tasting)	dulce	DOOL-*seh*
sweetheart	novio, m.	NOH-*byoh*
swim, to	nadar	*nah-*THAHR
Swiss (adj.)	suizo	SWEE-*soh*
syllable	sílaba, f.	SEE-*lah-bah*
sympathy (compassion)	compasión, f.	*kohm-pah-*SYOHN
table (furniture)	mesa, f.	MEH-*sah*
tablecloth	mantel, m.	*mahn-*TEHL
tailor	sastre, m.	SAHSS-*treh*
take, to	tomar	*toh-*MAHR
talk (conversation)	conversación, f.	*kohn-behr-sah-*SYOHN
talk, to	hablar	*ah-*BLAHR
tall (of persons)	alto	AHL-*toh*
tall (of things)	alto	AHL-*toh*
tap (faucet)	grifo, m.	GREE-*foh*
tape recorder	grabador de cinta, m.	*grah-bah-*THOHR *deh* SEEN-*tah*
tariff (duty)	tarifa, f.	*tah-*REE-*fah*
taste (flavor)	sabor, m.	*sah-*BOHR
taste (sample), to	probar	*proh-*BAHR
tax (n.)	impuesto, m.	*eem-*PWEHSS-*toh*
taxi	taxímetro, m.	*tahk-*SEE-*meh-troh*

ENGLISH	SPANISH	PRONUNCIATION
tea	té, m.	TEH
teach, to	enseñar	*ehn-seh-NYAHR*
teacher	maestro, m.	*mah-EHSS-troh*
tear (rip), to	rasgar	*rrahz-GAHR*
tease, to	embromar	*ehm-broh-MAHR*
telegraph, to	telegrafiar	*teh-leh-grah-FYAHR*
telephone	teléfono, m.	*teh-LEH-foh-noh*
telephone, to	telefonear	*teh-leh-foh-neh-AHR*
television	televisión, f.	*teh-leh-bee-SYOHN*
tell (inform), to	decir	*deh-SEER*
temperature	temperatura, f.	*tehm-peh-rah-TOO-rah*
temporary	provisional	*proh-bee-syoh-NAHL*
tenant	inquilino, m.	*een-kee-LEE-noh*
tent	tienda de cam-paña, f.	TYEHN-*dah deh* kahm-PAH-*nyah*
term (duration)	plazo, m.	PLAH-*soh*
term (expression)	término, m.	TEHR-*mee-noh*
terms (conditions)	condiciones, f. pl.	*kohn-dee-SYOH-nehss*
terrible	terrible	*teh-RREE-bleh*
test (educ.)	examen, m.	*ehk-SAH-mehn*
testify, to	atestiguar	*ah-tehss-tee-GWAHR*
testimony	testimonio, m.	*tehss-tee-MOH-nyoh*
textile (n.)	tejido, m.	*teh-HEE-thoh*
than	que	*keh*
thank, to	dar gracias a	DAHR GRAH-*syahss-ah*
thankful	agradecido	*ah-grah-theh-SEE-thoh*
thanks (gratitude)	gracias, f. pl.	GRAH-*syahss*

ENGLISH	SPANISH	PRONUNCIATION
then (at that time)	entonces	*ehn*-TOHN-*sehss*
then (in that case)	en tal caso	*ehn tahl* KAH-*soh*
then (subsequently)	luego	LWEH-*goh*
there (at that place)	allá	*ah*-YAH
therefore	por lo tanto	*pohr loh* TAHN-*toh*
thick (not thin)	espeso	*ehss*-PEH-*soh*
thief	ladrón, m.	*lah*-THROHN
thin (not fat)	flaco	FLAH-*koh*
thin (not thick)	delgado	*dehl*-GAH-*thoh*
thing (material object)	cosa, f.	KOH-*sah*
think (reason), to	pensar	*pehn*-SAHR
thirst	sed, f.	SEHTH
thirsty	sediento	*seh*-THYEHN-*toh*
thorough (complete)	completo	*kohm*-PLEH-*toh*
thought (idea)	idea, f.	*ee*-THEH-*ah*
thread (sewing thread)	hilo, m.	EE-*loh*
threaten, to	amenazar	*ah-meh-nah*-SAHR
throat	garganta, f.	*gahr*-GAHN-*tah*
through (by means of, prep.)	por medio de	*pohr* MEH-*thyoh deh*
through (from end to end of, prep.)	a través de	*ah trah*-BEHSS *deh*
throw, to	tirar	*tee*-RAHR
thumb	pulgar, m.	*pool*-GAHR
thunder	trueno, m.	TRWEH-*noh*
ticket (entitling card)	billete, m.	*bee*-YEH-*teh*
tide, high	marea alta, f.	*mah*-REH-*ah* AHL-*tah*
tide, low	marea baja, f.	*mah*-REH-*ah* BAH-*hah*
tie (necktie)	corbata, f.	*kohr*-BAH-*tah*

ENGLISH	SPANISH	PRONUNCIATION
tie (fasten), to	amarrar	*ah-mah*-RRAHR
time (hour determined by clock)	hora, f.	OH-*rah*
time (interval)	tiempo, m.	TYEHM-*poh*
timetable	horario, m.	*oh*-RAH-*ryoh*
tiny	diminuto	*dee-mee*-NOO-*toh*
tip (gratuity)	propina, f.	*proh*-PEE-*nah*
tire	neumático, m.	*neh-oo*-MAH-*tee-koh*
tired	cansado	*kahn*-SAH-*thoh*
title (name)	título, m.	TEE-*too-loh*
to (indicating destination, prep.)	a; hasta	*ah;* AHSS-*tah*
to (indicating direction, prep.)	a	*ah*
to (in order to, prep.)	para	*pah-rah*
toast (bread)	tostada, f.	*tohss*-TAH-*thah*
tobacco	tabaco, m.	*tah*-BAH-*koh*
today	hoy	OY
toe	dedo del pie, m.	DEH-*thoh dehl* PYEH
together	juntos	HOON-*tohss*
toilet (water closet)	inodoro, m.	*een-oh*-THOH-*roh*
tomorrow	mañana	*mah*-NYAH-*nah*
tongue	lengua, f.	LEHN-*gwah*
tonight	esta noche	EHSS-*tah* NOH-*cheh*
too (also)	también	*tahm*-BYEHN
too (overly)	demasiado	*deh-mah*-SYAH-*thoh*
tooth	diente, m.	DYEHN-*teh*
toothache	dolor de diente, m.	*doh*-LOHR *deh* DYEHN-*teh*
toothbrush	cepillo de diente, m.	*seh*-PEE-*yoh deh* DYEHN-*teh*

ENGLISH	SPANISH	PRONUNCIATION
tooth paste	pasta dentífrica, f.	PAHSS-*tah dehn*-TEE-*free-kah*
top (summit)	cima, f.	SEE-*mah*
total (complete)	total	toh-TAHL
total (sum)	suma, f.	SOO-*mah*
touch, to	tocar	toh-KAHR
tour	jira, f.	HEE-*rah*
toward	hacia	AH-*syah*
towel, hand	toalla, f.	toh-AH-*yah*
town	pueblo, m.	PWEH-*bloh*
toy	juguete, m.	hoo-GHEH-*teh*
track (rails)	vía, f.	BEE-*ah*
trade mark	marca de fábrica, f.	MAHR-*kah deh* FAH-*bree-kah*
traffic (flow of vehicles)	tráfico, m.	TRAH-*fee-koh*
train, railroad	tren, m.	TREHN
training (instruction)	instrucción, f.	*een-strook*-SYOHN
transit (passage)	tránsito, m.	TRAHN-*see-toh*
transport, to	transportar	*trahnss-pohr*-TAHR
transportation (conveying)	transporte, m.	*trahnss*-POHR-*teh*
travel, to	viajar	*byah*-HAHR
traveler	viajero, m.	*byah*-HEH-*roh*
tray	bandeja, f.	*bahn*-DEH-*hah*
treat (behave toward), to	tratar	*trah*-TAHR
treatment (behavior toward)	manera de tratar, f.	*mah*-NEH-*rah deh* *trah*-TAHR
treatment (medical care)	tratamiento, m.	*trah-tah*-MYEHN-*toh*
tree	árbol, m.	AHR-*bohl*
trial (court proceeding)	proceso, m.	*proh*-SEH-*soh*

ENGLISH	SPANISH	PRONUNCIATION
trick (ruse)	engaño, m.	*ehn*-GAH-*nyoh*
trip (journey)	viaje, m.	BYAH-*heh*
trip (stumble), to	tropezar	*troh-peh*-SAHR
trolley (street car)	tranvía, m.	*trahn*-BEE-*ah*
trouble (distress)	aflicción, f.	*ah-fleek*-SYOHN
trouble (exertion)	pena, f.	PEH-*nah*
trousers	pantalones, m. pl.	*pahn-tah*-LOH-*nehss*
truck (automobile)	camión, m.	*kah*-MYOHN
true	verdadero	*behr-thah*-THEH-*roh*
trunk (baggage)	baúl, m.	*bah*-OOL
trust (confidence)	confianza, f.	*kohn*-FYAHN-*sah*
trust (rely on), to	verdad, f.	*behr*-THAHTH
try (attempt), to	intentar	*een-tehn*-TAHR
tub (bathtub)	bañera, f.	*bah*-NYEH-*rah*
tuition (school fee)	derechos de enseñanza, m. pl.	*deh*-REH-*chohss deh ehn-seh*-NYAHN-*sah*
tumbler (glass)	vaso, m.	BAH-*soh*
tune (melody)	tonada, f.	*toh*-NAH-*thah*
turkey	pavo, m.	PAH-*boh*
turn (face about), to	volverse	*bohl*-BEHR-*seh*
turn (make rotate), to	hacer girar	*ah*-SEHR *hee*-RAHR
tweed (cloth)	mezclilla de lana, f.	*mehss*-KLEE-*yah deh* LAH-*nah*
twice	dos veces	DOHSS BEH-*sehss*
twilight	crepúsculo, m.	*kreh*-POOSS-*koo-loh*
twin (n.)	gemelo, m.	*heh*-MEH-*loh*
twist (wind), to	torcer	*tohr*-SEHR
type (kind)	tipo, m.	TEE-*poh*
type (typewrite), to	escribir en máquina	*ehss-kree*-BEER *ehn* MAH-*kee-nah*

ENGLISH	SPANISH	PRONUNCIATION
typewriter	máquina de escribir, f.	MAH-*kee-nah* deh *ehss-kree-*BEER
typhoid fever	fiebre tifoidea, f.	FYEH-*breh tee-foy-*THEH-*ah*
ugly	feo	FEH-*oh*
ulcer	úlcera, f.	OOL-*seh-rah*
umbrella	paraguas, m.	*pah-*RAH-*gwahss*
uncle	tío, m.	TEE-*oh*
under (prep.)	bajo	BAH-*hoh*
underground (below-ground, adj.)	subterráneo	*soob-teh-*RRAH-*neh-oh*
underneath (prep.)	debajo de	*deh-*BAH-*hoh deh*
understand, to	comprender	*kohm-prehn-*DEHR
underwear	ropa interior, f.	RROH-*pah een-teh-*RYOHR
uneasy (anxious)	inquieto	*een-*KYEH-*toh*
unemployed	desocupado	*deh-soh-koo-*PAH-*thoh*
unemployment	desempleo, m.	*deh-sehm-*PLEH-*oh*
unequal	desigual	*deh-see-*GWAHL
unexpected (adj.)	inesperado	*een-ehss-peh-*RAH-*thoh*
unfortunate	desventurado	*dehss-behn-too-*RAH-*thoh*
unhappy (sorrowful)	infeliz	*een-feh-*LEESS
United Nations	Naciones Unidas f. pl.	*nah-*SYOH-*nehss oo-*NEE-*thahss*
university	universidad, f.	*oo-nee-behr-see-*THAHTH
unjust (inequitable)	injusto	*een-*HOOSS-*toh*
unknown	desconocido	*dehss-koh-noh-*SEE-*thoh*
unless (conj.)	a menos que	*ah* MEH-*nohss keh*
unlucky	desgraciado	*dehz-grah-*SYAH-*thoh*

ENGLISH	SPANISH	PRONUNCIATION
unnecessary	innecesario	*een-neh-seh-*SAH-*ryoh*
unpaid (due)	no pagado	*noh pah-*GAH-*thoh*
unpleasant	desagradable	*deh-sah-grah-*THAH-*bleh*
until (before, prep.)	antes de	AHN-*tehss deh*
until (conj.)	hasta que	AHSS-*tah keh*
until (up to the time of, prep.)	hasta	AHSS-*tah*
up (adv.)	arriba	*ah-*RREE-*bah*
upon	sobre	SOH-*breh*
upstairs (at upper story, adv.)	arriba	*ah-*RREE-*bah*
upstairs (to upper story, adv.)	hacia arriba	AH-*syah ah-*RREE-*bah*
urgent	urgente	*oor-*HEHN-*teh*
use (utilization)	uso, m.	OO-*soh*
use (utilize), to	usar	*oo-*SAHR
useful	útil	OO-*teel*
useless	inútil	*een-*OO-*teel*
usual	usual	*oo-*SWAHL
utility (usefulness)	utilidad, f.	*oo-tee-lee-*THAHTH
vacant (untenanted)	vacante	*bah-*KAHN-*teh*
vacation (work holidays)	vacaciones, f. pl.	*bah-kah-*SYOH-*nehss*
vaccination	vacunación, f.	*bah-koo-nah-*SYOHN
vain (futile)	vano	BAH-*noh*
valuable	de valor	*deh bah-*LOHR
value	valor, m.	*bah-*LOHR
value (prize), to	valuar	*bah-*LWAHR
variety (assortment)	surtido, m.	*soor-*TEE-*thoh*
various (different)	varios	BAH-*ryohss*
veal	carne de ternera, f.	KAHR-*neh deh tehr-*NEH-*rah*
veal chop	chuleta de ternera, f.	*choo-*LEH-*tah deh tehr-*NEH-*rah*

ENGLISH	SPANISH	PRONUNCIATION
vegetable	legumbre, f.	*leh*-GOOM-*breh*
vehicle (conveyance)	vehículo, m.	*beh*-EE-*koo-loh*
venture (dare), to	atreverse	*ah-treh*-BEHR-*seh*
vertical (adj.)	vertical	*behr-tee*-KAHL
very (extremely)	muy	MWEE
vessel (ship)	barco, m.	BAHR-*koh*
vest	chaleco, m.	*chah*-LEH-*koh*
vicinity	vecindad, f.	*beh-seen*-DAHTH
victorious	victorioso	*beek-toh*-RYOH-*soh*
victory	victoria, f.	*beek*-TOH-*ryah*
Viennese (adj.)	vienés	*byeh*-NEHSS
view (opinion)	parecer, m.	*pah-reh*-SEHR
view (scene)	vista, f.	BEESS-*tah*
village	aldea, f.	*ahl*-DEH-*ah*
vine (grapevine)	vid, f.	BEETH
vinegar	vinagre, m.	*bee*-NAH-*greh*
visible	visible	*bee*-SEE-*bleh*
vision (eyesight)	vista, f.	BEESS-*tah*
visit (social call)	visita, f.	*bee*-SEE-*tah*
visit (call on), to	visitar	*bee-see*-TAHR
visitor	visita, f.	*bee*-SEE-*tah*
vital (essential)	vital	*bee*-TAHL
voice	voz, f.	BOHSS
volume (book)	volumen, m.	*boh*-LOO-*mehn*
vomit, to	vomitar	*boh-mee*-TAHR
vote, to	votar	*boh*-TAHR
vow	voto, m.	BOH-*toh*
voyage	viaje por mar, m.	BYAH-*heh pohr* MAHR
vulgar (ill-bred)	vulgar	*bool*-GAHR
wages	salario, m.	*sah*-LAH-*ryoh*
waist	cintura, f.	*seen*-TOO-*rah*
waiter	camarero, m.	*kah-mah*-REH-*roh*
wait for, to	esperar	*ehss-peh*-RAHR
wake (make awaken), to	despertar	*dehss-pehr*-TAHR
wake (rouse oneself), to	despertarse	*dehss-pehr*-TAHR-*seh*

ENGLISH	SPANISH	PRONUNCIATION
walk (stroll)	paseo, m.	*pah-*SEH*-oh*
walk, to	andar	*ahn-*DAHR
wall (inside)	pared, f.	*pah-*REHTH
wall (outside)	pared, f.	*pah-*REHTH
wander, to	vagar	*bah-*GAHR
want (desire), to	querer	*keh-*REHR
war	guerra, f.	GHEH*-rrah*
wardrobe (apparel)	vestuario, m.	*behss-*TWAH*-ryoh*
warm	caliente	*kah-*YEHN*-teh*
warm, to	calentar	*kah-lehn-*TAHR
warn, to	advertir	*ahd-behr-*TEER
wash (cleanse), to	lavar	*lah-*BAHR
wash (cleanse oneself), to	lavarse	*lah-*BAHR*-seh*
waste, to	derrochar	*deh-rroh-*CHAHR
watch (timepiece)	reloj, m.	*rreh-*LOH
watch (guard), to	vigilar	*bee-hee-*LAHR
watch (observe), to	observar	*ohb-sehr-*BAHR
water	agua, m.	AH*-gwah*
waterproof	impermeable	*eem-pehr-meh-*AH*-bleh*
way (route)	ruta, f.	RROO*-tah*
we	nosotros	*noh-*SOH*-trohss*
weak	débil	DEH*-beel*
wear (have on), to	llevar	*yeh-*BAHR
weather	tiempo, m.	TYEHM*-poh*
week	semana, f.	*seh-*MAH*-nah*
weekend (n.)	fin de semana, m.	FEEN *deh seh-*MAH*-nah*
weekly (adj.)	semanal	*seh-mah-*NAHL
weep, to	llorar	*yoh-*RAHR
weigh, to	pesar	*peh-*SAHR
weight (scale weight)	peso, m.	PEH*-soh*
welcome (n.)	bienvenida, f.	*byehn-beh-*NEE*-thah*

ENGLISH	SPANISH	PRONUNCIATION
welcome (receive hospitably), to	dar la bienvenida a	DAHR *lah byehn-beh-*NEE-*thah ah*
well (in health, adj.)	sano	SAH-*noh*
well (water pit, n.)	pozo, m.	POH-*soh*
west (n.)	oeste, m.	oh-EHSS-*teh*
western	occidental	*ohk-see-thehn-*TAHL
wet	mojado	*moh-*HAH-*thoh*
what (interrog. adj.)	qué	*keh*
what (interrog. pron.)	qué	*keh*
what (rel. pron.)	lo que	*loh keh*
wheel	rueda, f.	RWEH-*thah*
when (any time that, conj.)	cuando	KWAHN-*toh*
when (at the time that, conj.)	mientras (que)	MYEHN-*trahss (keh)*
when (at what time, adv.)	cuándo	KWAHN-*doh*
where (in, at the place that, conj.)	donde	DOHN-*deh*
where (in, at what place, adv.)	dónde	DOHN-*deh*
where (to what place, adv.)	adónde	*ah-*THOHN-*deh*
whether (either, conj.)	sea que . . . o que	SEH-*ah keh . . . oh keh*
whether (if, conj.)	si	*see*
while (during the time that, conj.)	mientras (que)	MYEHN-*trahss (keh)*
whisper (utter softly), to	cuchichear	*koo-chee-cheh-*AHR
whistle, to	silbar	*seel-*BAHR
white (adj.)	blanco	BLAHN-*koh*

ENGLISH	SPANISH	PRONUNCIATION
who (interrog. pron.)	quién	KYEHN
whole (entire, adj.)	entero	*ehn*-TEH-*roh*
whooping cough	tos ferina, f.	TOHSS *feh*-REE-*nah*
why	por qué	*pohr* KEH
wide (not narrow)	ancho	AHN-*choh*
widow	viuda, f.	BYOO-*thah*
widower	viudo, m.	BYOO-*thoh*
width	anchura, f.	*ahn*-CHOO-*rah*
wife	esposa, f.	*ehss*-POH-*sah*
will (power of choice)	voluntad, f.	*boh-loon*-TAHTH
win (be victor in), to	vencer	*behn*-SEHR
wind	viento, m.	BYEHN-*toh*
window	ventana, f.	*behn*-TAH-*nah*
windshield	parabrisa, m.	*pah-rah*-BREE-*sah*
wine (beverage)	vino, m.	BEE-*noh*
winter (n.)	invierno, m.	*een*-BYEHR-*noh*
wisdom	sabiduría, f.	*sah-bee-thoo-*REE-*ah*
wise	sabio	SAH-*byoh*
wish	deseo, m.	*deh*-SEH-*oh*
wish for, to	desear	*deh-seh*-AHR
wit (humor)	sal, f.	SAHL
with (prep.)	con	*kohn*
without (lacking, prep.)	sin	*seen*
woman	mujer, f.	*moo*-HEHR
wonder (ask oneself), to	preguntarse	*preh-goon*-TAHR-*seh*
wood (lumber)	madera, f.	*mah*-THEH-*rah*
wool (cloth)	paño, m.	PAH-*nyoh*
word	palabra, f.	*pah*-LAH-*brah*
work (labor)	trabajo, m.	*trah*-BAH-*hoh*
work (labor), to	trabajar	*trah-bah*-HAHR

ENGLISH	SPANISH	PRONUNCIATION
worker	trabajador, m.	*trah-bah-hah-*THOHR
world	mundo, m.	MOON-*doh*
worry (feel anxious), to	inquietarse	*een-kyeh-*TAHR-*seh*
worse (adj.)	peor	*peh-*OHR
worse (adv.)	peor	*peh-*OHR
worship, to (rel.)	adorar	*ah-thoh-*RAHR
worst (adv.)	(lo) peor	*(loh) peh-*OHR
worst (n.)	(lo) peor, n.	*(loh) peh-*OHR
worthless (value-less)	sin valor	*seen bah-*LOHR
worthy (deserving)	digno	DEEG-*noh*
wound (injury)	herida, f.	*eh-*REE-*thah*
wrist	muñeca, f.	*moo-*NYEH-*kah*
write, to	escribir	*ehss-kree-*BEER
writer (author)	escritor, m.	*ehss-kree-*TOHR
wrong (amiss, adv.)	mal	MAHL
wrong (erroneous, adj.)	incorrecto	*een-koh-*RREHK-*toh*
wrong (injustice)	injusticia, f.	*een-hooss-*TEE-*syah*
wrong (unjust, adj.)	injusto	*een-*HOOSS-*toh*
X-ray (examine), to	radiografiar	*rrah-thyoh-grah-*FYAHR
year	año, m.	AH-*nyoh*
yearly (adj.)	anual	*ah-*NWAHL
yellow (adj.)	amarillo	*ah-mah-*REE-*yoh*
yes	sí	SEE
yesterday	ayer	*ah-*YEHR
yet (now, until now, adv.)	todavía	*toh-thah-*BEE-*ah*
young (adj.)	joven	HOH-*behn*
youth (period of life)	juventud, f.	*hoo-behn-*TOOTH
youthful	joven	HOH-*behn*
zero (n.)	cero, m.	SEH-*roh*

ENGLISH	SPANISH	PRONUNCIATION

CARDINAL NUMBERS

ENGLISH	SPANISH	PRONUNCIATION
one	uno	OO-*noh*
two	dos	DOHSS
three	tres	TREHSS
four	cuatro	KWAH-*troh*
five	cinco	SEEN-*koh*
six	seis	SEHSS
seven	siete	SYEH-*teh*
eight	ocho	OH-*choh*
nine	nueve	NWEH-*beh*
ten	diez	DYEHSS
eleven	once	OHN-*seh*
twelve	doce	DOH-*seh*
thirteen	trece	TREH-*seh*
fourteen	catorce	*kah*-TOHR-*seh*
fifteen	quince	KEEN-*seh*
sixteen	dieciséis	*dyeh-see*-SEHSS
seventeen	diecisiete	*dyeh-see*-SYEH-*teh*
eighteen	dieciocho	*dyeh-see*-OH-*choh*
nineteen	diecinueve	*dyeh-see*-NWEH-*beh*
twenty	veinte	BEH-*een-teh*
twenty-one	veintiuno	*beh-een-tee*-OO-*noh*
twenty-two	veintidós	*beh-een-tee*-THOHSS
thirty	treinta	TREH-*een-tah*
forty	cuarenta	*kwah*-REHN-*tah*
fifty	cincuenta	*seen*-KWEHN-*tah*
sixty	sesenta	*seh*-SEHN-*tah*
seventy	setenta	*seh*-TEHN-*tah*
eighty	ochenta	*oh*-CHEHN-*tah*
ninety	noventa	*noh*-BEHN-*tah*
one hundred	cien	SYEHN
one hundred one	ciento uno	SYEHN-*toh* OO-*noh*

ENGLISH	SPANISH	PRONUNCIATION
two hundred	doscientos	*dohss-*SYEHN-*tohss*
two hundred one	doscientos uno	*dohss-*SYEHN-*tohss* OO-*noh*
one thousand	mil	MEEL
one thousand one	mil uno	MEEL OO-*noh*
two thousand	dos mil	DOHSS MEEL
two thousand one	dos mil uno	DOHSS MEEL OO-*noh*
one million	un millón	*oon mee-*YOHN
one billion	mil millones	MEEL *mee-*YOH-*nehss*

ORDINAL NUMBERS

first	primero	*pree-*MEH-*roh*
second	segundo	*seh-*GOON-*doh*
third	tercero	*tehr-*SEH-*roh*
fourth	cuarto	KWAHR-*toh*
fifth	quinto	KEEN-*toh*
sixth	sexto	SEHSS-*toh*
seventh	séptimo	SEHP-*tee-moh*
eighth	octavo	*ohk-*TAH-*boh*
ninth	noveno	*noh-*BEH-*noh*
tenth	décimo	DEH-*see-moh*
eleventh	undécimo	*oon-*DEH-*see-moh*
twelfth	duodécimo	*doo-oh-*THEH-*see-moh*

DAYS OF THE WEEK

Sunday	domingo, m.	*doh-*MEEN *goh*
Monday	lunes, m.	LOO-*nehss*
Tuesday	martes, m.	MAHR-*tehss*
Wednesday	miércoles, m.	MYEHR-*koh-lehss*
Thursday	jueves, m.	HWEH-*behss*
Friday	viernes, m.	BYEHR-*nehss*
Saturday	sábado, m.	SAH-*bah-thoh*

ENGLISH	SPANISH	PRONUNCIATION

MONTHS OF THE YEAR

ENGLISH	SPANISH	PRONUNCIATION
January	enero, m.	*eh-*NEH*-roh*
February	febrero, m.	*feh-*BREH*-roh*
March	marzo, m.	MAHR*-soh*
April	abril, m.	*ah-*BREEL
May	mayo, m.	MAH*-yoh*
June	junio, m.	HOO*-nyoh*
July	julio, m.	HOO*-lyoh*
August	agosto, m.	*ah-*GOHSS*-toh*
September	septiembre, m.	*seh-*TYEHM*-breh*
October	octubre, m.	*ohk-*TOO*-breh*
November	noviembre, m.	*noh-*BYEHM*-breh*
December	diciembre, m.	*dee-*SYEHM*-breh*